Joseph F. Hair Jr. • G. Tomas M. Hult
Christian M. Ringle • Marko Sarstedt
Nicholas P. Danks • Soumya Ray

Partial Least Squares Structural Equation Modeling (PLS-SEM) Using R

A Workbook

Joseph F. Hair Jr.
Mitchell College of Business
University of South Alabama
Mobile, AL
USA

G. Tomas M. Hult
Broad College of Business
Michigan State University
East Lansing, MI
USA

Christian M. Ringle
Department of Management
Science and Technology
Hamburg University of Technology
Hamburg, Germany

Marko Sarstedt
Otto-von-Guericke University Magdeburg
Magdeburg, Germany

Babeș-Bolyai University
Faculty of Economics and Business
Administration
Cluj, Romania

Nicholas P. Danks
Trinity Business School
Trinity College
Dublin, Ireland

Soumya Ray
National Tsing Hua University
Hsinchu, Taiwan

This book is an open access publication.

ISSN 2662-2866   ISSN 2662-2874 (electronic)
Classroom Companion: Business
ISBN 978-3-030-80518-0   ISBN 978-3-030-80519-7 (eBook)
https://doi.org/10.1007/978-3-030-80519-7

© The Editor(s) (if applicable) and The Author(s) 2021
Open Access This book is licensed under the terms of the Creative Commons Attribution 4.0 International License (http://creativecommons.org/licenses/by/4.0/), which permits use, sharing, adaptation, distribution and reproduction in any medium or format, as long as you give appropriate credit to the original author(s) and the source, provide a link to the Creative Commons license and indicate if changes were made.
The images or other third party material in this book are included in the book's Creative Commons license, unless indicated otherwise in a credit line to the material. If material is not included in the book's Creative Commons license and your intended use is not permitted by statutory regulation or exceeds the permitted use, you will need to obtain permission directly from the copyright holder.
The use of general descriptive names, registered names, trademarks, service marks, etc. in this publication does not imply, even in the absence of a specific statement, that such names are exempt from the relevant protective laws and regulations and therefore free for general use.
The publisher, the authors, and the editors are safe to assume that the advice and information in this book are believed to be true and accurate at the date of publication. Neither the publisher nor the authors or the editors give a warranty, expressed or implied, with respect to the material contained herein or for any errors or omissions that may have been made. The publisher remains neutral with regard to jurisdictional claims in published maps and institutional affiliations.

This Springer imprint is published by the registered company Springer Nature Switzerland AG
The registered company address is: Gewerbestrasse 11, 6330 Cham, Switzerland

Classroom Companion: Business

The Classroom Companion series in Business features foundational and introductory books aimed at students to learn the core concepts, fundamental methods, theories and tools of the subject. The books offer a firm foundation for students preparing to move towards advanced learning. Each book follows a clear didactic structure and presents easy adoption opportunities for lecturers.

More information about this series at http://www.springer.com/series/16374

Preface

In 2021, the third edition of our introductory book *A Primer on Partial Least Squares Structural Equation Modeling (PLS-SEM)* was published (Hair, Hult, Ringle, & Sarstedt, 2022). The book covers the latest developments in the field, including recent advances in model evaluation (e.g., inference testing in discriminant validity assessment, predictive power assessments using PLS$_{predict}$, and model comparisons), improved guidelines for minimum sample sizes, and new complementary methods and concepts such as necessary condition analysis and endogeneity. The book has been highly successful as evidenced in its citation count of more than 24,000 times according to Google Scholar (as of August 2021), and the translations into seven other languages, including in German (Hair et al., 2017), Italian (Hair et al., 2020), and Spanish (Hair et al., 2019). One of the book's features that has likely contributed to its popularity is our strong focus on pedagogical elements, most notably our reliance on a single running case study and the commercial SmartPLS 3 software (Ringle, Wende, & Becker, 2015), which stands out due to its frictionless design, allowing novice researchers to quickly specify and estimate PLS path models (Memon et al., 2021; Sarstedt & Cheah, 2019).

While SmartPLS constitutes the most frequently used software to conduct PLS-SEM analyses (Ghasemy, Teeroovengadum, Becker, & Ringle, 2020; Hair, Hollingsworth, Randolph, & Chong. 2017; Usakli & Kucukergin 2018), research has brought forward several packages for the R environment such as csem (Rademaker et al., 2020), SEMinR (Ray et al., 2021), and semPLS (Monecke & Leisch, 2012; Monecke & Leisch, 2013), whose use has recently gained traction. Among the R packages available on CRAN, Ray et al.'s (2021) SEMinR package brings a particularly friendly syntax to creating and estimating structural equation models using functions named appropriately for the facets of PLS path models that applied researchers are familiar with: "multi-item" versus "single-item," "constructs," "paths," and so on. The package also gives users intuitive functions for generating higher-order constructs and interaction terms, the flexibility to quickly implement and insert their own extensions such as missing data imputation methods or visualizations, and generate reports and figures for research output. It was logical, therefore, to prepare a version of the book that shares the methodological concepts and also features the R software as a method for estimating PLS path models. This book caters this aim.

We designed the text as a workbook for readers who have already been exposed to PLS-SEM by reading textbooks (e.g., Hair et al., 2022; Henseler, 2021; Ramayah, Cheah, Chuah, Ting, & Memon, 2016; Mehmetoglu & Venturini, 2021; Wong, 2019) or seminal articles (e.g., Chin, 1998; Hair, Ringle, & Sarstedt, 2011; Hair, Risher, Ringle, & Sarstedt, 2019; Henseler, Ringle, & Sinkovics, 2009; Sarstedt, Ringle, & Hair, 2022; Tenenhaus, Esposito Vinzi, Chatelin, & Lauro, 2005) on the method. Nevertheless, to enable readers with little background in PLS-SEM to quickly grasp the concepts, each chapter offers a concise overview of relevant topics and metrics relevant for executing PLS-SEM and interpreting the results. Accompanied by a rich set of references for further reading, rules of thumb in every chapter provide guidelines on best practices in the application of PLS-SEM. The focus, however, is on the in-depth description of the case study, which gives readers the "how-tos" of using SEMinR to obtain solutions and to report their results. Correspondingly, the workbook puts less emphasis on aspects related to model design and measurement model specification but, instead, introduces the R environment and particularly the SEMinR package in detail.

Nevertheless, the workbook incorporates many of the new features that have been introduced in the third edition of the *Primer on Partial Least Squares Structural Equation Modeling (PLS-SEM)* (Hair et al., 2022) and offers unique contents tailored to the SEMinR package. These include the following:

- An overview of the latest research on the nature of composite-based modeling, which is the conceptual foundation for PLS-SEM
- Details on the distinction between PLS-SEM and CB-SEM as well as the research goals and the model constellations, which are favorable toward the use of PLS-SEM
- Application of PLS-SEM with secondary (archival) data
- Guidelines for determining minimum sample sizes using the inverse square root method
- Detailed coverage of internal consistency reliability using rho_A and inference testing in discriminant validity assessment
- Latest research on bootstrapping settings and assessment
- Analyzing a model's out-of-sample predictive power using the $PLS_{predict}$ procedure
- Metrics for model comparisons (e.g., the Bayesian information criterion)
- Coverage of the latest literature on PLS-SEM

All examples in the edition apply to the newest version of the SEMinR package, which is available free of charge in CRAN (▶ https://CRAN.R-project.org/package=seminr; see also ▶ Chap. 3). The book chapters and learning support supplements are organized around the learning outcomes shown at the beginning of each chapter. Moreover, each chapter includes a single concise summary for the learning outcomes. The website ▶ https://www.pls-sem.com includes a series of support materials to facilitate learning and applying the PLS-SEM method and using the SEMinR package.

> Visit ▶ https://www.pls-sem.com for access to R markdown documents, which weave together descriptions and code that can be easily copied into the R console.

Additionally, the PLS-SEM Academy (▶ https://www.pls-sem-academy.com) offers video-based online courses based on this book. The courses include basic contents such as model specification and evaluation as well as advanced topics, including mediation, higher-order constructs, moderation, measurement invariance, multigroup analysis, and nonlinear effects.

Besides several hours of online video material presented by world-renowned instructors, the PLS-SEM Academy provides comprehensive lecturing slides that illustrate all analyses step-by-step. While the case study descriptions draw on the SmartPLS software, the concepts are fully applicable to the R software-based analyses using the SEMinR package. Registered users can claim course certificates after successful completion of each end of section exam.

> **Discounted PLS-SEM Academy Access**
>
> The PLS-SEM Academy offers all owners of this book a 15% discount on the purchase of access to its course offerings. All you have to do is send a photo of yourself with the book in your hand, your name and address to the e-mail address support@pls-sem-academy.com. A short time later you will receive a 15% discount code which you can use on the website ▶ https://www.pls-sem-academy.com. We hope you enjoy perfecting your PLS-SEM skills with the help of these courses and wish you every success in obtaining the certificates.

We would like to acknowledge the many insights and suggestions provided by the colleagues, students, and PLS-SEM users worldwide. Most notably, we thank Nicole Beachum (University of Alabama, Birmingham), Jan-Michael Becker (BI Norwegian Business School), Zakariya Belkhamza (Ahmed Bin Mohammed Military College), Charla Brown (Troy University), Roger Calantone (Michigan State University), Fabio Cassia (University of Verona), Gabriel Cepeda Carrión (University of Seville), Jacky Jun Hwa Cheah (Universiti Putra Malaysia), Adamantios Diamantopoulos (University of Vienna), Markus Eberl (Kantar), George Franke (University of Alabama), Anne Gottfried (University of Texas, Arlington), Siegfried P. Gudergan (University of Waikato), Saurabh Gupta (Kennesaw State University), Karl-Werner Hansmann (University of Hamburg), Dana Harrison (East Tennessee State University), Sven Hauff (Helmut Schmidt University), Mike Hollingsworth (Old Dominion University), Philip Holmes (Pensacola Christian College), Chris Hopkins (Auburn University), Lucas Hopkins (Florida State University), Maxwell K. Hsu (University of Wisconsin), Heungsun Hwang (McGill University), Ida Rosnita Ismail (Universiti Kebangsaan Malaysia), April Kemp (Southeastern Louisiana University), David Ketchen (Auburn University), Ned Kock (Texas A&M University), Marcel Lichters (TU Chemnitz), Benjamin Liengaard (Aarhus University), Chein-Hsin Lin (Da-Yeh University), Yide Liu (Macau University of Science and Technology), Francesca Magno (University of Bergamo), Lucy Matthews (Middle Tennessee State University), Jay Memmott (University of South Dakota), Mumtaz Ali Memon (NUST Business School), Adam Merkle (University of South Alabama), Ovidiu I. Moisescu (Babeș-Bolyai University), Zach Moore (University of Louisiana at Monroe), Arthur Money (Henley Business School), Christian Nitzl (Universität der Bundeswehr München), Torsten Pieper (University of North Carolina), Dorian Proksch (University of Twente), Lacramioara Radomir (Babeș-Bolyai University), Arun Rai (Georgia State University), Sascha Raithel (Freie Universität Berlin), S. Mostafa Rasoolimanesh (Taylor's University), Lauren Rich (University of West Florida), Nicole

Richter (University of Southern Denmark), Edward E. Rigdon (Georgia State University), Jeff Risher (Southeastern Oklahoma University), José Luis Roldán (University of Seville), Amit Saini (University of Nebraska-Lincoln), Phillip Samouel (University of Kingston), Francesco Scafarto (University of Rome "Tor Vergata"), Bruno Schivinski (University of London), Rainer Schlittgen (University of Hamburg), Manfred Schwaiger (Ludwig-Maximillians University), Pratyush N. Sharma (University of Alabama), Wen-Lung Shiau (Zhejiang University of Technology), Galit Shmueli (National Tsing Hua University), Donna Smith (Ryerson University), Toni M. Somers (Wayne State University), Detmar W. Straub (Georgia State University), Ramayah Thurasamy (Universiti Sains Malaysia), Hiram Ting (UCSI University), Ron Tsang (Agnes Scott College), Huiwen Wang (Beihang University), Sven Wende (SmartPLS GmbH), Anita Whiting (Clayton State University), David Williams (Dalton State University), and Lea Witta (University of Central Florida) for their helpful remarks.

Also, we thank the team of doctoral student and research fellows at Hamburg University of Technology and Otto-von-Guericke University Magdeburg—namely, Michael Canty, Svenja Damberg, Lena Frömbling, Frauke Kühn, Benjamin Maas, Mandy Pick, and Martina Schöniger—for their kind support. In particular, we would like to thank Susanne Adler who translated the book contents into R markdown documents, available on ► https://www.pls-sem.net. In addition, at Springer we thank Ruth Milewski and Prashanth Mahagaonkar for their support and great work. We hope the R software version of our book will expand knowledge of the capabilities and benefits of PLS-SEM to a much broader group of researchers and practitioners. Lastly, if you have any remarks, suggestions, or ideas to improve this book, please get in touch with us. We appreciate any feedback on the book's concept and contents!

Visit the companion site for this book at ► https://www.pls-sem.com.

Joseph F. Hair Jr.
Mobile, AL, USA

G. Tomas M. Hult
East Lansing, MI, USA

Christian M. Ringle
Hamburg, Germany

Marko Sarstedt
Magdeburg, Germany

Nicholas P. Danks
Dublin, Ireland

Soumya Ray
Hsinchu, Taiwan

References

Chin, W. W. (1998). The partial least squares approach to structural equation modeling. In G. A. Marcoulides (Ed.), *Modern methods for business research* (pp. 295–358). Mahwah, NJ: Erlbaum.

Ghasemy, M., Teeroovengadum, V., Becker, J.-M., & Ringle, C. M. (2020). This fast car can move faster: A review of PLS-SEM application in higher education research. *Higher Education, 80*, 1121–1152.

Hair, J. F., Hollingsworth, C. L., Randolph, A. B., & Chong, A. Y. L. (2017a). An updated and expanded assessment of PLS-SEM in information systems research. *Industrial Management & Data Systems, 117*(3), 442–458.

Hair, J. F., Hult, G. T. M., Ringle, C. M., & Sarstedt, M. (2022). *A primer on partial least squares structural equation modeling (PLS-SEM)* (3rd ed.). Thousand Oaks, CA: Sage.

Hair, J. F., Hult, G. T. M., Ringle, C. M., Sarstedt, M., Castillo Apraiz, J., Cepeda-Carrión, G., & Roldán, J. L. (2019a). *Manual de partial least squares structural equation modeling (PLS-SEM)*. (Seconda Edizione). Barcelona: OmniaScience.

Hair, J. F., Hult, G. T. M., Ringle, C. M., Sarstedt, M., Magno, F., Cassia, F., & Scafarto, F. (2020). *Le Equazioni Strutturali Partial Least Squares: Introduzione alla PLS-SEM*. (Seconda Edizione). Milano: Franco Angeli.

Hair, J. F., Hult, G. T. M., Ringle, C. M., Sarstedt, M., Richter, N. F., & Hauff, S. (2017b). *Partial Least Squares Strukturgleichungsmodellierung (PLS-SEM): Eine anwendungsorientierte Einführung*. München: Vahlen.

Hair, J. F., Ringle, C. M., & Sarstedt, M. (2011). PLS-SEM: Indeed a silver bullet. *Journal of Marketing Theory and Practice, 19*(2), 139–151.

Hair, J. F., Risher, J. J., Sarstedt, M., & Ringle, C. M. (2019b). When to use and how to report the results of PLS-SEM. *European Business Review, 31*(1), 2–24.

Henseler, J. (2021). *Composite-based structural equation modeling: Analyzing latent and emergent variables*. New York, NY: Guilford Press.

Henseler, J., Ringle, C. M., & Sinkovics, R. R. (2009). The use of partial least squares path modeling in international marketing. In R. R. Sinkovics & P. N. Ghauri (Eds.), *New challenges to international marketing*. (Advances in International Marketing, 20 (pp. 277–319). Bingley: Emerald.

Mehmetoglu, M., & Venturini, S. (2021). *Structural equation modelling with partial least squares using Stata and R*. London: Routledge.

Memon, M. A., Ramayah, T., Cheah, J.-H., Ting, H., Chuah, F., & Cham, T. H. (2021). PLS-SEM statistical programs: A review. *Journal of Applied Structural Equation Modeling, 5*(1), i–xiv.

Monecke, A., & Leisch, F. (2012). semPLS: Structural equation modeling using partial least squares. *Journal of Statistical Software, 48*(3), 1–32.

Monecke, A., & Leisch, F. (2013). *R package semPLS: Structural equation modeling using partial least squares version 1.0-10 [computer software]*. Retrieved from ▶ https://cran.r-project.org/web/packages/semPLS/

Rademaker, M. E., Schuberth, F., Schamberger, T., Klesel, M., Dijkstra, T. K., & Henseler, J. (2020). *R package cSEM: Composite-based structural equation modeling version 0.3.0 [computer software]*. Retrieved from: ▶ https://cran.r-project.org/web/packages/cSEM/

Ramayah, T., Cheah, J.-H., Chuah, F., Ting, H., & Memon, M. A. (2016). *Partial least squares structural equation modeling (PLS-SEM) using SmartPLS 3.0: An updated and practical guide to statistical analysis*. Kuala Lumpur: Pearson Malaysia.

Ray, S., Danks, N. P., Calero Valdez, A. (2021). *R package seminr: Domain-specific language for building and estimating structural equation models version 2.1.0 [computer software]*. Retrieved from: ▶ https://cran.r-project.org/web/packages/seminr/

Ringle, C. M., Wende, S., & Becker, J.-M. (2015). *SmartPLS 3 [computer software]*. Bönningstedt: SmartPLS. Retrieved from ▶ https://www.smartpls.com

Sarstedt, M., & Cheah, J. H. (2019). Partial least squares structural equation modeling using SmartPLS: A software review. *Journal of Marketing Analytics, 7*(3), 196–202.

Sarstedt, M., Hair, J. F., & Ringle, C. M. (2022). Partial least squares structural equation modeling. In C. Homburg, M. Klarmann, & A. Vomberg (Eds.), *Handbook of Market Research*. Cham: Springer.

Tenenhaus, M., Esposito Vinzi, V., Chatelin, Y.-M., & Lauro, C. (2005). PLS path modeling. *Computational Statistics & Data Analysis, 48*(1), 159–205.

Usakli, A., & Kucukergin, K. G. (2018). Using partial least squares structural equation modeling in hospitality and tourism: Do researchers follow practical guidelines? *International Journal of Contemporary Hospitality Management, 30*(11), 3462–3512.

Wong, K. K.-K. (2019). *Mastering partial least squares structural equation modeling (PLS-SEM) with SmartPLS in 38 hours*. Bloomington, IN: iUniverse.

Contents

1	**An Introduction to Structural Equation Modeling**	1
2	**Overview of R and RStudio**	31
3	**The SEMinR Package**	49
4	**Evaluation of Reflective Measurement Models**	75
5	**Evaluation of Formative Measurement Models**	91
6	**Evaluation of the Structural Model**	115
7	**Mediation Analysis**	139
8	**Moderation Analysis**	155

Supplementary Information

Appendix A: The PLS-SEM Algorithm	174
Appendix B: Assessing the Reflectively Measured Constructs in the Corporate Reputation Model	177
Glossary	182
Index	195

About the Authors

Joseph F. Hair Jr.
is Cleverdon Chair of Business, and director of the PhD degree in business administration, Mitchell College of Business, University of South Alabama. He previously held the Copeland Endowed Chair of Entrepreneurship and was director of the Entrepreneurship Institute, Ourso College of Business Administration, Louisiana State University. Joe was recognized by Clarivate Analytics in 2018, 2019, and 2020 for being in the top 1% globally of all business and economics professors based on his citations and scholarly accomplishments, which exceed 251,000 over his career. Professor Hair has authored more than 75 books, including *Multivariate Data Analysis (8th edition, 2019; cited 150,000+ times)*, *MKTG (13th edition, 2020)*, *Essentials of Business Research Methods (2020)* and *Essentials of Marketing Research* (4th edition, 2020). He also has published numerous articles in scholarly journals and was recognized as the *Academy of Marketing Science Marketing Educator of the Year*. As a popular guest speaker, Professor Hair often presents seminars on research techniques, multivariate data analysis, and marketing issues for organizations in Europe, Australia, China, India, and South America. He has a new book on *Essentials of Marketing Analytics*, 2021 (McGraw-Hill).

G. Tomas M. Hult
is professor and Byington Endowed Chair at Michigan State University (USA), and holds a visiting chaired professorship at Leeds University Business School (United Kingdom) and a visiting professorship at Uppsala University (Sweden). Professor Hult is a member of the Expert Networks of the World Economic Forum and United Nations/UNCTAD's World Investment Forum and is also part of the Expert Team at the American Customer Satisfaction Index (ACSI). Professor Hult was recognized in 2016 as the *Academy of Marketing Science/CUTCO-Vector Distinguished Marketing Educator*; he is an elected fellow of the Academy of International Business; and he ranks in the top-10 scholars in marketing per the prestigious *World Ranking of Scientists*. At Michigan State University, Professor Hult was recognized with the Beal Outstanding Faculty Award in 2019 (MSU's highest award "for outstanding total service to the University"), and he has also been recognized with the John Dunning AIB Service Award for outstanding service to AIB—as the longest serving executive director in AIB's history (2004–2019) (the most prestigious service award given by the Academy of International Business). Professor Hult regularly teaches doctoral seminars

on multivariate statistics, structural equation modeling, and hierarchical linear modeling worldwide. He is a dual citizen of Sweden and the United States. More information about Professor Hult can be found at ▶ http://www.tomashult.com.

Christian M. Ringle

is a chaired professor of management at the Hamburg University of Technology (Germany). His research addresses management of organizations, human resource management, and methods development for business analytics and their application to business research. His contributions in these fields have been published in journals such as *International Journal of Research in Marketing, Information Systems Research, Journal of the Academy of Marketing Science, MIS Quarterly, Organizational Research Methods,* and *The International Journal of Human Resource Management*. Since 2018, he has been named member of Clarivate Analytics' Highly Cited Researchers List. In 2014, Professor Ringle co-founded SmartPLS (▶ https://www.smartpls.com), a software tool with a graphical user interface for the application of the partial least squares structural equation modeling (PLS-SEM) method. Besides supporting consultancies and international corporations, he regularly teaches doctoral seminars on business analytics, machine learning methods, multivariate statistics, the PLS-SEM method, and the use of SmartPLS worldwide. More information about Professor Christian M. Ringle can be found at ▶ https://www.tuhh.de/hrmo/team/prof-dr-c-m-ringle.html.

Marko Sarstedt

is a chaired professor of marketing at the Ludwig-Maximilians-University Munich (Germany) and an adjunct professor at Babeș-Bolyai University, Romania. His main research interest is the advancement of research methods to enhance the understanding of consumer behavior. His research has been published in *Nature Human Behavior, Journal of Marketing Research, Journal of the Academy of Marketing Science, Multivariate Behavioral Research, Organizational Research Methods, MIS Quarterly,* and *Psychometrika,* among others. His research ranks among the most frequently cited in the social sciences. Professor Sarstedt has won numerous best paper and citation awards, including five *Emerald Citations of Excellence Awards* and two *AMS William R. Darden Awards*. According to the 2020 F.A.Z. ranking, he is among the most influential researcher in Germany, Austria, and Switzerland. Professor Sarstedt has been named member of Clarivate Analytics' Highly Cited Researchers List, which includes the "world's most impactful scientific researchers."

Nicholas P. Danks
is an assistant professor of business analytics at Trinity College, Dublin. His research focuses on structural equation modeling, partial least squares, predictive methodology, and programming. Nicholas is a co-author and the primary maintainer of SEMinR, an open-source package for the R Statistical Environment for the estimation and evaluation of structural equation models. He received a William R. Darden Best Marketing Research Paper Award at the conference of the Academy of Marketing Science. His research has been published in the Human Resource Management Journal, *Journal of Business Research*, and *Decision Sciences*.

Soumya Ray
Soumya Ray is an associate professor at the Institute of Service Science at National Tsing Hua University. He is the co-creator of the SEMinR package for structural equation modeling for the R platform. His research interests include online user behavior and applied methods, and his work has been published in *Information Systems Research*, *Journal of Management Information Systems*, *Decisions Sciences*, and others. His teaching and development interests include systems architecture, information security, and computational statistics.

An Introduction to Structural Equation Modeling

Contents

1.1 What Is Structural Equation Modeling? – 3

1.2 Principles of Structural Equation Modeling – 4
1.2.1 Path Models with Latent Variables – 4
1.2.2 Testing Theoretical Relationships – 7
1.2.3 Measurement Theory – 7
1.2.4 Structural Theory – 8

1.3 PLS-SEM and CB-SEM – 8

1.4 Considerations When Applying PLS-SEM – 11
1.4.1 Key Characteristics of the PLS-SEM Method – 11

© The Author(s) 2021
J. F. Hair Jr. et al., *Partial Least Squares Structural Equation Modeling (PLS-SEM) Using R*, Classroom Companion: Business, https://doi.org/10.1007/978-3-030-80519-7_1

1.4.2　Data Characteristics – 15
1.4.3　Model Characteristics – 20

1.5　Guidelines for Choosing Between PLS-SEM and CB-SEM – 22

References – 24

> **Learning Objectives**
> After reading this chapter, you should:
> 1. Understand the principles of structural equation modeling (SEM)
> 2. Describe the basic elements of a structural equation model
> 3. Comprehend the basic concepts of partial least squares structural equation modeling (PLS-SEM)
> 4. Explain the differences between covariance-based structural equation modeling (CB-SEM) and PLS-SEM and when to use each of the approaches

1.1 What Is Structural Equation Modeling?

First-generation multivariate data analysis techniques, such as multiple regression, logistic regression, and analysis of variance, belong to the core set of statistical methods employed by researchers to empirically test hypothesized relationships between variables of interest. Numerous researchers in various scientific disciplines have applied these methods to generate findings that have significantly shaped the way we see the world today. These techniques have three important limitations in common, namely (1) the postulation of a simple model structure, (2) requiring that all variables can be considered observable, and (3) the assumption that all variables are measured without error (Haenlein & Kaplan, 2004).

With regard to the first limitation, multiple regression analysis and its extensions postulate a simple model structure involving one layer of dependent and independent variables. Causal chains, such as "A leads to B leads to C" or more complex nomological networks involving a large number of intervening variables, can only be estimated piecewise with these methods rather than simultaneously, which can have severe consequences for the quality of the results (Sarstedt, Hair, Nitzl, Ringle, & Howard, 2020).

With regard to the second limitation, regression-type methods are restricted to processing observable variables, such as age or sales (in units or dollars). Theoretical concepts, which are "abstract, unobservable properties or attributes of a social unit of entity" (Bagozzi & Philipps, 1982, p. 465), can only be considered after prior stand-alone validation by means of, for example, a confirmatory factor analysis (CFA). The ex post inclusion of measures of theoretical concepts, however, comes with various shortcomings.

With regard to the third limitation and related to the previous point, one has to bear in mind that each observation of the real world is accompanied by a certain degree of **measurement error**, which can be systematic or random. First-generation techniques are, strictly speaking, only applicable when measured variables contain neither systematic nor random error. This situation is, however, rarely encountered in reality, particularly when the aim is to estimate relationships among measures of theoretical concepts. Since the social sciences, and many other fields of scientific inquiry, routinely deal with theoretical concepts, such as perceptions, attitudes, and intentions, these limitations of first-generation techniques are fundamental.

To overcome these limitations, researchers have increasingly been turning to **second-generation techniques**. These methods, referred to as **structural equation modeling (SEM),** enable researchers to simultaneously model and estimate complex relationships among multiple dependent and independent variables. The concepts under consideration are typically unobservable and measured indirectly by multiple indicators. In estimating the relationships, SEM accounts for measurement error in observed variables. As a result, the method obtains a more precise measurement of the theoretical concepts of interest (Cole & Preacher, 2014). We will discuss these aspects in the following sections in greater detail.

Two popular methods dominate SEM in practice: **covariance-based SEM (CB-SEM)** and **partial least squares SEM (PLS-SEM**, also called **PLS path modeling**). CB-SEM is primarily used to confirm (or reject) theories and their underlying hypotheses. This approach confirms/rejects hypotheses by determining how closely a proposed theoretical model can reproduce the covariance matrix for an observed **sample** dataset. In contrast, PLS has been introduced as a "causal–predictive" approach to SEM (Jöreskog & Wold, 1982, p. 270), which focuses on explaining the variance in the model's dependent variables (Chin et al., 2020).

PLS-SEM is evolving rapidly as a statistical modeling technique. Over the last few decades, there have been numerous introductory articles on this methodology (e.g., Chin, 1998; Haenlein & Kaplan, 2004; Hair et al., 2020; Hair, Howard, & Nitzl, 2020; Hair, Risher, Sarstedt, & Ringle, 2019; Nitzl & Chin, 2017; Rigdon, 2013; Roldán & Sánchez-Franco, 2012; Tenenhaus, Esposito Vinzi, Chatelin, & Lauro, 2005; Wold, 1985) as well as review articles examining how researchers across different disciplines have used the method (◘ Table 1.1). In light of the increasing maturation of the field, researchers have also started exploring the knowledge infrastructure of methodological research on PLS-SEM by analyzing the structures of authors, countries, and co-citation networks (Hwang, Sarstedt, Cheah, & Ringle, 2020; Khan et al., 2019).

The remainder of this chapter first provides a brief introduction of measurement and structural theory as a basis for presenting the PLS-SEM method. In describing the PLS-SEM method's characteristics, we also discuss distinguishing features vis-à-vis CB-SEM. Finally, we outline considerations when using PLS-SEM and highlight situations that favor its use compared to CB-SEM.

1.2 Principles of Structural Equation Modeling

1.2.1 Path Models with Latent Variables

Path models are diagrams used to visually display the hypotheses and variable relationships that are examined when SEM is applied (Hair, Page, & Brunsveld, 2020; Hair, Ringle, & Sarstedt, 2011). An example of a path model is shown in ◘ Fig. 1.1.

Constructs (i.e., variables that are not directly measurable), also referred to as **latent variables**, are represented in path models as circles or ovals (Y_1 to Y_4). The **indicators**, also called items or manifest variables, are the directly measured vari-

1.2 · Principles of Structural Equation Modeling

Table 1.1 Review articles on the use of PLS-SEM

Disciplines	References
Accounting	Lee, Petter, Fayard, and Robinson (2011) Nitzl (2016)
Construction management	Zeng, Liu, Gong, Hertogh, and König (2021)
Entrepreneurship	Manley, Hair, Williams, and McDowell (2020)
Family business	Sarstedt, Ringle, Smith, Reams, and Hair (2014)
Higher education	Ghasemy, Teeroovengadum, Becker, & Ringle, (2020)
Hospitality and tourism	Ali, Rasoolimanesh, Sarstedt, Ringle, and Ryu (2018) do Valle, P. O.,, and Assaker, G. (2016) Usakli and Kucukergin (2018)
Human resource management	Ringle et al. (2020)
International business research	Richter, Sinkovics, Ringle, and Schlägel (2016)
Knowledge management	Cepeda Carrión, Cegarra-Navarro, and Cillo (2019)
Management	Hair, Sarstedt, Pieper, and Ringle (2012)
Marketing	Hair, Sarstedt, Ringle, and Mena (2012)
Management information systems	Hair, Hollingsworth, Randolph, and Chong (2017) Ringle et al. (2012)
Operations management	Bayonne, Marin-Garcia, and Alfalla-Luque (2020) Peng and Lai (2012)
Psychology	Willaby, Costa, Burns, MacCann, and Roberts (2015)
Software engineering	Russo and Stol (2021)
Supply chain management	Kaufmann and Gaeckler (2015)

Source: Hair, Hult, Ringle, & Sarstedt (2022), Chap. 1; used with permission by Sage

ables that contain the raw data. They are represented in path models as rectangles (x_1 to x_{10}). Relationships between constructs, as well as between constructs and their assigned indicators, are depicted as arrows. In PLS-SEM, the arrows are always single headed, thus representing directional relationships. Single-headed arrows are considered predictive relationships and, with strong theoretical support, can be interpreted as causal relationships.

A PLS path model consists of two elements. First, there is a **structural model** (also called the **inner model** in the context of PLS-SEM) that links together the constructs (circles or ovals). The structural model also displays the relationships (paths) between the constructs. Second, there are the **measurement models** (also referred to as the **outer models** in PLS-SEM) of the constructs that display the relationships between the constructs and the indicator variables (rectangles). In ◘ Fig. 1.1, there are two types of measurement models: one for the **exogenous**

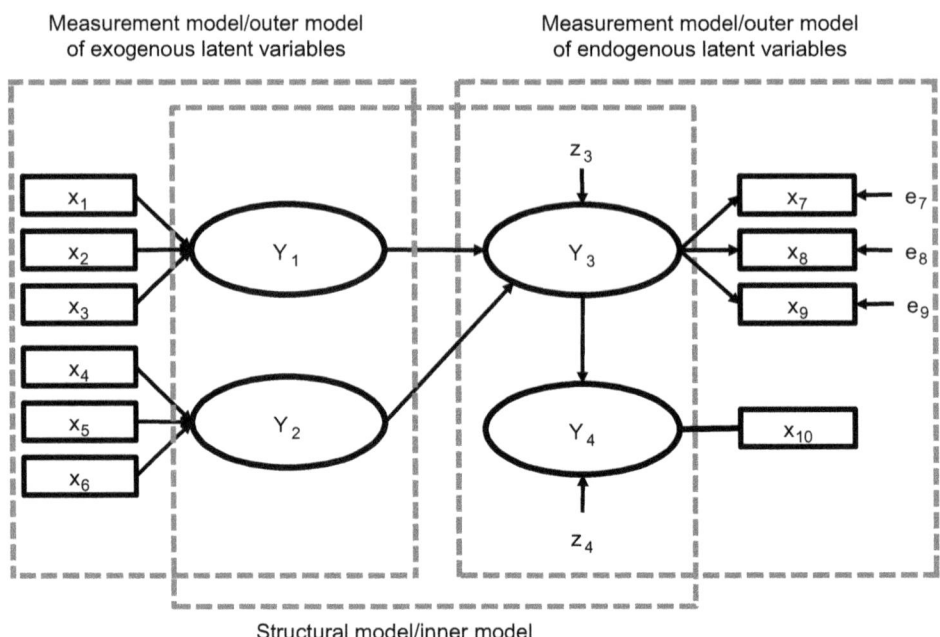

● Fig. 1.1 A simple path model. (Source: Hair et al., 2022, Chap. 1; used with permission by Sage)

latent variables (i.e., those constructs that only explain other constructs in the model) and one for the **endogenous latent variables** (i.e., those constructs that are being explained in the model). Rather than referring to measurement models of exogenous and endogenous latent variables, researchers often refer to the measurement model of one specific latent variable. For example, x_1 to x_3 are the indicators used in the measurement model of Y_1, while Y_4 only includes the x_{10} indicator in the measurement model.

The **error terms** (e.g., e_7 or e_8; ● Fig. 1.1) are connected to the (endogenous) constructs and (reflectively) measured variables by single-headed arrows. Error terms represent the unexplained variance when path models are estimated (i.e., the difference between the model's in-sample prediction of a value and an observed value of a manifest or latent variable). Error terms e_7 to e_9 in ● Fig. 1.1 are connected to those indicators whose relationships point from the construct (Y_3) to the indicators (i.e., reflectively measured indicators).

In contrast, the formatively measured indicators x_1 to x_6, where the relationship goes from the indicator to the construct (Y_1 and Y_2), do not have error terms (Sarstedt, Hair, Ringle, Thiele, & Gudergan, 2016). Finally, for the single-item construct Y_4, the direction of the relationships between the construct and the indicator is not relevant, as construct and item are equivalent. For the same reason, there is no error term connected to x_{10}. The structural model also contains error terms. In ● Fig. 1.1, z_3 and z_4 are associated with the endogenous latent variables Y_3 and Y_4 (note that error terms on constructs and measured variables are labeled differently). In contrast, the exogenous latent variables (Y_1 and Y_2) that only explain

1.2.2 Testing Theoretical Relationships

Path models are developed based on theory and are often used to test theoretical relationships. **Theory** is a set of systematically related hypotheses developed following the scientific method that can be used to explain and predict outcomes. Thus, hypotheses are individual conjectures, whereas theories are multiple hypotheses that are logically linked together and can be tested empirically. Two types of theory are required to develop path models: measurement theory and structural theory. Measurement theory specifies which indicators and how these are used to measure a certain theoretical concept. In contrast, structural theory specifies how the constructs are related to one another in the structural model.

Testing theory using PLS-SEM follows a two-step process (Hair, Black, Babin, & Anderson, 2019). We first test the measurement theory to confirm the reliability and validity of the measurement models. After the measurement models are confirmed, we move on to testing the structural theory. The logic is that we must first confirm the measurement theory before testing the structural theory, because structural theory cannot be confirmed if the measures are unreliable or invalid.

1.2.3 Measurement Theory

Measurement theory specifies how the latent variables (constructs) are measured. Generally, there are two different ways to measure unobservable variables. One approach is referred to as reflective measurement, and the other is formative measurement. Constructs Y_1 and Y_2 in ◘ Fig.1.1 are modeled based on a **formative measurement model**. Note that the directional arrows are pointing from the indicator variables (x_1 to x_3 for Y_1 and x_4 to x_6 for Y_2) to the construct, indicating a predictive (causal) relationship in that direction.

In contrast, Y_3 in ◘ Fig. 1.1 is modeled based on a **reflective measurement model**. With reflective indicators, the direction of the arrows is from the construct to the indicator variables, indicating the assumption that the construct "causes" the measurement (more precisely, the covariation) of the indicator variables. As indicated in ◘ Fig. 1.1, reflective measures have an error term associated with each indicator, which is not the case with formative measures. The latter are assumed to be error-free (Diamantopoulos, 2006). Finally, note that Y_4 is measured using a single item rather than multi-item measures. Therefore, the relationship between construct and indicator is undirected.

Deciding whether to measure the constructs reflectively versus formatively and whether to use multiple items or a single-item measure is fundamental when developing path models. Hair, Hult, Ringle, and Sarstedt (2022; Chap. 2) explain these approaches to modeling constructs in more detail.

1.2.4 Structural Theory

Structural theory shows how the latent variables are related to one another (i.e., it shows the constructs and their path relationships in the structural model). The location and sequence of the constructs are either based on theory or the researcher's experience and accumulated knowledge or both. When path models are developed, the sequence is from left to right. The variables on the left side of the path model are independent variables, and any variable on the right side is a dependent variable. Moreover, variables on the left are shown as sequentially preceding and predicting the variables on the right. However, when variables are in the middle of the path model (between the variables that serve only as independent or dependent variables – Y_3; ◘ Fig. 1.1), they serve as both independent and dependent variables in the structural model.

When latent variables only serve as independent variables, they are called exogenous latent variables (Y_1 and Y_2). When latent variables only serve as dependent variables (Y_4) or as both independent and dependent variables (Y_3), they are called endogenous latent variables (◘ Fig. 1.1). Any latent variable that has only single-headed arrows going out of it is an exogenous latent variable. In contrast, endogenous latent variables can have either single-headed arrows going both into and out of them (Y_3) or only going into them (Y_4). Note that the exogenous latent variables Y_1 and Y_2 do not have error terms, since these constructs are the entities (independent variables) that are explaining the dependent variables in the path model.

1.3 PLS-SEM and CB-SEM

There are two main approaches to estimating the relationships in a structural equation model (Hair et al., 2011; Hair, Black, et al., 2019). One is CB-SEM, and the other is PLS-SEM, the latter being the focus of this book. Each is appropriate for a different research context, and researchers need to understand the differences in order to apply the correct method (Marcoulides & Chin, 2013; Rigdon, Sarstedt, & Ringle, 2017). Finally, some researchers have argued for using regressions based on sum scores, instead of some type of indicator weighting as is done by PLS-SEM. The sum scores approach offers practically no value compared to the PLS-SEM weighted approach and in fact can produce erroneous results (Hair et al., 2017). For this reason, in the following sections, we only briefly discuss sum scores and instead focus on the PLS-SEM and CB-SEM methods.

A crucial conceptual difference between PLS-SEM and CB-SEM relates to the way each method treats the latent variables included in the model. CB-SEM represents a **common factor-based SEM** method that considers the constructs as common factors that explain the covariation between its associated indicators. This approach is consistent with the measurement philosophy underlying reflective measurement, in which the indicators and their covariations are regarded as manifestations of the underlying construct. In principle, CB-SEM can also accommodate formative measurement models, even though the method follows a common factor model estimation approach. To estimate this model type, however, researchers must follow rules that require specific constraints on the model to ensure model identification (Bollen & Davies, 2009; Diamantopoulos & Riefler, 2011), which means that the method can calculate estimates for all model parameters. As Hair, Sarstedt, Ringle, and Mena (2012, p. 420) note, "[t]hese constraints often contradict theoretical considerations, and the question arises whether model design should guide theory or vice versa."

PLS-SEM, on the other hand, assumes the concepts of interest can be measured as composites (Jöreskog & Wold, 1982), which is why PLS is considered a **composite-based SEM** method (Hwang et al., 2020). Model estimation in PLS-SEM involves linearly combining the indicators of a measurement model to form composite variables. The composite variables are assumed to be comprehensive representations of the constructs, and, therefore, valid proxies of the conceptual variables being examined (e.g., Hair & Sarstedt, 2019). The composite-based approach is consistent with the measurement philosophy underlying formative measurement, but this does not imply that PLS-SEM is only capable of estimating formatively specified constructs. The reason is that the estimation perspective (i.e., forming composites to represent conceptual variables) should not be confused with the measurement theory perspective (i.e., specifying measurement models as reflective or formative). The way a method like PLS-SEM estimates the model parameters needs to be clearly distinguished from any measurement theoretical considerations on how to operationalize constructs (Sarstedt et al., 2016). Researchers can include reflectively and formatively specified measurement models that PLS-SEM can straightforwardly estimate.

In following a composite-based approach to SEM, PLS relaxes the strong assumption of CB-SEM that all of the covariation between the sets of indicators is explained by a common factor (Henseler et al., 2014; Rigdon, 2012; Rigdon et al., 2014). At the same time, using weighted composites of indicator variables facilitates accounting for measurement error, thus making PLS-SEM superior compared to multiple regression using **sum scores**, where each indicator is weighted equally.

It is important to note that the composites produced by PLS-SEM are not assumed to be identical to the theoretical concepts, which they represent. They are explicitly recognized as approximations (Rigdon, 2012). As a consequence, some scholars view CB-SEM as a more direct and precise method to empirically measure theoretical concepts (e.g., Rönkkö, McIntosh, & Antonakis, 2015), while PLS-SEM provides approximations. Other scholars contend, however, that such a view is quite shortsighted, since common factors derived in CB-SEM are also not necessarily equivalent to the theoretical concepts that are the focus of the research (Rigdon, 2012; Rigdon et al., 2017; Rossiter, 2011; Sarstedt et al., 2016). Rigdon, Becker, and Sarstedt (2019a) show that common factor models can be subject to considerable degrees of metrological uncertainty. **Metrological uncertainty** refers to the dispersion of the measurement values that can be attributed to the object or concept being measured (JCGM/WG1, 2008). Numerous sources contribute to metrological uncertainty such as definitional uncertainty or limitations related to the measurement scale design, which go well beyond the simple standard errors produced by CB-SEM analyses (Hair & Sarstedt, 2019). As such, uncertainty is a validity threat to measurement and has adverse consequences for the replicability of study findings (Rigdon, Sarstedt, & Becker, 2020). While uncertainty also applies to composite-based SEM, the way researchers treat models in CB-SEM analyses typically leads to a pronounced increase in uncertainty (Rigdon & Sarstedt, 2021). More precisely, in an effort to improve model fit, researchers typically reduce the number of indicators per construct, which in turn increases uncertainty (Hair, Matthews, Matthews, & Sarstedt, 2017; Rigdon et al., 2019a). These issues do not necessarily imply that composite models are superior, but they cast considerable doubt on the assumption of some researchers that CB-SEM constitutes the gold standard when measuring unobservable concepts. In fact, researchers in various fields of science show increasing appreciation that common factors may not always be the right approach to measure concepts (e.g., Rhemtulla, van Bork, & Borsboom, 2020; Rigdon, 2016). Similarly, Rigdon, Becker, and Sarstedt (2019b) show that using sum scores can significantly increase the degree of metrological uncertainty, which questions this measurement practice.

Apart from differences in the philosophy of measurement, the differing treatment of latent variables and, more specifically, the availability of **construct scores** also have consequences for the methods' areas of application. Specifically, while it is possible to estimate latent variable scores within a CB-SEM framework, these estimated scores are not unique. That is, an infinite number of different sets of latent variable scores that will fit the model equally well are possible. A crucial consequence of this **factor (score) indeterminacy** is that the correlations between a common factor and any variable outside the factor model are themselves indeterminate (Guttman, 1955). That is, they may be high or low, depending on which set of factor scores one chooses. As a result, this limitation makes CB-SEM grossly unsuitable for **prediction** (e.g., Dijkstra, 2014; Hair & Sarstedt, 2021). In contrast, a major advantage of PLS-SEM is that it always produces a single specific (i.e., determinate) score for each composite of each observation, once the indicator weights/loadings are established. These determinate scores are proxies of the theoretical concepts being measured, just as factors are proxies for the conceptual variables in CB-SEM (Rigdon et al., 2017; Sarstedt et al., 2016).

Using these proxies as input, PLS-SEM applies ordinary least squares regression with the objective of minimizing the error terms (i.e., the residual variance) of the endogenous constructs. In short, PLS-SEM estimates coefficients (i.e., path model relationships) with the goal of maximizing the R^2 values of the endogenous (target) constructs. This feature achieves the (in-sample) prediction objective of PLS-SEM (Hair & Sarstedt, 2021), which is therefore the preferred method when the research objective is theory development and explanation of variance (prediction of the constructs). For this reason, PLS-SEM is also regarded a **variance-based SEM** approach. Specifically, the logic of the PLS-SEM approach is that all of the indicators' variance should be used to estimate the model relationships, with particular focus on prediction of the dependent variables (e.g., McDonald, 1996). In contrast, CB-SEM divides the total variance into three types – common, unique, and error variance – but utilizes only common variance (i.e., the variance shared with other indicators in the same measurement model) for the model estimation (Hair, Black, et al., 2019). That is, CB-SEM only explains the covariation between measurement and structural model indicators (Jöreskog, 1973) and does not focus on predicting dependent variables (Hair, Matthews, et al., 2017).

> **Attention**
> PLS-SEM is similar but not equivalent to **PLS regression**, another popular multivariate data analysis technique (Abdi, 2010; Wold, Sjöström, & Eriksson, 2001). PLS regression is a regression-based approach that explores the linear relationships between multiple independent variables and a single or multiple dependent variable(s). PLS regression differs from regular regression, however, because, in developing the regression model, the method derives composite factors from the multiple independent variables by means of principal component analysis. PLS-SEM, on the other hand, relies on prespecified networks of relationships between constructs as well as between constructs and their measures (see Mateos-Aparicio, 2011, for a more detailed comparison between PLS-SEM and PLS regression).

1.4 Considerations When Applying PLS-SEM

1.4.1 Key Characteristics of the PLS-SEM Method

Several considerations are important when deciding whether or not to apply PLS-SEM. These considerations also have their roots in the method's characteristics. The statistical properties of the PLS-SEM algorithm have important features associated with the characteristics of the data and model used. Moreover, the properties of the PLS-SEM method affect the evaluation of the results. Four critical issues are relevant to the application of PLS-SEM (Hair et al., 2011; Hair, Risher, et al., 2019): (1) data characteristics, (2) model characteristics, (3) model estimation, and (4) model evaluation. ◘ Table 1.2 summarizes the key characteristics of the PLS-SEM method. An initial overview of these issues is provided in this chapter. For a more detailed explanation, see Hair et al. (2022).

PLS-SEM works efficiently with small sample sizes and complex models (Cassel, Hackl, & Westlund, 1999; Hair, Sarstedt, & Ringle, 2019). In addition, different from maximum likelihood-based CB-SEM, which requires normally distributed data, PLS-SEM makes no distributional assumptions (i.e., it is nonparametric). PLS-SEM can easily handle reflective and formative measurement models, as well as single-item constructs, with no identification problems. It can therefore be applied in a wide variety of research situations. When applying PLS-SEM, researchers also benefit from high efficiency in parameter estimation, which is manifested in the method's greater **statistical power** in comparison to that of CB-SEM. Greater statistical power means that PLS-SEM is more likely to render a specific relationship significant when it is in fact present in the population. The same holds for the comparison with regression using sum score data, which is also characterized by lower statistical power than PLS-SEM (Hair, Hollingsworth, et al., 2017).

Table 1.2 Key characteristics of PLS-SEM

Data characteristics

Sample size	No identification issues with small sample sizes Achieves high levels of statistical power with small sample sizes Larger sample sizes increase the precision (i.e., consistency) of PLS-SEM estimations
Distribution	No distributional assumptions; PLS-SEM is a nonparametric method Influential outliers and collinearity may influence the results
Missing values	Highly robust as long as missing values are below a reasonable level (less than 5%)
Scale of measurement	Works with metric data and quasi-metric (ordinal) scaled variables The standard PLS-SEM algorithm accommodates binary-coded variables, but additional considerations are required when they are used as control variables and moderators and in the analysis of data from discrete choice experiments

Model characteristics

Number of items in each construct's measurement model	Handles constructs measured with single- and multi-item measures
Relationships between constructs and their indicators	Easily incorporates reflective and formative measurement models
Model complexity	Handles complex models with many structural model relationships
Model setup	No causal loops (no circular relationships) are allowed in the structural model

Model estimation

Objective	Aims at maximizing the amount of unexplained variance in the dependent measures (i.e., the R^2 values)
Efficiency	Converges after a few iterations (even in situations with complex models and/or large sets of data) to the optimum solution (i.e., the algorithm is very efficient)
Nature of constructs	Viewed as proxies of the latent concept under investigation, represented by composites
Construct scores	Estimated as linear combinations of their indicators (i.e., they are determinate) Used for predictive purposes Can be used as input for subsequent analyses Not affected by data limitations and inadequacies
Parameter estimates	Structural model relationships are generally underestimated, and measurement model relationships are generally overestimated compared to solutions obtained using data from common factor models Unbiased and consistent when estimating data from composite models High levels of statistical power compared to alternative methods, such as CB-SEM and multiple regression with sum scores

1.4 · Considerations When Applying PLS-SEM

□ Table 1.2 (continued)

Model evaluation	
Evaluation of the overall model	The concept of fit – as defined in CB-SEM – does not apply to PLS-SEM. Efforts to introduce model fit measures have generally proven unsuccessful
Evaluation of the measurement models	Reflective measurement models are assessed on the grounds of indicator reliability, internal consistency reliability, convergent validity, and discriminant validity Formative measurement models are assessed on the grounds of convergent validity, indicator collinearity, and the significance and relevance of indicator weights
Evaluation of the structural model	Collinearity among sets of predictor constructs Significance and relevance of path coefficients Criteria available to assess the model's in-sample (i.e., explanatory) power and out-of-sample predictive power ($PLS_{predict}$)

Additional analyses	Methodological research has substantially extended the original PLS-SEM method by introducing advanced modeling, assessment, and analysis procedures. Some examples include:
	  Confirmatory tetrad analysis
	  Confirmatory composite analysis
	  Discrete choice modeling
	  Endogeneity assessment
	  Higher-order constructs
	  Latent class analysis
	  Measurement model invariance
	  Mediation analysis
	  Model selection
	  Moderating effects, including moderated mediation
	  Multigroup analysis
	  Necessary condition analysis
	  Nonlinear effects

Source: Adapted and extended from Hair et al. (2011). Copyright © 2011 by M.E. Sharpe, Inc. Reprinted by permission of the publisher (Taylor & Francis Ltd., ► http://www.tandfonline.com)

There are, however, several limitations of PLS-SEM. In its basic form, the technique cannot be applied when structural models contain causal loops or circular relationships between the latent variables (i.e., non-recursive models). Early extensions of the basic PLS-SEM algorithm that have not yet been implemented in standard PLS-SEM software packages, however, enable the handling of circular relationships (Lohmöller, 1989). Furthermore, since PLS-SEM does not have an established global goodness-of-fit measure, its use for theory testing and confirmation is more limited in certain situations. Recent research has attempted to promote common goodness-of-fit measures within a PLS-SEM framework (Schuberth, Henseler, & Dijkstra, 2018) but with very limited success. The concept of model fit – as defined in CB-SEM – is not applicable to PLS-SEM because of the methods' different functioning principles (Hair, Sarstedt, & Ringle, 2019). Instead, PLS-SEM-based model estimation and assessment follow a causal–predictive paradigm, in which the objective is to test the predictive power of a model, derived from theory and logic. As such, the method strikes a balance between machine learning methods, which are fully predictive in nature and CB-SEM, which focuses on confirmation and model fit (Richter, Cepeda Carrión, Roldán, & Ringle, 2016). Its causal–predictive nature makes PLS-SEM particularly appealing for research in fields that aim to derive recommendations for practice. For example, recommendations in managerial implication sections in business research journals always include predictive statements ("our results suggest that managers should…"). Making such statements requires a prediction focus on model estimation and evaluation (Sarstedt & Danks, 2021). PLS-SEM perfectly emphasizes this need as the method sheds light on the mechanisms (i.e., the structural model relationships) through which the predictions are generated (Hair, 2020; Hair & Sarstedt, 2019, 2021).

In early writing, researchers noted that PLS estimation is "deliberately approximate" to factor-based SEM (Hui & Wold, 1982, p. 127), a characteristic previously referred to as the **PLS-SEM bias** (e.g., Chin, Marcolin, & Newsted, 2003). A number of studies have used simulations to demonstrate the alleged PLS-SEM bias (e.g., Goodhue, Lewis, & Thompson, 2012; McDonald, 1996; Rönkkö & Evermann, 2013). According to prior research on the PLS-SEM bias, measurement model estimates are biased upward, whereas structural model estimates are biased downward compared to CB-SEM results. The studies conclude that parameter estimates will approach what has been labeled the "true" parameter values when both the number of indicators per construct and sample size increase (Hui & Wold, 1982). However, all the abovementioned simulation studies used CB-SEM as the benchmark against which the PLS-SEM estimates were evaluated with the assumption that they should be the same. Because PLS-SEM is a composite-based approach, which uses the total variance to estimate parameters, differences can be expected in such an assessment (Lohmöller, 1989; Schneeweiß, 1991). Not surprisingly, the very same issues apply when composite models are used to estimate CB-SEM results. In fact, Sarstedt et al. (2016) show that the bias produced by CB-SEM is far more severe than that of PLS-SEM, when applying the method to the wrong type of model (i.e., estimating composite models with CB-SEM versus estimating common factor models with PLS-SEM). Apart from these conceptual concerns, simulation studies show that the differences between PLS-SEM and CB-SEM estimates, when assuming the latter as a standard of comparison, are very small, provided that measurement models meet minimum recommended standards in terms of measurement quality (i.e., reliability and validity). Specifically, when the measurement models have four or more indicators and indicator loadings meet the common standards (≥ 0.70), there are practically no differences between the two methods in terms of parameter accuracy (e.g., Reinartz, Haenlein, & Henseler, 2009; Sarstedt et al., 2016). Thus, the extensively discussed PLS-SEM bias is of no practical relevance for the vast majority of applications (e.g., Binz Astrachan, Patel, & Wanzenried, 2014).

Finally, methodological research has substantially extended the original PLS-SEM method by introducing advanced modeling, assessment, and analysis procedures. Examples include different types of robustness checks (Sarstedt et al., 2020), higher-order constructs (Sarstedt, Hair, Cheah, Becker, & Ringle, 2019), discrete choice modeling (Hair, Sarstedt, & Ringle, 2019), necessary condition analysis and related methods (Rasoolimanesh, Ringle, Sarstedt, & Olya, 2021; Richter, Schubring, Hauff, Ringle, & Sarstedt, 2020), and out-of-sample prediction metrics (Hair, 2020). Hair, Sarstedt, Ringle, and Gudergan (2018) offer an introduction into several of these advanced topics.

In the following, we discuss aspects related to data characteristics (e.g., minimum sample size requirements) and model characteristics (e.g., model complexity).

1.4.2 Data Characteristics

Data characteristics, such as minimum sample size requirements, non-normal data, and scales of measurement (i.e., the use of different scale types), are among the most often stated reasons for applying PLS-SEM across numerous disciplines (e.g., Ghasemy, Teeroovengadum, Becker, & Ringle, 2020; Hair, Sarstedt, Ringle, & Mena, 2012; Ringle et al., 2020). While some of the arguments are consistent with the method's capabilities, others are not. In the following sections, we discuss these and also aspects related data characteristics.

1.4.2.1 Minimum Sample Size Requirements

Small sample size is likely the most often abused reason stated for using PLS-SEM, with some researchers obtaining model solutions with unacceptably low sample sizes (Goodhue et al., 2012; Marcoulides & Saunders, 2006). These researchers oftentimes believe there is some "magic" in the PLS-SEM approach that allows them to use a very small sample to obtain results representing the effects that exist in large populations of several million elements or individuals. No multivariate analysis technique, including PLS-SEM, has this kind of "magic" inferential capability (Petter, 2018).

PLS-SEM can certainly obtain solutions with smaller samples, but the population's nature determines the situations in which small sample sizes are acceptable (Rigdon, 2016). For example, in business-to-business research, populations are often restricted in size. Assuming that other situational characteristics are equal, the more heterogeneous the population, the larger the sample size needed to achieve an acceptable accuracy (Cochran, 1977). If basic sampling theory guidelines are not considered (Sarstedt, Bengart, Shaltoni, & Lehmann, 2018), questionable results are produced.

In addition, when applying multivariate analysis techniques, the technical dimension of the sample size becomes relevant. Adhering to the minimum sample size guidelines ensures the results of a statistical method, such as PLS-SEM, have adequate statistical power. In these regards, an analysis based on an insufficient sample size may not reveal an effect that exists in the underlying population (which results in committing a type II error). Moreover, executing statistical analyses based on minimum sample size guidelines will ensure the results of the statistical method are robust and the model is generalizable to another sample from that same population. Thus, an insufficient sample size may lead to PLS-SEM results that differ from those of another larger sample. In the following, we focus on the PLS-SEM method and its technical requirements of the minimum sample size.

The overall complexity of a structural model has little influence on the **minimum sample size requirements** for PLS-SEM. The reason is the PLS-SEM algorithm does not compute all relationships in the structural model at the same time. Instead, it uses ordinary least squares regressions to estimate the model's partial regression relationships. Two early studies systematically evaluated the performance of PLS-SEM with small sample sizes and concluded that the method performed well (e.g., Chin & Newsted, 1999; Hui & Wold, 1982). More recently, simulation studies by Hair et al. (2017) and Reinartz et al. (2009) indicate that PLS-SEM is the method of choice when the sample size is small. Moreover, compared with its covariance-based counterpart, PLS-SEM has higher levels of statistical power in situations with complex model structures and smaller sample sizes. Similarly, Henseler et al. (2014) show that results can be obtained with PLS-SEM when other methods do not converge or provide inadmissible solutions. For example, problems often are encountered when using CB-SEM on complex models, especially when the sample size is limited. Finally, CB-SEM encounters identification and convergence issues when formative measures are involved (e.g., Diamantopoulos & Riefler, 2011).

Unfortunately, some researchers believe sample size considerations do not play a role in the application of PLS-SEM. This idea has been fostered by the often-cited 10-time rule (Barclay, Higgins, & Thompson, 1995), which suggests the sample size should be equal to 10 times the number of independent variables in the most complex regression in the PLS path model (i.e., considering both measurement and structural models). This rule of thumb is equivalent to saying the minimum sample size should be 10 times the maximum number of arrowheads pointing at a latent variable anywhere in the PLS path model. While this rule offers a rough guideline, the minimum sample size requirement should consider the statistical power of the estimates. To assess statistical power, researchers can consider power tables (Cohen, 1992) or power analyses using programs, such as G*Power (Faul, Erdfelder, Buchner, & Lang, 2009), which is available free of charge at ▶ http://www.gpower.hhu.de/. These approaches do not explicitly consider the entire model but instead use the most complex regression in the (formative) measurement models and structural model of a PLS path model as a point of reference for assessing the statistical power. In doing so, researchers typically aim at achieving a power level of 80%. However, the minimum sample size resulting from these calculations may still be too small (Kock & Hadaya, 2018).

Addressing these concerns, Kock and Hadaya (2018) proposed the **inverse square root method**, which considers the probability that the ratio of a path coefficient and its standard error will be greater than the critical value of a test statistic for a specific significance level. The results depend, therefore, on only one path coefficient and are dependent neither on the size of the most complex regression in the (formative) models nor on the size of the overall model. Assuming a common power level of 80% and significance levels of 1%, 5%, and 10%, the minimum sam-

1.4 · Considerations When Applying PLS-SEM

ple size (n_{min}) is given by the following equations, respectively, where p_{min} is the value of the path coefficient with the minimum magnitude in the PLS path model:

$$\text{Significance level} = 1\%: n_{min} > \left(\frac{3.168}{|p_{min}|}\right)^2.$$

$$\text{Significance level} = 5\%: n_{min} > \left(\frac{2.486}{|p_{min}|}\right)^2.$$

$$\text{Significance level} = 10\%: n_{min} > \left(\frac{2.123}{|p_{min}|}\right)^2.$$

For example, assuming a significance level of 5% and a minimum path coefficient of 0.2, the minimum sample size is given by

$$n_{min} > \left(\frac{2.486}{0.2}\right)^2 = 154.505.$$

This result needs to be rounded to the next integer, so the minimum sample size is 155.

The inverse square root method is rather conservative, in that it slightly overestimates the sample size required to render an effect significant at a given power level. Most importantly, the method is characterized by its ease of use, since it can be readily implemented.

Nevertheless, two considerations are important when using the inverse square root method. First, by using the smallest statistical path coefficient as the point of reference, the method can be misleading as researchers will not expect marginal effects to be significant. For example, assuming a 5% significance level and a minimum path coefficient of 0.01 would require a sample size of 61,802! Hence, researchers should choose a higher path coefficient as input, depending on whether the model produces either overall weak or strong effects or the smallest relevant (to be detected) effect.

Second, by relying on model estimates, the inverse square root method follows a retrospective approach. As a result, this assessment approach can be used as a basis for additional data collection or adjustments in the model. If possible, however, researchers should follow a prospective approach by trying to derive the minimum expected effect size prior to data analysis. To do so, researchers can draw on prior research involving a comparable conceptual background or models with similar complexity or, preferably, the results of a pilot study, which tested the hypothesized model using a smaller sample of respondents from the same population. For example, if the pilot study produced a minimum path coefficient of 0.15, this value should be chosen as input for computing the required sample size for the main study.

☐ **Table 1.3** Minimum sample sizes for different levels of minimum path coefficients (p_{min}) and a power of 80%

p_{min}	Significance level		
	1%	5%	10%
0.05–0.1	1004	619	451
0.11–0.2	251	155	113
0.21–0.3	112	69	51
0.31–0.4	63	39	29
0.41–0.5	41	25	19

Source: Hair et al. (2022), Chap. 1; used with permission by Sage

In most cases, however, researchers have only limited information regarding the expected effect sizes, even if a pilot study has been conducted. Hence, it is reasonable to consider ranges of effect sizes rather than specific values to determine the sample size required for a specific study. ☐ Table 1.3 shows the minimum sample size requirement for different significance levels and varying ranges of p_{min}. In deriving the minimum sample size, it is reasonable to consider the upper boundary of the effect range as reference, since the inverse square root method is rather conservative. For example, when assuming that the minimum path coefficient expected to be significant is between 0.11 and 0.20, one would need approximately 155 observations to render the corresponding effect significant at 5%. Similarly, if the minimum path coefficient expected to be significant is between 0.31 and 0.40, then the recommended sample size would be 39.

1.4.2.2 Missing Value Treatment

As with other statistical analyses, missing values should be dealt with when using PLS-SEM. For reasonable limits (i.e., less than 5% values missing per indicator), **missing value treatment** options, such as mean replacement, the EM (expectation–maximization) algorithm, and nearest neighbor (e.g., Hair, Black, et al., 2019), generally result in only slightly different PLS-SEM estimates (Grimm & Wagner, 2020). Alternatively, researchers can opt for deleting all observations with missing values, which decreases variation in the data and may introduce biases when certain groups of observations have been deleted systematically.

1.4.2.3 Non-normal Data

The use of PLS-SEM has two other key advantages associated with data characteristics (i.e., distribution and scales). In situations where it is difficult or impossible to meet the stricter requirements of more traditional multivariate techniques (e.g., normal data distribution), PLS-SEM is always the preferred method. PLS-SEM's greater flexibility is described by the label "soft modeling," coined by Wold (1982), who developed the method. It should be noted, however, that "soft" is attributed only to the distributional assumptions and not to the concepts, models, or estimation techniques (Lohmöller, 1989). PLS-SEM's statistical properties provide very robust model estimations with data that have normal as well as extremely non-normal (i.e., skewness and/or kurtosis) distributional properties (Hair, Hollingsworth, et al., 2017; Hair, Matthews, et al., 2017; Reinartz et al., 2009). It must be remembered, however, that influential observations, outliers, and collinearity do influence the ordinary least squares regressions in PLS-SEM and researchers should evaluate the data and results for these issues (Hair, Black, et al., 2019).

1.4.2.4 Scales of Measurement

The PLS-SEM algorithm generally requires variables to be measured on a **metric scale** (**ratio scale** or **interval scale**) for the measurement model indicators. But the method also works well with ordinal scales with equidistant data points (i.e., quasi-metric scales; Sarstedt & Mooi, 2019; Chap. 3.6) and with binary-coded data. The use of binary-coded data is often a means of including categorical control variables (Hair et al., 2022) or moderators in PLS-SEM models. In short, binary indicators can be included in PLS-SEM models but require special attention. For example, using PLS-SEM in discrete choice experiments, where the aim is to explain or to predict a binary dependent variable, requires specific designs and estimation routines (Hair, Ringle, Gudergan, Fischer, Nitzl, & Menictas, 2019).

1.4.2.5 Secondary Data

Secondary data are data that have already been gathered, often for a different research purpose some time ago (Sarstedt & Mooi, 2019; Chap. 3.2.1). Secondary data are increasingly available to explore real-world phenomena. Research based on secondary data typically focuses on a different objective than in a standard CB-SEM analysis, which is strictly confirmatory in nature. More precisely, secondary data are mainly used in exploratory research to propose causal–predictive relationships in situations that have little clearly defined theory (Hair, Matthews, et al., 2017; Hair, Hollingsworth, et al., 2017). Such settings require researchers to place greater emphasis on examining all possible relationships rather than achieving model fit (Nitzl, 2016). By its nature, this process creates large, complex models that can hardly be analyzed with the CB-SEM method. In contrast, due to its less stringent data requirements, PLS-SEM offers the flexibility needed for the interplay between theory and data (Nitzl, 2016). Or, as Wold (1982, p. 29) notes, "soft modeling is primarily designed for research contexts that are simultaneously data-rich and theory-skeletal." Furthermore, the increasing popularity of secondary data analysis (e.g., by using data that stem from company databases, social media, customer tracking, national statistical bureaus, or publicly available survey data) shifts the research focus from strictly confirmatory to predictive and causal–predictive modeling. Such research settings are a perfect fit for the prediction-oriented PLS-SEM approach and even more so when assessing out-of-sample prediction (Shmueli, et al., 2019).

PLS-SEM also proves valuable for analyzing secondary data from a measurement theory perspective. First, unlike survey measures, which are usually crafted to confirm a well-developed theory, measures used in secondary data sources are typ-

> **Table 1.4** Data considerations when applying PLS-SEM
>
> - The 10-time rule is not a reliable indication of sample size requirements in PLS-SEM. While statistical power analyses provide a more reliable minimum sample size estimate, researchers should primarily draw on the inverse square root method, which is superior in terms of precision and ease of use
> - When the construct measures meet recommended guidelines in terms of reliability and validity, results from CB-SEM and PLS-SEM are generally similar
> - PLS-SEM can handle extremely non-normal data (e.g., data with high levels of skewness)
> - Most missing value treatment procedures (e.g., mean replacement, pairwise deletion, EM, and nearest neighbor) can be used for reasonable levels of missing data (less than 5% missing per indicator) with limited effect on the analysis results
> - PLS-SEM works with metric, quasi-metric, and categorical (i.e., dummy-coded) scaled data, although there are certain limitations. Processing of data from discrete choice experiments requires specific designs and estimation routines
> - Due to its flexibility in handling different data and measurement types, PLS-SEM is the method of choice when analyzing secondary data
>
> Source: Hair et al. (2022), Chap. 1; used with permission by Sage

ically not created and refined over time for confirmatory analyses. Thus, achieving model fit is very unlikely with secondary data measures in most research situations when using CB-SEM. Second, researchers who use secondary data do not have the opportunity to revise or refine the measurement model to achieve fit. Third, a major advantage of PLS-SEM when using secondary data is that it permits the unrestricted use of single-item and formative measures. This is extremely valuable for research involving secondary data, because many measures included in corporate databases are artifacts, such as financial ratios and other firm-fixed factors (Henseler, 2017). Such artifacts typically are reported in the form of formative indices whose estimation dictates the use of PLS-SEM.

Table 1.4 summarizes key considerations related to data characteristics.

1.4.3 Model Characteristics

PLS-SEM is very flexible in its modeling properties. In its basic form, the PLS-SEM algorithm requires all models to not include circular relationships or loops of relationships between the latent variables in the structural model. Although causal loops are sometimes specified in business research, this characteristic does not limit the applicability of PLS-SEM, if such models are required as Lohmöller's (1989) extensions of the basic PLS-SEM algorithm allow for handling such model types. Other model specification requirements that constrain the use of CB-SEM, such as distribution and identification assumptions, are generally not relevant with PLS-SEM.

Measurement model difficulties are one of the major obstacles to obtaining a solution with CB-SEM. For instance, estimation of complex models with many latent variables and/or indicators is often impossible with CB-SEM. In contrast,

1.4 · Considerations When Applying PLS-SEM

PLS-SEM can easily be applied in such situations, since this method is not constrained by identification and other technical issues. Consideration of reflective and formative measurement models is a key issue in the application of SEM (Bollen & Diamantopoulos, 2017). PLS-SEM can easily handle both formative and reflective measurement models and is (therefore) considered the primary approach when the hypothesized model incorporates formative measures. CB-SEM can accommodate formative indicators, but to ensure model identification, they must follow distinct specification rules (Diamantopoulos & Riefler, 2011). In fact, the requirements often prevent running the analysis as originally planned. In contrast, PLS-SEM does not have such requirements and handles formative measurement models without any limitation. This also applies to model settings in which endogenous constructs are measured formatively. The applicability of CB-SEM to such model settings has been subject to considerable debate (Cadogan & Lee, 2013; Rigdon, 2014), but due to PLS-SEM's multistage estimation process (Tenenhaus et al., 2005), which separates measurement from structural model estimation, the inclusion of formatively measured endogenous constructs is not an issue in PLS-SEM (Rigdon et al., 2014). The only problematic issue is when high levels of collinearity exist between the indicator variables of a formative measurement model.

Different from CB-SEM, PLS-SEM facilitates easy specification of interaction terms to map moderation effects in a path model. This makes PLS-SEM the method of choice in simple moderation models and more complex conditional process models, which combine moderation and mediation effects (Sarstedt, Hair, et al., 2020). Similarly, higher-order constructs, which allow specifying a construct simultaneously on different levels of abstraction (Sarstedt et al., 2019), can readily be implemented in PLS-SEM.

Finally, PLS-SEM is capable of estimating very complex models. For example, if theoretical or conceptual assumptions support large models and sufficient data are available (i.e., meeting minimum sample size requirements), PLS-SEM can handle models of almost any size, including those with dozens of constructs and hundreds of indicator variables. As noted by Wold (1985), PLS-SEM is virtually without competition when path models with latent variables are complex in their structural relationships. ◘ Table 1.5 summarizes rules of thumb for PLS-SEM model considerations.

◘ **Table 1.5** Model considerations when choosing PLS-SEM

- PLS-SEM offers much flexibility in handling different measurement model setups. For example, PLS-SEM can handle reflective and formative measurement models as well as single-item measures without additional requirements or constraints
- The method allows for the specification of advanced model elements, such as interaction terms and higher-order constructs
- Model complexity is generally not an issue for PLS-SEM. As long as appropriate data meet minimum sample size requirements, the complexity of the structural model is virtually unrestricted

Source: Hair et al. (2022), Chap. 1; used with permission by Sage)

1.5 Guidelines for Choosing Between PLS-SEM and CB-SEM

Summarizing the previous discussions and drawing on Hair, Risher, et al. (2019), ◘ Table 1.6 displays the rules of thumb applied when deciding whether to use CB-SEM or PLS-SEM. As can be seen, PLS-SEM is not recommended as a universal alternative to CB-SEM. Both methods differ from a statistical point of view, are designed to achieve different objectives, and rely on different measurement philosophies. Neither of the techniques is generally superior to the other, and neither of them is appropriate for all situations (Petter, 2018). Hence, to answer the question of when to use PLS-SEM versus CB-SEM, researchers should focus on the characteristics and objectives that distinguish the two methods (Hair, Sarstedt, Ringle, & Mena, 2012). Broadly speaking, with its strong focus on model fit and in light of its extensive data requirements, CB-SEM is particularly suitable for testing a theory in the confinement of a concise theoretical model. However, if the primary research objective is prediction and explanation of target constructs (Rigdon, 2012), PLS-SEM should be given preference (Hair, Sarstedt, & Ringle, 2019; Hair, Hollingsworth, Randolph, & Chong, 2017).

In general, the strengths of PLS-SEM are CB-SEM's limitations and vice versa, although PLS-SEM is increasingly being applied for scale development and confir-

◘ **Table 1.6** Rules of thumb for choosing between PLS-SEM and CB-SEM

Use PLS-SEM when
The analysis is concerned with testing a theoretical framework from a prediction perspective, particularly out-of-sample prediction
The structural model is complex and includes many constructs, indicators, and/or model relationships
The research objective is to better understand increasing complexity by exploring theoretical extensions of established theories (exploratory research for theory development)
The path model includes one or more formatively measured constructs
The research consists of financial ratios or similar types of artifacts
The research is based on secondary data, which may lack a comprehensive substantiation on the grounds of measurement theory
A small population restricts the sample size (e.g., business-to-business research), but note that PLS-SEM also works very well with large sample sizes
Distribution issues are a concern, such as lack of normality
The research requires latent variable scores for follow-up analyses
Use CB-SEM when
The goal is theory testing and confirmation
Error terms require additional specification, such as the covariation
The structural model has circular relationships
The research requires a global goodness-of-fit criterion

Source: Adapted from Hair, Risher, et al. (2019). Copyright © 2019 by Emerald Publishing. Reprinted by permission of the publisher (Emerald Publishing; ► https://www.emeraldgrouppublishing.com)

1.5 · Guidelines for Choosing Between PLS-SEM and CB-SEM

mation (Hair, Howard, & Nitzl, 2020). It is important that researchers understand the different applications each approach was developed for and use them accordingly. Researchers need to apply the SEM technique that best suits their research objective, data characteristics, and model setup (Roldán & Sánchez-Franco, 2012).

Summary

SEM is a second-generation multivariate data analysis method, which facilitates analyzing the relationships among constructs, each measured by one or more indicator variables. The primary advantage of SEM is its ability to measure complex model relationships while accounting for measurement error inherent in the indicators. There are two types of SEM methods – CB-SEM and PLS-SEM. The two method types differ in the way they estimate the model parameters and their assumptions regarding the nature of measurement. Compared to CB-SEM, PLS-SEM emphasizes prediction, while simultaneously relaxing the demands regarding the data and specification of relationships. PLS-SEM aims at maximizing the endogenous latent variables' explained variance by estimating partial model relationships in an iterative sequence of ordinary least squares regressions. In contrast, CB-SEM estimates model parameters, such that the discrepancy between the estimated and sample covariance matrices is minimized. Instead of following a common factor model logic in estimating concept proxies as CB-SEM does, PLS-SEM calculates composites of indicators that serve as proxies for the concepts under research. The method is not constrained by identification issues, even if the model becomes complex – a situation that typically restricts CB-SEM use – and does not rely on distributional assumptions. Moreover, PLS-SEM can better handle formative measurement models and has advantages when sample sizes are relatively small as well as when analyzing secondary data. Researchers should consider the two SEM approaches as complementary and apply the SEM technique that best suits their research objective, data characteristics, and model setup.

❓ Exercise

Please answer the following questions:
1. When would SEM methods be more advantageous than first-generation techniques in understanding relationships between variables?
2. Why should social science researchers consider using SEM instead of multiple regression?
3. What are the most important considerations in deciding whether to use CB-SEM or PLS-SEM?
4. Under what circumstances is PLS-SEM the preferred method over CB-SEM?
5. Why is an understanding of theory important when deciding whether to use PLS-SEM or CB-SEM?
6. Why is PLS-SEM's prediction focus a major advantage of the method?

References

Abdi, H. (2010). Partial least squares regression and projection on latent structure regression (PLS-Regression). *WIREs Computational Statistics, 2*(1), 97–106.

Ali, F., Rasoolimanesh, S. M., Sarstedt, M., Ringle, C. M., & Ryu, K. (2018). An assessment of the use of partial least squares structural equation modeling (PLS-SEM) in hospitality research. *The International Journal of Contemporary Hospitality Management, 30*(1), 514–538.

Bagozzi, R. P., & Philipps, L. W. (1982). Representing and testing organizational theories: A holistic construal. *Administrative Science Quarterly, 27*(3), 459–489.

Barclay, D. W., Higgins, C. A., & Thompson, R. (1995). The partial least squares approach to causal modeling: Personal computer adoption and use as illustration. *Technology Studies, 2*(2), 285–309.

Bayonne, E., Marin-Garcia, J. A., & Alfalla-Luque, R. (2020). Partial least squares (PLS) in operations management research: Insights from a systematic literature review. *Journal of Industrial Engineering and Management, 13*(3), 565–597.

Binz Astrachan, C. B., Patel, V. K., & Wanzenried, G. (2014). A comparative study of CB-SEM and PLS-SEM for theory development in family firm research. *Journal of Family Business Strategy, 5*(1), 116–128.

Bollen, K. A., & Davies, W. R. (2009). Causal indicator models: Identification, estimation, and testing. *Structural Equation Modeling, 16*(3), 498–522.

Bollen, K. A., & Diamantopoulos, A. (2017). In defense of causal-formative indicators: A minority report. *Psychological Methods, 22*(3), 581–596.

Cadogan, J. W., & Lee, N. (2013). Improper use of endogenous formative variables. *Journal of Business Research, 66*(2), 233–241.

Cassel, C., Hackl, P., & Westlund, A. H. (1999). Robustness of partial least squares method for estimating latent variable quality structures. *Journal of Applied Statistics, 26*(4), 435–446.

Cepeda Carrión, G., Cegarra-Navarro, J.-G., & Cillo, V. (2019). Tips to use partial least squares structural equation modelling (PLS-SEM) in knowledge management. *Journal of Knowledge Management, 23*(1), 67–89.

Chin, W. W. (1998). The partial least squares approach to structural equation modeling. In G. A. Marcoulides (Ed.), *Modern methods for business research* (pp. 295–358). Mahwah, NJ: Erlbaum.

Chin, W. W., Cheah, J.-H., Liu, Y., Ting, H., Lim, X.-J., & Cham, T. H. (2020). Demystifying the role of causal-predictive modeling using partial least squares structural equation modeling in information systems research. *Industrial Management & Data Systems, 120*(12), 2161–2209.

Chin, W. W., Marcolin, B. L., & Newsted, P. R. (2003). A partial least squares latent variable modeling approach for measuring interaction effects: Results from a Monte Carlo simulation study and an electronic-mail emotion/adoption study. *Information Systems Research, 14*(2), 189–217.

Chin, W. W., & Newsted, P. R. (1999). Structural equation modeling analysis with small samples using partial least squares. In R. H. Hoyle (Ed.), *Statistical strategies for small sample research* (pp. 307–341). Thousand Oaks, CA: Sage.

Cochran, W. G. (1977). *Sampling techniques.* New York, NY: Wiley.

Cohen, J. (1992). A power primer. *Psychological Bulletin, 112*(1), 155–159.

Cole, D. A., & Preacher, K. J. (2014). Manifest variable path analysis: Potentially serious and misleading consequences due to uncorrected measurement error. *Psychological Methods, 19*(2), 300–315.

Diamantopoulos, A. (2006). The error term in formative measurement models: Interpretation and modeling implications. *Journal of Modelling in Management, 1*(1), 7–17.

Diamantopoulos, A., & Riefler, P. (2011). Using formative measures in international marketing models: A cautionary tale using consumer animosity as an example. In M. Sarstedt, M. Schwaiger, & C. R. Taylor (Eds.), *Measurement and research methods in international marketing (Advances in International Marketing, 22)* (pp. 11–30). Bingley: Emerald.

Dijkstra, T. K. (2014). PLS' Janus face—Response to Professor Rigdon's "Rethinking partial least squares modeling: In praise of simple methods". *Long Range Planning, 47*(3), 146–153.

do Valle, P. O., & Assaker, G. (2016). Using partial least squares structural equation modeling in tourism research: A review of past research and recommendations for future applications. *Journal of Travel Research, 55*(6), 695–708.

References

Faul, F., Erdfelder, E., Buchner, A., & Lang, A.-G. (2009). Statistical power analyses using G*Power 3.1: Tests for correlation and regression analyses. *Behavior Research Methods, 41*(4), 1149–1160.

Ghasemy, M., Teeroovengadum, V., Becker, J.-M., & Ringle, C. M. (2020). This fast car can move faster: A review of PLS-SEM application in higher education research. *Higher Education, 80*, 1121–1152.

Goodhue, D. L., Lewis, W., & Thompson, R. (2012). Does PLS have advantages for small sample size or non-normal data? *MIS Quarterly, 36*(3), 981–1001.

Grimm, M. S., & Wagner, R. (2020). The impact of missing values on PLS, ML and FIML model fit. *Archives of Data Science, Series A, 6*(1), 04.

Guttman, L. (1955). The determinacy of factor score matrices with implications for five other basic problems of common-factor theory. *British Journal of Statistical Psychology, 8*(2), 65–81.

Haenlein, M., & Kaplan, A. M. (2004). A beginner's guide to partial least squares analysis. *Understanding Statistics, 3*(4), 283–297.

Hair, J. F. (2020). Next generation prediction metrics for composite-based PLS-SEM. *Industrial Management & Data Systems, 121*(1), 5–11.

Hair, J. F., Binz Astrachan, C., Moisescu, O. I., Radomir, L., Sarstedt, M., Vaithilingam, S., & Ringle, C. M. (2020). Executing and interpreting applications of PLS-SEM: Updates for family business researchers. *Journal of Family Business Strategy, 12*(3), 100392.

Hair, J. F., Black, W. C., Babin, B. J., & Anderson, R. E. (2019). *Multivariate data analysis* (8th ed.). London: Cengage Learning.

Hair, J. F., Hollingsworth, C. L., Randolph, A. B., & Chong, A. Y. L. (2017). An updated and expanded assessment of PLS-SEM in information systems research. *Industrial Management & Data Systems, 117*(3), 442–458.

Hair, J. F., Howard, M. C., & Nitzl, C. (2020). Assessing measurement model quality in PLS-SEM using confirmatory composite analysis. *Journal of Business Research, 109*, 101–110.

Hair, J. F., Hult, G. T. M., Ringle, C. M., & Sarstedt, M. (2022). *A primer on partial least squares structural equation modeling (PLS-SEM)* (3rd ed.). Thousand Oaks, CA: Sage.

Hair, J. F., Matthews, L., Matthews, R., & Sarstedt, M. (2017). PLS-SEM or CB-SEM: Updated guidelines on which method to use. *International Journal of Multivariate Data Analysis, 1*(2), 107–123.

Hair, J. F., Page, M. J., & Brunsveld, N. (2020). *Essentials of business research methods* (4th ed.). New York, NY: Routledge.

Hair, J. F., Ringle, C. M., Gudergan, S. P., Fischer, A., Nitzl, C., & Menictas, C. (2019). Partial least squares structural equation modeling-based discrete choice modeling: An illustration in modeling retailer choice. *Business Research, 12*(1), 115–142.

Hair, J. F., Ringle, C. M., & Sarstedt, M. (2011). PLS-SEM: Indeed a silver bullet. *Journal of Marketing Theory and Practice, 19*(2), 139–151.

Hair, J. F., Risher, J. J., Sarstedt, M., & Ringle, C. M. (2019). When to use and how to report the results of PLS-SEM. *European Business Review, 31*(1), 2–24.

Hair, J. F., & Sarstedt, M. (2019). Composites vs. factors: Implications for choosing the right SEM method. *Project Management Journal, 50*(6), 1–6.

Hair, J. F., & Sarstedt, M. (2021). Explanation plus prediction – The logical focus of project management research. *Project Management Journal, 52*(4), 319–322.

Hair, J. F., Sarstedt, M., Pieper, T., & Ringle, C. M. (2012). The use of partial least squares structural equation modeling in strategic management research: A review of past practices and recommendations for future applications. *Long Range Planning, 45*(5–6), 320–340.

Hair, J. F., Sarstedt, M., & Ringle, C. M. (2019). Rethinking some of the rethinking of partial least squares. *European Journal of Marketing, 53*(4), 566–584.

Hair, J. F., Sarstedt, M., Ringle, C. M., & Gudergan, S. P. (2018). *Advanced issues in partial least squares structural equation modeling (PLS-SEM)*. Thousand Oaks, CA: Sage.

Hair, J. F., Sarstedt, M., Ringle, C. M., & Mena, J. A. (2012). An assessment of the use of partial least squares structural equation modeling in marketing research. *Journal of the Academy of Marketing Science, 40*(3), 414–433.

Henseler, J. (2017). Bridging design and behavioral research with variance-based structural equation modeling. *Journal of Advertising, 46*(1), 178–192.

Henseler, J., Dijkstra, T. K., Sarstedt, M., Ringle, C. M., Diamantopoulos, A., Straub, D. W., Ketchen, D. J., Hair, J. F., Hult, G. T. M., & Calantone, R. J. (2014). Common beliefs and reality about partial least squares: Comments on Rönkkö & Evermann (2013). *Organizational Research Methods, 17*(1), 182–209.

Hui, B. S., & Wold, H. (1982). Consistency and consistency at large of partial least squares estimates. In K. G. Jöreskog & H. Wold (Eds.), *Systems under indirect observation, part II* (pp. 119–130). Amsterdam: North-Holland.

Hwang, H., Sarstedt, M., Cheah, J.-H., & Ringle, C. M. (2020). A concept analysis of methodological research on composite-based structural equation modeling: Bridging PLSPM and GSCA. *Behaviormetrika, 47*(1), 219–241.

JCGM/WG1 (2008). Joint committee for guides in metrology/working group on the expression of uncertainty in measurement (JCGM/WG1): Evaluation of measurement data - guide to the expression of uncertainty in measurement. Retrieved from https://www.bipm.org/utils/common/documents/jcgm/JCGM_100_2008_E.pdf. Access date: 26 Feb 2021

Jöreskog, K. G. (1973). A general method for estimating a linear structural equation system. In A. S. Goldberger & O. D. Duncan (Eds.), *Structural equation models in the social sciences* (pp. 255–284). New York, NJ: Seminar Press.

Jöreskog, K. G., & Wold, H. (1982). The ML and PLS techniques for modeling with latent variables: Historical and comparative aspects. In H. Wold & K. G. Jöreskog (Eds.), *Systems under indirect observation, part I* (pp. 263–270). Amsterdam: North-Holland.

Kaufmann, L., & Gaeckler, J. (2015). A structured review of partial least squares in supply chain management research. *Journal of Purchasing and Supply Management, 21*(4), 259–272.

Khan, G., Sarstedt, M., Shiau, W.-L., Hair, J. F., Ringle, C. M., & Fritze, M. (2019). Methodological research on partial least squares structural equation modeling (PLS-SEM): A social network analysis. *Internet Research, 29*(3), 407–429.

Kock, N., & Hadaya, P. (2018). Minimum sample size estimation in PLS-SEM: The inverse square root and gamma-exponential methods. *Information Systems Journal, 28*(1), 227–261.

Lee, L., Petter, S., Fayard, D., & Robinson, S. (2011). On the use of partial least squares path modeling in accounting research. *International Journal of Accounting Information Systems, 12*(4), 305–328.

Lohmöller, J.-B. (1989). *Latent variable path modeling with partial least squares*. Heidelberg: Physica.

Manley, S. C., Hair, J. F., Williams, R. I., & McDowell, W. C. (2020). Essential new PLS-SEM analysis methods for your entrepreneurship analytical toolbox. *International Entrepreneurship and Management Journal,* forthcoming.

Marcoulides, G. A., & Chin, W. W. (2013). You write but others read: Common methodological misunderstandings in PLS and related methods. In H. Abdi, W. W. Chin, V. Esposito Vinzi, G. Russolillo, & Trinchera (Eds.), *New perspectives in partial least squares and related methods* (pp. 31–64). New York, NY: Springer.

Marcoulides, G. A., & Saunders, C. (2006). PLS: A silver bullet? *MIS Quarterly, 30*(2), iii–ix.

Mateos-Aparicio, G. (2011). Partial least squares (PLS) methods: Origins, evolution, and application to social sciences. *Communications in Statistics–Theory and Methods, 40*(13), 2305–2317.

McDonald, R. P. (1996). Path analysis with composite variables. *Multivariate Behavioral Research, 31*(2), 239–270.

Nitzl, C. (2016). The use of partial least squares structural equation modelling (PLS-SEM) in management accounting research: Directions for future theory development. *Journal of Accounting Literature, 37*(December), 19–35.

Nitzl, C., & Chin, W. W. (2017). The case of partial least squares (PLS) path modeling in managerial accounting research. *Journal of Management Control, 28*, 137–156.

Peng, D. X., & Lai, F. (2012). Using partial least squares in operations management research: A practical guideline and summary of past research. *Journal of Operations Management, 30*(6), 467–480.

Petter, S. (2018). "Haters gonna hate": PLS and information systems research. *ACM SIGMIS Database: the DATABASE for Advances in Information Systems, 49*(2), 10–13.

Rasoolimanesh, S. M., Ringle, C. M., Sarstedt, M., & Olya, H. (2021). The combined use of prediction-oriented approaches: Partial least squares-structural equation modeling and fuzzyset quali-

References

tative comparative analysis. *International Journal of Contemporary Hospitality Management*, 33(5), 1571–1592.

Reinartz, W., Haenlein, M., & Henseler, J. (2009). An empirical comparison of the efficacy of covariance-based and variance-based SEM. *International Journal of Research in Marketing*, 26(4), 332–344.

Rhemtulla, M., van Bork, R., & Borsboom, D. (2020). Worse than measurement error: Consequences of inappropriate latent variable measurement models. *Psychological Methods*, 25(1), 30–45.

Richter, N. F., Cepeda Carrión, G., Roldán, J. L., & Ringle, C. M. (2016). European management research using partial least squares structural equation modeling (PLS-SEM): Editorial. *European Management Journal*, 34(6), 589–597.

Richter, N. F., Schubring, S., Hauff, S., Ringle, C. M., & Sarstedt, M. (2020). When predictors of outcomes are necessary: Guidelines for the combined use of PLS-SEM and NCA. *Industrial Management & Data Systems*, 120(12), 2243–2267.

Richter, N. F., Sinkovics, R. R., Ringle, C. M., & Schlägel, C. (2016). A critical look at the use of SEM in International Business Research. *International Marketing Review*, 33(3), 376–404.

Rigdon, E. E. (2012). Rethinking partial least squares path modeling: In praise of simple methods. *Long Range Planning*, 45(5–6), 341–358.

Rigdon, E. E. (2013). Partial least squares path modeling. In G. R. Hancock & R. D. Mueller (Eds.), *Structural equation modeling: A second course* (2nd ed., pp. 81–116). Charlotte, NC: Information Age.

Rigdon, E. E. (2014). Rethinking partial least squares path modeling: Breaking chains and forging ahead. *Long Range Planning*, 47(3), 161–167.

Rigdon, E. E. (2016). Choosing PLS path modeling as analytical method in European management research: A realist perspective. *European Management Journal*, 34(6), 598–605.

Rigdon, E. E., Becker, J.-M., Rai, A., Ringle, C. M., Diamantopoulos, A., Karahanna, E., Straub, D. W., & Dijkstra, T. K. (2014). Conflating antecedents and formative indicators: A comment on Aguirre-Urreta and Marakas. *Information Systems Research*, 25(4), 780–784.

Rigdon, E. E., Becker, J.-M., & Sarstedt, M. (2019a). Factor indeterminacy as metrological uncertainty: Implications for advancing psychological measurement. *Multivariate Behavioral Research*, 54(3), 429–443.

Rigdon, E. E., Becker, J.-M., & Sarstedt, M. (2019b). Parceling cannot reduce factor indeterminacy in factor analysis: A research note. *Psychometrika*, 84(3), 772–780.

Rigdon, E. E., Sarstedt, M., & Becker, J.-M. (2020). Quantify uncertainty in behavioral research. *Nature Human Behaviour*, 4(4), 329–331.

Rigdon, E. E., & Sarstedt, M. (2021). Accounting for uncertainty in the measurement of unobservable marketing phenomena. In H. Baumgartner & B. Weijters (Eds.), *Review of marketing research*, forthcoming.

Rigdon, E. E., Sarstedt, M., & Ringle, C. M. (2017). On comparing results from CB-SEM and PLS-SEM: Five perspectives and five recommendations. *Marketing ZFP*, 39(3), 4–16.

Ringle, C. M., Sarstedt, M., Mitchell, R., & Gudergan, S. P. (2020). Partial least squares structural equation modeling in HRM research. *International Journal of Human Resource Management*, 31(12), 1617–1643.

Ringle, C. M., Sarstedt, M., & Straub, D. W. (2012). A critical look at the use of PLS-SEM in *MIS Quarterly*. *MIS Quarterly*, 36(1), iii–xiv.

Roldán, J. L., & Sánchez-Franco, M. J. (2012). Variance-based structural equation modeling: Guidelines for using partial least squares in information systems research. In M. Mora, O. Gelman, A. L. Steenkamp, & M. Raisinghani (Eds.), *Research methodologies, innovations and philosophies in software systems engineering and information systems* (pp. 193–221). Hershey, PA: IGI Global.

Rönkkö, M., & Evermann, J. (2013). A critical examination of common beliefs about partial least squares path modeling. *Organizational Research Methods*, 16(3), 425–448.

Rönkkö, M., McIntosh, C. N., & Antonakis, J. (2015). On the adoption of partial least squares in psychological research: Caveat emptor. *Personality and Individual Differences*, 87(December), 76–84.

Rossiter, J. R. (2011). *Measurement for the social sciences: The C-OAR-SE method and why it must replace psychometrics*. Berlin: Springer.

Russo, D., & Stol, K.-J. (2021). PLS-SEM for software engineering research: An introduction and survey. *ACM Computing Surveys*, 54(4), Article 78.

Sarstedt, M., Bengart, P., Shaltoni, A. M., & Lehmann, S. (2018). The use of sampling methods in advertising research: A gap between theory and practice. *International Journal of Advertising*, 37(4), 650–663.

Sarstedt, M., Hair, J. F., Cheah, J.-H., Becker, J.-M., & Ringle, C. M. (2019). How to specify, estimate, and validate higher-order models. *Australasian Marketing Journal*, 27(3), 197–211.

Sarstedt, M., Hair, J. F., Nitzl, C., Ringle, C. M., & Howard, M. C. (2020). Beyond a tandem analysis of SEM and PROCESS: Use PLS-SEM for mediation analyses! *International Journal of Market Research*, 62(3), 288–299.

Sarstedt, M., Hair, J. F., Ringle, C. M., Thiele, K. O., & Gudergan, S. P. (2016). Estimation issues with PLS and CB-SEM: Where the bias lies! *Journal of Business Research*, 69(10), 3998–4010.

Sarstedt, M., & Mooi, E. A. (2019). *A concise guide to market research: The process, data, and methods using IBM SPSS statistics* (3rd ed.). Berlin: Springer.

Sarstedt, M., Ringle, C. M., Cheah, J.-H., Ting, H., Moisescu, O. I., & Radomir, L. (2020). Structural model robustness checks in PLS-SEM. *Tourism Economics*, 26(4), 531–554.

Sarstedt, M., & Danks, N. (2021). Prediction in HRM research—A gap between rhetoric and reality. *Human Resource Management Journal*, forthcoming.

Sarstedt, M., Ringle, C. M., Smith, D., Reams, R., & Hair, J. F. (2014). Partial least squares structural equation modeling (PLS-SEM): A useful tool for family business researchers. *Journal of Family Business Strategy*, 5(1), 105–115.

Schneeweiß, H. (1991). Models with latent variables: LISREL versus PLS. *Statistica Neerlandica*, 45(2), 145–157.

Schuberth, F., Henseler, J., & Dijkstra, T. K. (2018). Confirmatory composite analysis. *Frontiers in Psychology*, 9, 2541.

Tenenhaus, M., Esposito Vinzi, V., Chatelin, Y.-M., & Lauro, C. (2005). PLS path modeling. *Computational Statistics & Data Analysis*, 48(1), 159–205.

Usakli, A., & Kucukergin, K. G. (2018). Using partial least squares structural equation modeling in hospitality and tourism: Do researchers follow practical guidelines? *International Journal of Contemporary Hospitality Management*, 30(11), 3462–3512.

Willaby, H., Costa, D., Burns, B., MacCann, C., & Roberts, R. (2015). Testing complex models with small sample sizes: A historical overview and empirical demonstration of what partial least squares (PLS) can offer differential psychology. *Personality and Individual Differences*, 84, 73–78.

Wold, H. (1982). Soft modeling: The basic design and some extensions. In K. G. Jöreskog & H. Wold (Eds.), *Systems under indirect observations, part II* (pp. 1–54). Amsterdam: North-Holland.

Wold, H. (1985). Partial least squares. In S. Kotz & N. L. Johnson (Eds.), *Encyclopedia of statistical sciences* (pp. 581–591). New York, NY: John Wiley.

Wold, S., Sjöström, M., & Eriksson, L. (2001). PLS-regression: A basic tool of chemometrics. *Chemometrics and Intelligent Laboratory Systems*, 58(2), 109–130.

Zeng, N., Liu, Y., Gong, P., Hertogh, M., & König, M. (2021). Do right PLS and do PLS right: A critical review of the application on PLS in construction management research. *Frontiers of Engineering Management*, 8(3), 356–369.

Suggested Readings

Chin, W. W. (1998). The partial least squares approach to structural equation modeling. In G. A. Marcoulides (Ed.), *Modern methods for business research* (pp. 295–358). Mahwah, NJ: Erlbaum.

Hair, J. F., Binz Astrachan, C., Moisescu, O. I., Radomir, L., Sarstedt, M., Vaithilingam, S., & Ringle, C. M. (2020). Executing and interpreting applications of PLS-SEM: Updates for family business researchers. *Journal of Family Business Strategy*, 12(3), 100392.

Suggested Readings

Jöreskog, K. G., & Wold, H. (1982). The ML and PLS techniques for modeling with latent variables: Historical and comparative aspects. In H. Wold & K. G. Jöreskog (Eds.), *Systems under indirect observation, part I* (pp. 263–270). Amsterdam: North-Holland.

Lohmöller, J.-B. (1989). *Latent variable path modeling with partial least squares*. Heidelberg: Physica.

Rigdon, E. E. (2012). Rethinking partial least squares path modeling: In praise of simple methods. *Long Range Planning, 45*(5–6), 341–358.

Sarstedt, M., Hair, J. F., Ringle, C. M., Thiele, K. O., & Gudergan, S. P. (2016). Estimation issues with PLS and CBSEM: Where the bias lies! *Journal of Business Research, 69*(10), 3998–4010.

Tenenhaus, M., Esposito Vinzi, V., Chatelin, Y.-M., & Lauro, C. (2005). PLS path modeling. *Computational Statistics & Data Analysis, 48*(1), 159–205.

Wold, H. (1982). Soft modeling: The basic design and some extensions. In K. G. Jöreskog & H. Wold (Eds.), *Systems under indirect observations, part II* (pp. 1–54). Amsterdam: North-Holland.

Open Access This chapter is licensed under the terms of the Creative Commons Attribution 4.0 International License (http://creativecommons.org/licenses/by/4.0/), which permits use, sharing, adaptation, distribution and reproduction in any medium or format, as long as you give appropriate credit to the original author(s) and the source, provide a link to the Creative Commons license and indicate if changes were made.

The images or other third party material in this chapter are included in the chapter's Creative Commons license, unless indicated otherwise in a credit line to the material. If material is not included in the chapter's Creative Commons license and your intended use is not permitted by statutory regulation or exceeds the permitted use, you will need to obtain permission directly from the copyright holder.

Overview of R and RStudio

Contents

2.1 Introduction – 32

2.2 Explaining Our Syntax – 32

2.3 Computational Statistics Using Programming – 33

2.4 Introducing R and RStudio – 34
2.4.1 Installing R and RStudio – 35
2.4.2 Layout of RStudio – 36

2.5 Organizing Your Projects – 37

2.6 Packages – 39

2.7 Writing R Scripts – 41

2.8 How to Find Help in RStudio – 41

References – 46

© The Author(s) 2021
J. F. Hair Jr. et al., *Partial Least Squares Structural Equation Modeling (PLS-SEM) Using R*, Classroom Companion: Business,
https://doi.org/10.1007/978-3-030-80519-7_2

Learning Objectives
After reading this chapter, you will understand:
1. The syntax and formatting for code used throughout this textbook.
2. Why computational statistical languages are so powerful and useful.
3. The layout and interface of R and RStudio.
4. How to manage R scripts and projects.
5. How to install and use packages.
6. How to seek help when bugs or errors are encountered.

2.1 Introduction

This chapter introduces the two software packages that will be used throughout this textbook. Software **packages** are a series of software functions and features with a similar purpose bundled into a single set. First, we introduce the R statistical computing language (R Core Team, 2021), which is the software language we will use to import and clean data as well as create and analyze PLS path models. We will then introduce the RStudio (RStudio Team, 2021) application, which is an integrated development environment that enables you to easily and productively conduct computational analyses using the R language. We will explain how to download and install the software required, how to interact with the software, and how to store your data and code.

We then offer a basic introduction to writing analytic scripts in R. This textbook will not serve as a comprehensive resource for learning R, so we will share further resources for learning this programming language and helpful documentation on the Internet. Additionally, we will provide examples of R code throughout this textbook, so we start by looking at the syntax and formatting that we will use to distinguish code from regular text.

2.2 Explaining Our Syntax

Throughout this textbook, it will be necessary to discuss various elements of the code when explaining how to perform analytic operations using R. For the sake of clarity, we will use a distinguishable formatting and syntax of code in either code blocks or embedded in the text. Code in the R language will be formatted as follows: `vector <- c(1, 2, 3, 4, 5)`. To distinguish code embedded in the text from regular text, the code will be bolded; and to distinguish arguments from regular code, the arguments will be italicized (*weights* =, *data* =). Furthermore, construct and variable names in the text will be italicized to distinguish them (e.g., *QUAL* and *qual_1*). We will use a similar format when code is used in a larger block. ◘ Table 2.1 provides a summary of the syntax and format of code that we use in this textbook. You may want to refer back to it when we show larger blocks of code.

2.3 · Computational Statistics Using Programming

□ Table 2.1 Syntax conventions used in this textbook (source: authors' own table)

Syntax	Example
Code, objects, and functions in text	`summary()`, `vector <- c(1, 2, 3, 4, 5)`
Arguments in text	`weights =`, `data =`
Construct and variable names in text	*QUAL* and *qual_1*
Comments in code block	`# Estimating the model`
Code, variables, functions, construct, and indicator names in code block	`summary()`, `corp_rep_data`, *QUAL*, and *qual_1*
Arguments in code block	`weights =`, `data =`

The code block below also includes comments that describe the purpose of the following line of code. Comments are not run by the programming language and only serve as communication to other users of the code about the purpose. Comments in the R language begin with a pound symbol ("#"), and we will display them in gray (again, see the code block below).

```
# Create a vector of integers
vector <- c(1, 2, 3, 4, 5)
```

2.3 Computational Statistics Using Programming

Data analytics using computationally intensive methods is becoming an increasingly important, strategic capability for companies to transform the data collected during business activities into information that can assist effective decision-making and policy creation. Similarly, academic research is rapidly adopting computational methods, involving the implementation of analytic techniques for inferential analysis and machine learning into computer programs (Hair & Sarstedt, 2021). Thus, researchers who learn and adopt computational methods will have the advantage of being able to apply and adapt the latest techniques to their research, while also being competent and conversant with industry trends.

We expect that many quantitative researchers are already familiar with certain types of software to analyze data: spreadsheet software, such as Apache OpenOffice Calc (▶ https://www.openoffice.org/product/calc.html) or Microsoft Excel (▶ https://www.microsoft.com/microsoft-365/excel), and more graphical, menu-driven software like IBM SPSS (▶ https://www.ibm.com/products/spss-statistics) and Statistica (▶ https://www.statsoft.de/de/software/statistica). Spreadsheet software has long been of value to business researchers, since a familiar ledger or balance book metaphor is adopted that predates computers. Spreadsheets are advantageous for smaller datasets, since they make it easy for users to manipulate data in tabular form and obtain quick results in the same interface as their data.

Graphical, menu-driven software has also become popular during recent decades, since it is easier to learn and process for many users and provides rich visualizations. Both of these advantages allow software like SPSS and Tableau (▶ https://www.tableau.com) to facilitate communication between stakeholders and conduct data exploration interactively in meetings.

Computational analytics using programming syntax has been present since the earliest days of computing, but has recently gained new popularity from the advent of big data analytics, artificial intelligence, and the larger data science movement. By programming in a syntactic language, such as R or Python (Van Rossum & Drake, 1995), analysts can apply complex methods that are not easy to parameterize with spreadsheet or graphical, menu-driven software. Computation offers analysts the ability to run simulations that test particular scenarios and create novel solutions and custom visualizations, which were not considered by others, or are rather specific to one's own use case. Moreover, the code that analysts generate serves as a manifest – or recipe – of their workflow that can be shared with other analysts or even deployed into online products and platforms. Finally, having code allows others to test, repeat, or replicate analyses in perfect detail – steps that are vital to modern applications of the scientific process (Rigdon, Sarstedt, & Becker, 2020). It is not surprising, therefore, that computational methods have become an integral component of the data science revolution in both industry and academia.

2.4 Introducing R and RStudio

R is a free, open-source software, which enables users to write and execute code that analyzes data. Readers should note that the name "R" can refer to both the programming language and the primary software that runs code written in this language. However, unless otherwise specified, in this book, R refers to the language. Further, **open source** refers to the kind of software whose underlying code is made freely available and is generally open to suggested improvements or new features built by others. The open-source nature of the R software makes code written in the R language highly reproducible, shareable, testable, scalable, and deployable to larger automated applications. An ever-expanding community of R users supports, tests, documents, and provides add-on resources for each other.

R (R Core Team, 2021) is an alternate implementation of the earlier S programming language, which was first developed by Ross Ihaka and Robert Gentleman in 1991 (Hornik & Leisch, 2002). The R language had been developed for several years, became free and open source in 1995, and started to gain attention with the first stable release on the Comprehensive R Archive Network (CRAN; ▶ http://www.r-project.org) in February 2000. CRAN serves as a vetted repository where reliable add-on packages of R code libraries can be freely contributed to or downloaded by R users around the world (packages are discussed in more detail in ▶ Sect. 2.6). The SEMinR package for PLS-SEM (Ray, Danks, & Valdez, 2021) we use in this book is also available on CRAN.

The R language was designed with computational statistics in mind. In its simplest form, it can be run from your operating system's command line or from the R

2.4 · Introducing R and RStudio

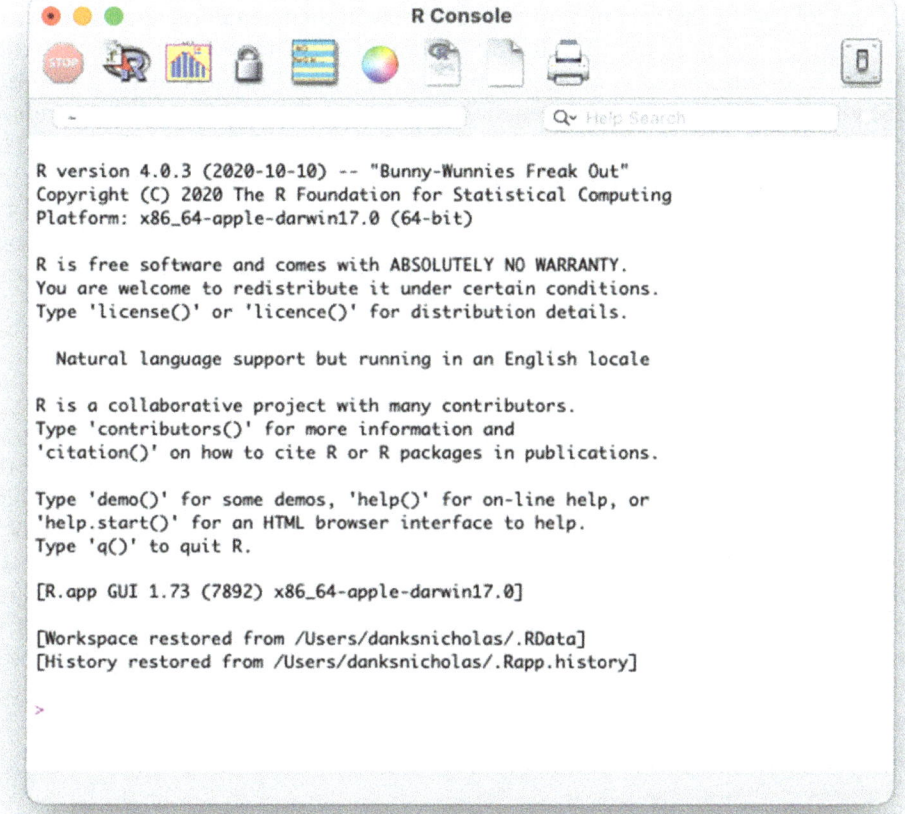

Fig. 2.1 The R console. (Source: authors' screenshot from R)

console (Fig. 2.1). However, we recommend using R from the convenience of an **integrated development environment (IDE)**, such as RStudio. An IDE is a programming environment that offers tools such as project management, tabs for easily managing multiple script files, and additional developer tools. We discuss the layout of the RStudio IDE in more detail in the next section. Throughout this book, we will demonstrate the use of R from within the RStudio IDE.

2.4.1 Installing R and RStudio

Before installing RStudio, the R software for executing code in the programming language must be installed on your operating system. The latest version of the R software for your operating system is available from the CRAN archive at the ► http://www.r-project.org website. Once you visit that website, click on the **Download R** link, select the mirror website closest to your location, and then choose the download file made for your operating system. Execute the download file and follow the instructions; the R software will then install on your computer.

Next, you will need to install RStudio from this website (▶ http://www.rstudio.com/). To do so, hover your mouse pointer over the **Products** menu and select **RStudio** from the dropdown menu. On the next page, click on the **Download RStudio Desktop** button, and once again click **Download RStudio Desktop**. The website will offer you the relevant version for your operating system. Execute the download file and follow the instructions. The RStudio IDE will then install on your computer. With both the R software and RStudio software installed on your computer, you can proceed to become familiar with the RStudio layout and interface.

2.4.2 Layout of RStudio

The RStudio desktop in its standard form comes with a layout of four primary windows: (1) In the upper-left corner is the source window; (2) in the upper right are the environment, history, connections, build, and git windows; (3) in the bottom left are the console and terminal windows; and (4) in the bottom right are the files, plots, packages, help, and viewer windows (◨ Fig. 2.2). Note that the source window only shows when data have been loaded. We will discuss this step in ▶ Chap. 3. Some of these windows are only available when settings have been enabled. For example, the git tab is only available when version control has been enabled and the build tab is only available when a package is being built. ◨ Table 2.2 describes the various windows and their uses in more detail.

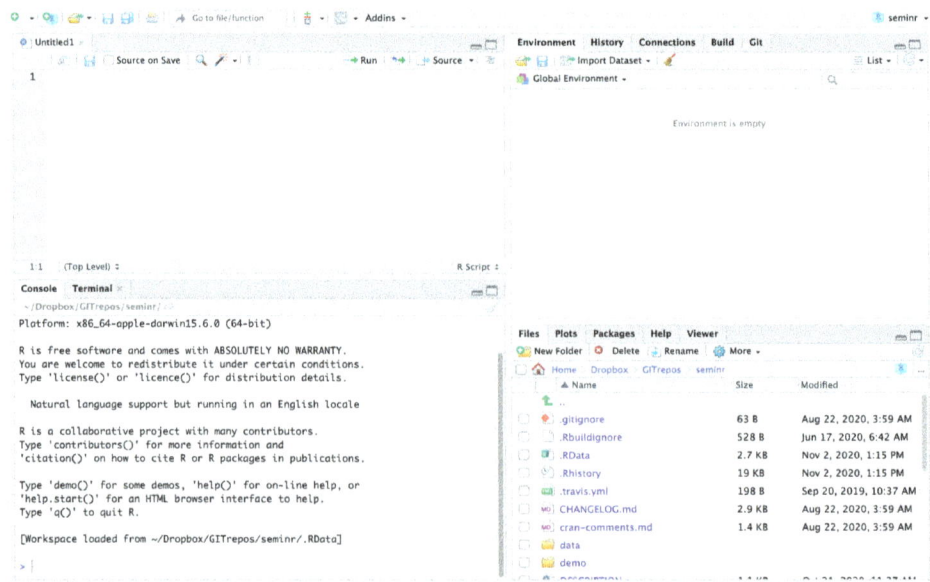

◨ **Fig. 2.2** The RStudio IDE desktop layout. (Source: authors' screenshot from RStudio)

◘ **Table 2.2** Table of the RStudio IDE desktop tabs, layout, and purpose

Tab	Window	Purpose
Connections, build, and git	Upper right	These tabs are beyond the scope of this textbook
Console	Lower left	The console tab provides a R console for entering commands and printing output
Environment	Upper right	The environment contains all objects created and saved to the local R workspace. These objects are interactive and can be loaded into the source window
Files	Lower right	The files tab provides a file explorer to navigate, duplicate, move, and copy files
Help	Lower right	The help tab provides help on packages, functions, and topics. Help can be searched using the search option, or specific help files can be accessed using the ? operator
History	Upper right	History records all keystrokes and commands entered into the console. Command history can be copied from here to the source or console tab
Packages	Lower right	The packages tab provides a list of available packages, their version number, and whether they have been sourced into the environment
Plots	Lower right	The plots tab provides an output location for plots, which can be navigated using the left and right arrows
Source	Upper left	The active source code files are displayed in the source window. Files can be edited and saved. Data objects can also be inspected in the source window
Terminal	Lower left	The terminal tab provides a console for entering commands to the operating system
Viewer	Lower right	The viewer tab is used to view local web content

Source: authors' own table

2.5 Organizing Your Projects

Organizing projects is much like organizing your documents in regular folders on your computer. The only major difference is you will need to remember where files are stored when loading files into or saving files out of the R environment. That is, you need to know the address of the file relative to the file you are editing. Often, users of R will create a catchall project (named workspace), in which they store their R script files, data files, and output files for multiple analyses or projects. This approach can quickly lead to chaos – the mixing of projects and the overwriting of crucial code and data files. Instead, we recommend you create separate projects and

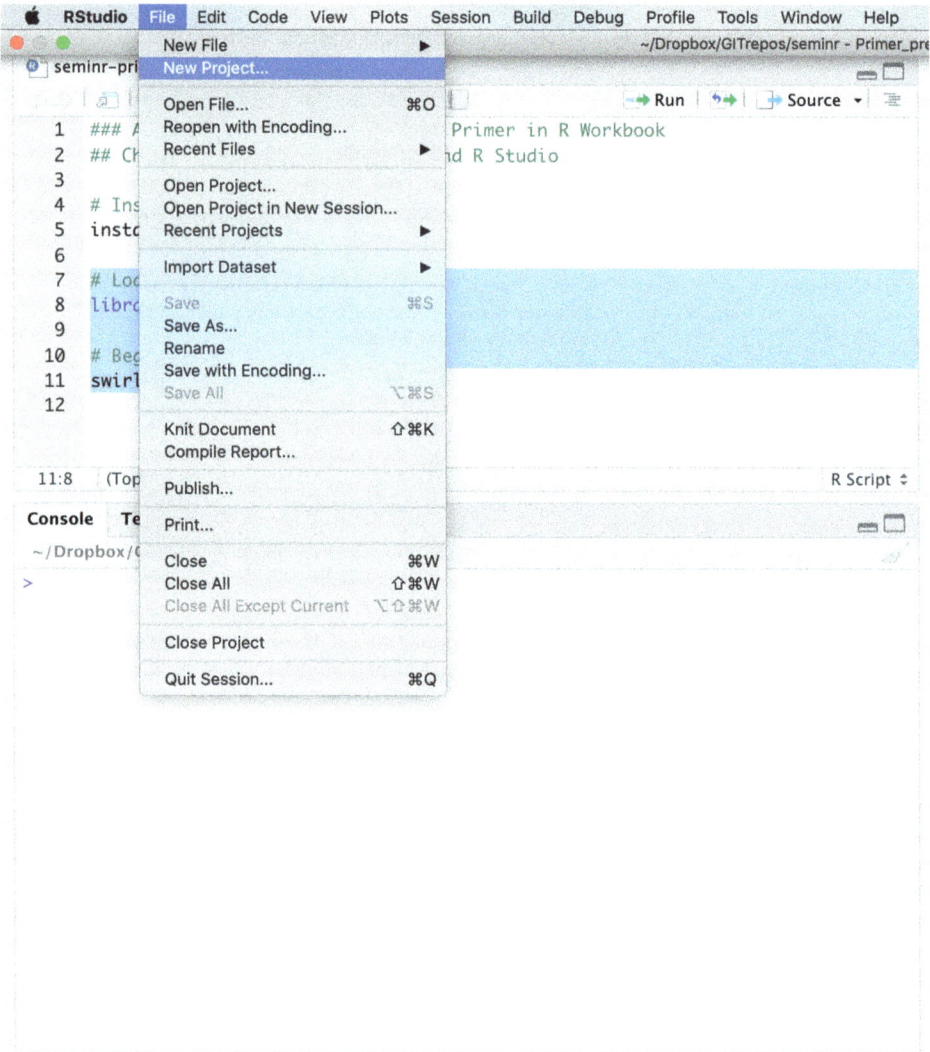

● **Fig. 2.3** Creating a new project in RStudio. (Source: authors' screenshot from RStudio)

organize them carefully, so that you keep the contents of each project separately and provide some order to your workflow.

To begin a new project in RStudio, click on the **File** dropdown menu, and select **New Project…** (● Fig. 2.3). The **Create Project** window will then open and guide you through creating a new project. When you create your first project, you need to set up a **New Directory** which stores all your project files. Next, click on **New Project**. In the dialog box that follows, specify a project name under **Directory name** and choose a folder in which the project files should be stored. Finally, click on **Create Project**.

An important feature of an R project is that the working directory, in which the project will be conducted, is specified. If at any time you wish to change the work-

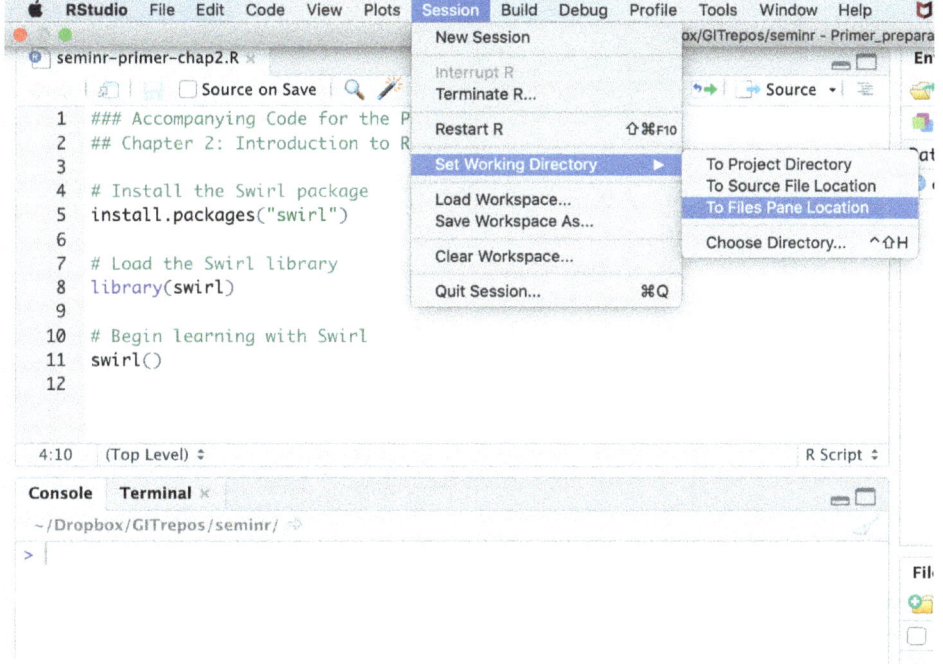

□ **Fig. 2.4** Changing the working directory. (Source: authors' screenshot from RStudio)

ing directory, this can be done by clicking on the **Session** dropdown menu, selecting **Set Working Directory,** and then specifying the correct location (□ Fig. 2.4).

R project details are stored in an .Rproj file in the project directory. In addition, the environment containing any objects saved to memory is stored in the .Rdata file, and the history of keystrokes and commands run in the console is stored in an .Rhistory file. Thus, a snapshot is kept of your activity in the project, which is reloaded every time you reopen the project. Note, however, that the packages required to run your code need to be reloaded every time you reopen a project and are not stored in the snapshot.

2.6 Packages

R includes a lot of preinstalled **packages** containing many of the standard functions and algorithms you will use in your statistical computations. Examples of such standard functions are `mean()` and `sd()` for calculating the mean and standard deviation of a vector, respectively, or `lm()` for generating linear regression models. While you should be able to fulfill much of your computational needs with the standard packages bundled in R, you might need to install further software libraries containing newer or more complicated algorithms. Such software libraries are bundled as packages that, when installed, add a new range of functions and operations. Examples of popular packages are `dplyr`, `ggplot`, and, of course, the package used in this book, `seminr`.

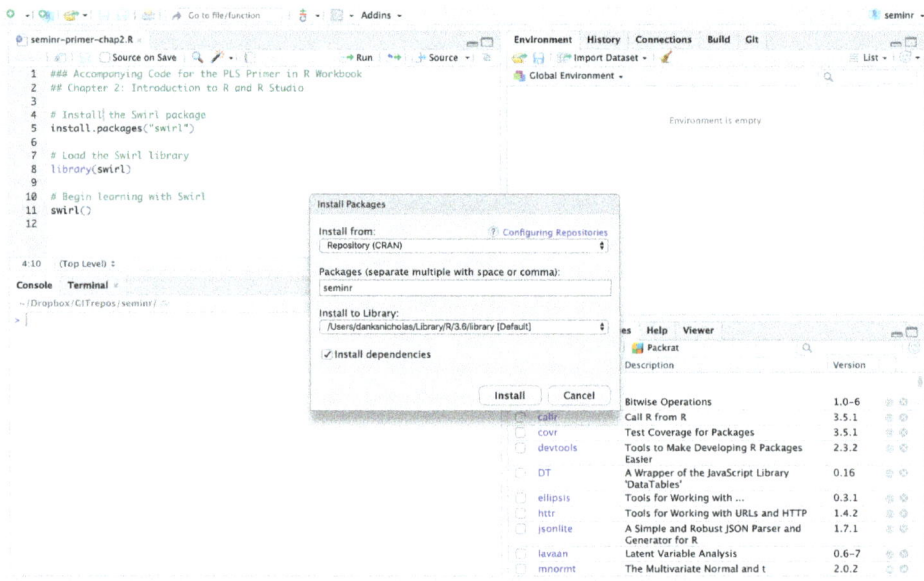

Fig. 2.5 Installing packages from the RStudio IDE. (Source: authors' screenshot from RStudio)

A majority of packages are hosted on CRAN. The packages hosted on CRAN have met certain criteria to qualify for being published in the CRAN archive, such as having documentation, being tested, and kept up to date with the latest versions of R. These packages can be installed from the command line or from the packages tab (Fig. 2.1 and   Table 2.2). Note that you will need internet access to install packages from CRAN. To install new packages, select the **Packages** tab in the lower right window of the RStudio IDE, click the **Install** button, set **Install from** to **Repository (CRAN)**, and enter the package name in the **Packages** field: "seminr" (Fig. 2.5). Next, click on **Install**.

Packages can also be installed from the command line using the `install.packages()` function. In this case, we wish to install the `swirl` package, which teaches you R programming (see ▶ Sect. 2.7 for more details on the `swirl` package). We therefore set the *pkgs* parameter equal to `"swirl"`.

```
# Install the Swirl package
install.packages(pkgs = "swirl")
```

Note that packages are installed to the local software library on your computer but are not loaded into the RStudio local environment. Once a package is installed, it will be available for computation in R but has to be loaded using the `library()` function prior to use. Packages must be loaded in each session if you wish to use the functions in this library. If the package is not loaded in a new session (i.e., after opening and rerunning R), the features will not be available in your session until you load the package by using the `library()` function.

```
# Load the Swirl package into the environment
library(swirl)
```

2.7 Writing R Scripts

Computational analyses are conducted by writing a series of instructions to the computer on how to import data, modify data, run algorithms for analyzing the data, and then report the results of those analyses. These instructions take the form of **R scripts** that are typically entered into a file, which contains all the scripts related to a single analysis or computation. These R script files have the suffix .R and are stored in your project directory.

To successfully conduct such analyses, you need to learn the form and function of the scripts that R can process. As indicated above, a key reason for using a free, open-source software, like R, is the community support and resources typically found for such software. A simple Internet search with keywords "R coding lesson" should provide hundreds of high-quality resources. We recommend swirl (▶ https://swirlstats.com/), which teaches you R programming by offering simple and useful lessons. This package helps the user become experienced at working with R's command-based interface and can be downloaded and used from the R console command line.

```
# Begin learning with Swirl
swirl()
```

In addition to online tutorials and code lessons, there are many free e-books describing both introductory and advanced usage of R and RStudio. A good archive for textbooks is available at the CRAN website (▶ https://www.r-project.org/other-docs.html). We highly recommend the book *R for Data Science* (Wickham & Grolemund, 2016). As we continue with this chapter and the textbook, we assume that you have studied the basics of using R and are comfortable with the language. We now turn our attention to overcoming the various challenges you might encounter, while writing R scripts and when using the SEMinR package.

2.8 How to Find Help in RStudio

Due to the complexity of a programming language – and the almost endless number of software libraries that can be installed adding to the functions and resources available to you – it can become difficult to keep track of how functions are called, what arguments they take, and what output they provide. Packages have a range of files that are designed to document and demonstrate the use of the functions they provide. These files take the form of R documentation, vignettes, and demonstration files. In this section, we discuss how to access information on using a function by inspecting these documents.

All packages submitted to CRAN are required to have sufficient documentation to describe the functions they add to your software library. For each function, there should be a matching R documentation file that can be accessed. **R documentation** describes the purpose, input, implementation, and output of a function and provides examples applying the syntax. The contents of an R document are described in ◘ Table 2.3. This documentation can be accessed in the **help** tab in the lower right window of the RStudio IDE. Help topics and functions can be

◘ **Table 2.3** Excerpt of contents of the R documentation for **read.csv()**

Section	Description	Example	
Description	A brief description of the function's purpose	Reads a file in table format and creates a data frame from it, which includes cases corresponding to lines and variables to fields	
Usage	The usage of the function	read.csv(file, header = TRUE, sep =",", quote ="\"", dec =".", fill = TRUE, comment.char ="",...)	
Arguments	The arguments that must be assigned to the function to execute and their corresponding description	File	The name of the file, which the data are to be read from
		header	A logical value indicating whether the file contains the names of the variables as its first line. If missing, the value is determined from the file format: header is set to TRUE if, and only if, the first row contains one fewer field than the number of columns
		Sep	The field separator character. Values on each line of the file are separated by this character. If sep = "" (the default for read.table), the separator is "white space" that is one or more spaces, tabs, new lines, or carriage returns
		quote	The set of quoting characters. To disable quoting altogether, use quote = ""
		Dec	The character used in the file for decimal points
		...	Further arguments to be passed to read table
Examples	An example for executing the function	## using count.fields to handle unknown maximum number of fields ## when fill = TRUE test1 <- c(1:5, "6,7", "8,9,10") tf <- tempfile() writeLines(test1, tf) read.csv(tf, fill = TRUE) # 1 column	

Source: authors' own table

2.8 · How to Find Help in RStudio

searched for in the search field of the help window or from the command line in the console window using the **?** operator. For example, we can search for help on the **read.csv()** function by typing the following into the console window in RStudio:

```
# Searching for help using the ? operator
?read.csv
```

In ◘ Fig. 2.6, we can see an excerpt of the contents of the R documentation for **read.csv()**. This information will be displayed in the **help** tab in the lower right window of the RStudio IDE and provides us with details on the purpose, arguments, and usage of the function and a demonstration example. When encountering a new function or an error, the R documentation is the first place to look in. For a full list of available R documentation topics for a package, click on the **Pack-**

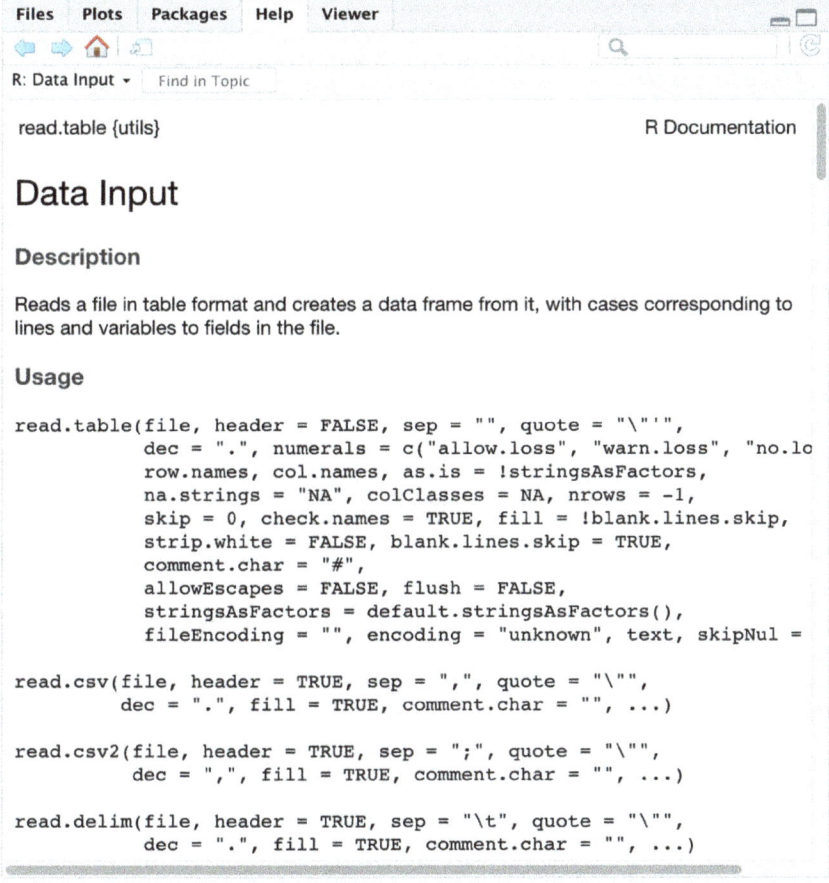

◘ Fig. 2.6 R documentation for the **read.csv()** function. (Source: authors' screenshot from RStudio)

SEMinR

Soumya Ray & Nicholas Danks

Dec 31, 2020

- Introduction
- Setup
- Data
- Measurement model description
  - Specifying measurement models with constructs
  - Describe individual constructs as composite or reflective
  - Converting composite models into reflective models
  - Specifying construct measurement items
  - Item associations (CBSEM only)
  - Interaction terms
- Structural model description
  - Specify structural model of relationships between constructs
  - Specify structural paths with
- Model Estimation
  - Consistent PLS (PLSc) estimation for common factors
  - Bootstrapping PLS models for significance
- Reporting the model estimation results
  - Reporting the estimated model
  - Reporting results of a bootstrapped PLS
  - Reporting confidence intervals for direct and mediated bootstrapped structural paths
  - Reporting data descriptive statistics and construct descriptive statistics
- References

Introduction

SEMinR brings a friendly syntax to creating and estimating structural equation models (SEM). The syntax allows applied practitioners of SEM to use terminology that is very close to their familiar modeling terms (e.g., reflective, composite, interactions) instead of specifying underlying

Fig. 2.7 The SEMinR vignette. (Source: authors' screenshot from RStudio)

ages tab in the bottom right window and select the package name (highlighted in blue). The **Help** tab will then open with the full list of documentation available for that package.

Another very important document to consult for help using a package or function is the vignette. **Vignettes** are designed as an all-purpose user's guide for the package – they describe the problem that the package seeks to solve and how it is used. This document usually describes the functioning of the package in detail and provides examples and demonstrations of the problems and solutions. You can access a list of vignettes installed by calling the `vignette()` function. This will output a list of available vignettes to an R vignette tab in the top left window of RStudio. You can then run `vignette("SEMinR")` to access a particular vignette – in this case, the vignette for the package SEMinR (**Fig. 2.7**).

```
# Check all vignettes available in R
vignette()

# Load the SEMinR vignette
vignette("SEMinR")
```

2.8 · How to Find Help in RStudio

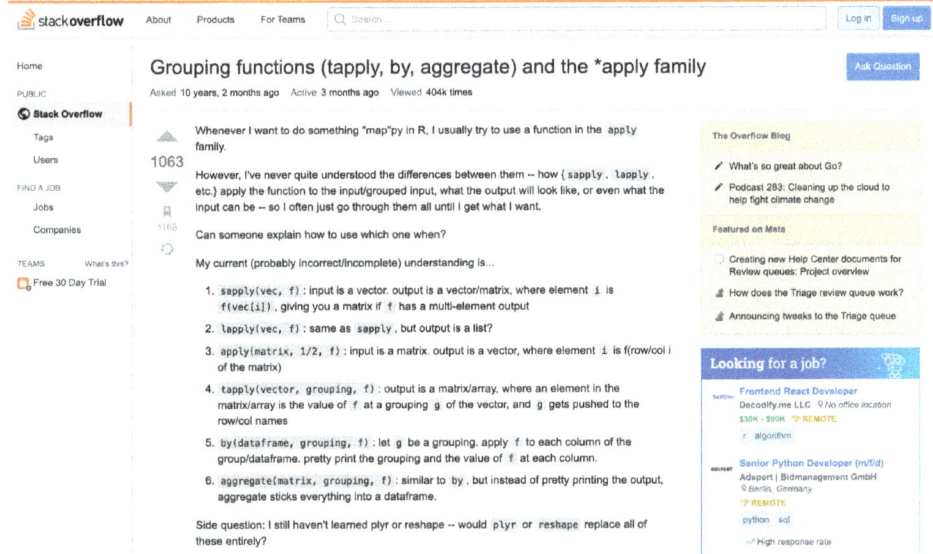

■ **Fig. 2.8** Finding help online using Stack Overflow. (Source: authors' screenshot from ▶ https://stackoverflow.com/)

Another source of help is using the demonstration code that comes bundled with most R packages. These demonstration files typically include an example dataset and model to demonstrate the purpose of the package's functions. To check all available demonstration files, use the **demo()** function. For the specific demonstration of the European Customer Satisfaction Index (ECSI) model (Eklöf & Westlund, 2002) in the SEMinR package, as originally presented by Tenenhaus, Esposito Vinzi, Chatelin, and Lauro (2005), use **demo("seminr-pls-ecsi")**.

```
# Check all demos available in R
demo()

# Load the SEMinR ECSI demo
demo("seminr-pls-ecsi")
```

A final invaluable source of help can be found by accessing the greater R community on platforms such as Stack Overflow (▶ https://stackoverflow.com/). These ask-and-answer forums put you in touch with seasoned veterans who can provide useful tips and other options for executing all your favorite R packages and functions. Members of these communities typically respond quickly and can provide excellent advice and solutions (■ Fig. 2.8).

Summary
In this chapter, we introduced the R statistical programming language and its popular development environment, RStudio. You should now be familiar with the layout and functionality of RStudio, creating, downloading, and managing projects and RScript files. If you encounter a bug or a function that is unfamiliar, you should now have the requisite tools (and knowledge) for seeking out appropriate help. We strongly recommend the careful study of an introductory program to learning the R language. We also recommend the **swirl** package for learning R and provide some ideas to assist you in finding supplementary resources and gaining access to useful material.

Exercise
In this chapter, we recommend the use of the **swirl** package to learn basic coding concepts and become familiar with the popular functions in R (see ▶ Sects. 2.6 and 2.7 on installing and loading **swirl**). Please complete the following lessons in the **swirl** package:
1. Basic building blocks
2. Workspaces and files
3. Sequences of numbers
4. Vectors
5. Missing values
6. Subsetting vectors
7. Matrices and data frames
8. Logic
9. Functions

References

Core Team, R. (2021). *R: A language and environment for statistical computing [computer software]*. Vienna: R Foundation for Statistical Computing. Retrieved from https://www.R-project.org/

Eklöf, J. A., & Westlund, A. H. (2002). The pan-European customer satisfaction index program: Current work and the way ahead. *Total Quality Management, 13*(8), 1099–1106.

Hair, J. F., & Sarstedt, M. (2021). Data, measurement, and causal inferences in machine learning: Opportunities and challenges for marketing. *Journal of Marketing Theory & Practice, 29*(1), 65–77.

Hornik, K., & Leisch, F. (2002). Vienna and R: Love, marriage and the future. In R. Dutter (Ed.), *Festschrift 50 Jahre Österreichische Statistische Gesellschaft* (pp. 61–70). Vienna: Österreichische Statistische Gesellschaft.

Ray, S., Danks, N. P., & Valdez, A.C. (2021). Seminr: Building and Estimating Structural Equation models [computer software]. R package version 2.1.0. Retrieved from: https://cran.r-project.org/web/packages/seminr/index.html

Rigdon, E. E., Sarstedt, M., & Becker, J.-M. (2020). Quantify uncertainty in behavioral research. *Nature Human Behaviour, 4*, 329–331.

RStudio Team. (2021). *RStudio: Integrated development for R [computer software]*. Boston, MA: RStudio, PBC. Retrieved from: http://www.rstudio.com/

Tenenhaus, M., Esposito Vinzi, V., Chatelin, Y.-M., & Lauro, C. (2005). PLS path modeling. *Computational Statistics & Data Analysis, 48*(1), 159–205.

Van Rossum, G., & Drake, F. L. (1995). *Python reference manual*. Amsterdam: Centrum voor Wiskunde en Informatica.

Wickham, H., & Grolemund, G. (2016). *R for data science*. Sebastopol, CA: O'Reilly Media. Retrieved from: https://r4ds.had.co.nz/

Suggested Readings

Grolemund, G. (2014). *Hands-on programming with R: Write your own functions and simulations*. Sebastopol, CA: O'Reilly Media.

Wickham, H. (2019). *Advanced R*. Boca Raton, FL: CRC press. Retrieved from: https://adv-r.hadley.nz/

Wickham, H., & Grolemund, G. (2016). *R for data science*. Sebastopol, CA: O'Reilly Media. Retrieved from: https://r4ds.had.co.nz/

Open Access This chapter is licensed under the terms of the Creative Commons Attribution 4.0 International License (http://creativecommons.org/licenses/by/4.0/), which permits use, sharing, adaptation, distribution and reproduction in any medium or format, as long as you give appropriate credit to the original author(s) and the source, provide a link to the Creative Commons license and indicate if changes were made.

The images or other third party material in this chapter are included in the chapter's Creative Commons license, unless indicated otherwise in a credit line to the material. If material is not included in the chapter's Creative Commons license and your intended use is not permitted by statutory regulation or exceeds the permitted use, you will need to obtain permission directly from the copyright holder.

The SEMinR Package

Contents

3.1 The Corporate Reputation Model – 52

3.2 Loading and Cleaning the Data – 53

3.3 Specifying the Measurement Models – 56

3.4 Specifying the Structural Model – 59

3.5 Estimating the Model – 59

3.6 Summarizing the Model – 62

3.7 Bootstrapping the Model – 64

3.8 Plotting, Printing, and Exporting Results to Articles – 66

References – 73

Learning Objectives
After reading this chapter, you should understand:
1. Loading and cleaning data for use in model estimation
2. Specifying measurement models in SEMinR syntax
3. Specifying the structural model in SEMinR syntax
4. Estimating a PLS path model using SEMinR syntax
5. Summarizing a PLS path model in SEMinR
6. Bootstrapping a PLS path model in SEMinR
7. Accessing the contents of the summary objects
8. Exporting the PLS-SEM results for reporting

SEMinR is a software package developed for the R statistical environment (R Core Team, 2021) that brings a user-friendly syntax to creating and estimating structural equation models. SEMinR is open source, which means that anyone can inspect, modify, and enhance the source code. SEMinR is distributed under a GNU General Public License version 3 (GPL-3), implying it is completely free for personal, academic, and commercial use – as long as any changes made to it, or applications built using it, are also open source.

SEMinR is hosted on GitHub (▶ https://github.com/sem-in-r/seminr). We encourage users to follow the GitHub page for SEMinR and contribute to this project or use the *issues* feature to report bugs or problems. Users of SEMinR can also interact with the developers and each other at the Facebook group (▶ https://www.facebook.com/groups/seminr). Participants regularly discuss recent developments, best practices, and tutorials on basic functionality of SEMinR. We also encourage you to follow this Facebook group for updates on bugs, issues, and new features.

The SEMinR syntax enables applied practitioners of PLS-SEM to use terminology that is very close to their familiar modeling terms (e.g., reflective, composite, and interactions), instead of specifying underlying matrices and covariances. Specifically, the syntax was designed to:
- Provide a domain-specific language to build and estimate PLS path models in R
- Use both variance-based PLS-SEM and covariance-based SEM (CB-SEM) to estimate composite and common factor models (▶ Chap. 1)
- Simply and quickly specify model relationships and more complex model elements, such as interaction terms (see ▶ Chap. 8) and higher-order constructs (Sarstedt, Hair Jr, Cheah, Becker, & Ringle, 2019)

SEMinR uses its own PLS-SEM estimation engine and integrates with the lavaan package (Rosseel, 2012) for CB-SEM estimation. SEMinR supports the state of the art of PLS-SEM and beyond. The development team regularly improves the program, incorporates new methods, and supports the users with useful reporting options in their analyses.

In ▶ Chap. 2, we introduced R and RStudio. After reading that chapter, you should now be familiar with writing scripts, creating objects, and installing packages. In this chapter, we discuss how to use the SEMinR package. The first step is to install the SEMinR package and load it into the RStudio environment (◘ Fig. 3.1). SEMinR was built using R version 4.0.3 – depending on how recently you installed R and RStudio, you might need to update these software files to the latest version before installing SEMinR. Refer to ▶ Chap. 2 for instructions on installing the latest versions of R and RStudio.

```
# Download and install the SEMinR package
# You only need to do this once to equip
# Rstudio on your computer with SEMinR
install.packages("seminr")

# Make the SEMinR library ready to use
# You must do this every time you restart Rstudio and wish to
use SEMinR
library(seminr)
```

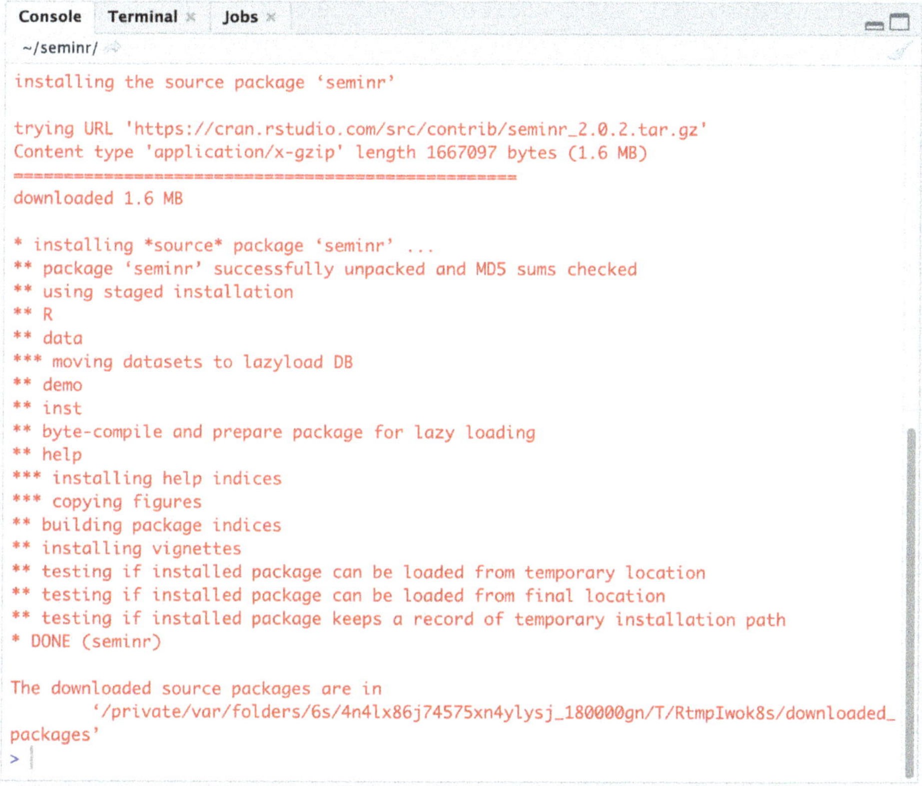

```
~/seminr/
installing the source package 'seminr'

trying URL 'https://cran.rstudio.com/src/contrib/seminr_2.0.2.tar.gz'
Content type 'application/x-gzip' length 1667097 bytes (1.6 MB)
==================================================
downloaded 1.6 MB

* installing *source* package 'seminr' ...
** package 'seminr' successfully unpacked and MD5 sums checked
** using staged installation
** R
** data
*** moving datasets to lazyload DB
** demo
** inst
** byte-compile and prepare package for lazy loading
** help
*** installing help indices
*** copying figures
** building package indices
** installing vignettes
** testing if installed package can be loaded from temporary location
** testing if installed package can be loaded from final location
** testing if installed package keeps a record of temporary installation path
* DONE (seminr)

The downloaded source packages are in
        '/private/var/folders/6s/4n4lx86j74575xn4ylysj_180000gn/T/RtmpIwok8s/downloaded_packages'
>
```

◘ **Fig. 3.1** Installing and loading the SEMinR package. (Source: authors' screenshot from RStudio)

3.1 The Corporate Reputation Model

With the SEMinR package installed and loaded to the environment, we now introduce the example dataset and model that will be used throughout this textbook. We draw on Eberl's (2010) corporate reputation model, which is also used in *A Primer on Partial Least Squares Structural Equation Modeling (PLS-SEM)* (Hair, Hult, Ringle, & Sarstedt, 2022). The goal of the model is to explain the effects of corporate reputation on customer satisfaction (*CUSA*) and, ultimately, customer loyalty (*CUSL*). Corporate reputation represents a company's overall evaluation by its stakeholders (Helm, Eggert, & Garnefeld, 2010). This construct is measured using two dimensions. One dimension represents cognitive evaluations of the company, which is the company's competence (*COMP*). The second dimension captures affective judgments, which determine the company's likeability (*LIKE*). Research has shown that the model performs favorably (in terms of convergent validity and predictive validity) compared to alternative reputation measures (Sarstedt, Wilczynski, & Melewar, 2013).

In summary, the simple corporate reputation model has two main theoretical components: (1) the target constructs of interest – namely, *CUSA* and *CUSL* (endogenous constructs) – and (2) the two corporate reputation dimensions *COMP* and *LIKE* (exogenous constructs), which are key determinants of the target constructs. ◘ Figure 3.2 shows the constructs and their relationships.

Each of these constructs is measured by means of multiple indicators, except satisfaction. For instance, the endogenous construct *COMP* is reflectively measured by three indicator variables, *comp_1*, *comp_2*, and *comp_3*. Respondents answered on a scale from 1 (totally disagree) to 7 (completely agree) to evaluate the statements that these three items represent (◘ Table 3.1). Two other constructs in the simple model (*CUSL* and *LIKE*) can be described in a similar manner, and the third (*CUSA*) has only a single indicator. ◘ Table 3.1 summarizes the indicator wordings for the four constructs considered in this simple corporate reputation

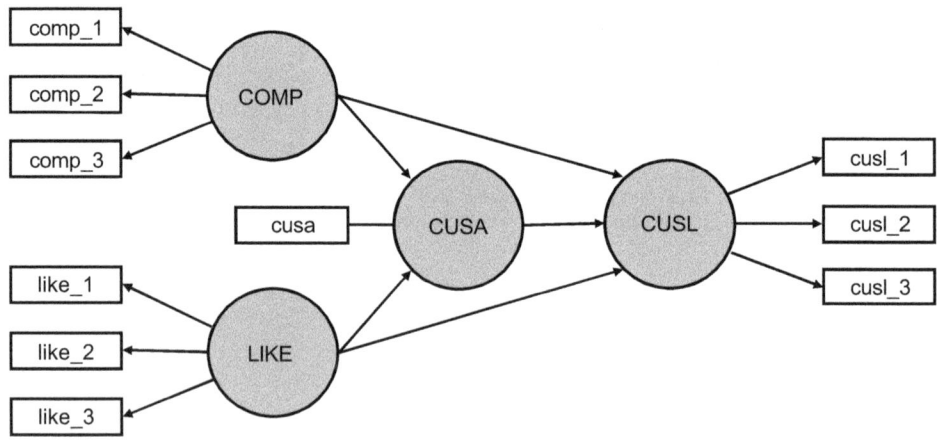

◘ **Fig. 3.2** Simple corporate reputation model. (Source: authors' own figure)

3.2 · Loading and Cleaning the Data

Table 3.1 Indicators for the reflectively measured constructs of corporate reputation model

Competence (*COMP*)	
comp_1	[The company] is a top competitor in its market
comp_2	As far as I know, [the company] is recognized worldwide
comp_3	I believe [the company] performs at a premium level
Likeability (*LIKE*)	
like_1	[The company] is a company I can better identify with than other companies
like_2	[The company] is a company I would regret more not having if it no longer existed than I would other companies
like_3	I regard [the company] as a likeable company
Customer satisfaction (*CUSA*)	
cusa	I am satisfied with [the company]
Customer loyalty (*CUSL*)	
cusl_1	I would recommend [company] to friends and relatives
cusl_2	If I had to choose again, I would choose [company] as my mobile phone service provider
cusl_3	I will remain a customer of [company] in the future

Source: Hair et al. (2022), Chap. 2; used with permission by Sage

model. In ► Chap. 5, we will extend the simple model by adding four formatively measured constructs.

Now that you are familiar with the reputation model, we will demonstrate the syntax used by SEMinR. Briefly, there are four steps to specify and estimate a structural equation model using SEMinR:
1. Loading and cleaning the data
2. Specifying the measurement models
3. Specifying the structural model
4. Estimating, bootstrapping, and summarizing the model

3.2 Loading and Cleaning the Data

When estimating a PLS-SEM model, SEMinR expects you to have already loaded your data into an object. This data object is usually a `data.frame` class object, but SEMinR will also accept a `matrix` class object. For more information about these objects, you can access the R documentation using the `?` operator (e.g., `?matrix`). The `read.csv()` function allows you to load data into R if the data file is in a .csv (comma-separated value) or .txt (text) format. Note that there are other packages that can be used to load data in Microsoft Excel's .xlsx format or other popular data formats.

Comma-separated value (CSV) files are a type of text file, whose lines contain the data of each subject or case of your dataset. The values in each line correspond to the different variables of interest (e.g., the first, second, or third value of a line corresponds with the first, second, or third variable in the dataset, from left to right). These values are typically separated by commas but can also be separated by other special characters (e.g., semicolons). The first line of the file typically consists of variable names, called the header line, and is also separated by commas or other special characters. Thus, a variable will have its name in the first row at a certain position (e.g., fifth data entry), and its values will be in all the following lines of data at the same position (e.g., also at the fifth data entry position). Files in a .csv format are a popular way of storing datasets, and we will use it as an example in this chapter. Many software packages, such as Microsoft Excel and SPSS, can export data into a .csv format.

We can load data from a .csv file using the `read.csv()` function. Remember that you can use the ? operator to find help about a function in R (e.g., use `?read.csv`) at any time. ◘ Table 3.2 shows several arguments for the `read.csv()` function as included in the help file.

In this section, we will demonstrate how to load a .csv file into the RStudio global environment. The file we will use is called Corporate Reputation Data.csv and can be downloaded from the book's website at ▶ https://www.pls-sem.net/downloads/. Once you have downloaded the Corporate Reputation Data.csv file, transfer it to your R project working directory as discussed in ▶ Chap. 2. If you inspect the Corporate Reputation Data.csv file in a text editor, it should appear as in the screenshot in ◘ Fig. 3.3. Note that this .csv file uses semicolons instead of commas to separate variable names and values.

In ◘ Fig. 3.3, we see that this sample data has a header row consisting of the variable names (columns). In addition, the semicolon (;) is used as a separator

◘ **Table 3.2** A (shortened) list of arguments for the `read.csv()` function

Argument	Value
`file`	The name of the file to be uploaded from the working directory
`header`	A logical value indicating whether the file contains column headers as the first line. Default is "TRUE"
`sep`	The character used as a separator between fields in the data file. Default is a comma ","
`dec`	The character used in the file for decimal points. Default is a period "."

Note: Use `?read.csv()` for the full documentation
Source: authors' own table

3.2 · Loading and Cleaning the Data

```
serviceprovider;servicetype;csor_1;csor_2;csor_3;csor_4;csor_5;csor_global;attr_1;attr_2;attr_3
;attr_global;perf_1;perf_2;perf_3;perf_4;perf_5;perf_global;qual_1;qual_2;qual_3;qual_4;qual_5;
qual_6;qual_7;qual_8;qual_global;like_1;like_2;like_3;comp_1;comp_2;comp_3;cusl_1;cusl_2;cusl_3
;cusa;age;education;occupation;nphh;sample_type;mga_1;mga_2;mga_3;mga_4
3;2;3;3;3;3;3;5;1;3;5;5;4;2;5;6;6;5;6;4;2;4;4;2;5;6;3;1;2;4;5;5;5;3;3;5;2;3;11;5;1;2;1;1;1
3;2;2;5;6;4;6;6;6;6;6;6;6;6;6;6;6;6;6;6;6;5;6;6;5;6;6;6;6;6;7;6;7;7;7;7;6;3;-99;2;1;2;1;1;1
3;2;3;1;2;2;4;4;5;6;5;6;4;4;2;5;4;5;3;4;3;4;3;5;4;4;5;5;5;5;4;5;2;7;7;5;6;2;3;11;2;1;2;1;1;1
3;2;3;3;5;3;5;5;3;7;5;7;5;5;5;3;3;6;6;5;6;6;7;5;4;5;6;7;6;5;6;6;4;4;7;7;7;6;3;4;11;1;1;2;1;1;1
3;2;4;3;4;4;4;4;6;6;6;6;5;6;7;6;5;7;6;5;7;7;6;6;6;7;7;6;6;7;6;4;6;6;7;7;6;2;2;12;5;1;2;1;1;1
3;2;3;3;4;3;3;4;4;1;5;5;6;6;4;5;6;6;5;5;5;6;3;4;6;6;7;7;3;4;4;7;7;7;6;2;2;11;1;1;2;1;1;1
1;1;7;5;7;3;3;7;5;7;3;7;4;7;6;5;4;7;5;5;6;4;7;7;4;4;7;4;1;7;7;5;7;7;7;7;7;1;2;11;3;1;1;1;2;1
1;1;4;1;3;3;2;4;4;1;5;5;5;6;6;4;7;6;3;2;1;6;5;1;5;6;4;3;4;6;6;6;6;5;4;6;4;5;2;3;3;1;1;1;2;1
3;1;7;5;6;4;6;7;6;3;7;7;7;7;4;6;7;7;7;6;7;6;7;6;7;7;7;5;7;5;7;6;5;7;7;6;1;1;11;4;1;1;1;1;1
3;2;4;1;5;2;4;5;5;1;6;6;6;5;4;6;6;6;5;6;7;7;4;7;7;6;6;6;6;5;5;6;6;7;6;3;2;2;2;1;2;1;1;1;1
1;1;4;6;4;4;4;6;4;1;3;4;4;6;4;4;4;6;6;6;7;5;6;6;6;4;7;4;4;4;4;4;4;4;2;1;3;2;4;6;4;1;1;1;2;1
1;1;4;3;4;4;3;4;4;2;5;5;4;3;4;3;4;4;6;5;5;5;4;4;5;3;6;4;6;5;3;6;2;4;5;6;4;2;2;11;3;1;1;1;2;1
2;2;4;2;3;2;2;4;4;1;4;4;3;5;4;3;4;5;4;2;4;3;4;3;3;4;4;2;4;4;3;3;4;4;5;5;4;5;3;5;4;1;2;2;1;1
1;2;4;4;4;4;3;4;7;4;5;7;7;7;6;7;7;7;4;3;5;3;5;5;4;7;7;3;4;7;5;7;7;7;7;7;5;6;2;-99;2;1;2;1;2;1
1;2;5;3;5;4;1;5;4;1;6;6;4;7;7;6;7;7;1;2;1;3;2;5;5;6;6;6;4;7;3;7;7;4;1;1;5;3;1;3;5;1;2;1;2;1
1;2;3;2;3;1;1;3;4;4;2;4;3;4;4;4;6;4;4;5;5;4;4;3;3;5;5;3;2;3;3;3;3;4;4;4;3;2;-99;1;1;2;1;2;1
1;1;6;3;2;3;4;6;7;1;3;7;7;7;6;3;4;7;7;7;6;6;1;7;2;7;7;3;5;3;6;7;6;2;1;3;4;2;2;2;4;1;1;1;2;1
1;1;5;5;5;4;5;5;5;1;6;6;5;6;6;6;5;6;6;4;6;5;6;6;5;6;6;7;6;6;7;6;6;7;6;6;2;2;4;1;1;1;2;1
2;2;3;1;3;1;3;3;4;3;3;4;3;5;5;7;6;7;7;7;7;1;7;3;5;7;7;5;6;6;6;7;7;6;7;7;7;4;2;6;2;1;2;2;1;1
1;2;5;5;4;4;5;5;7;3;6;7;3;4;5;5;6;6;6;4;5;6;6;6;7;5;7;6;6;5;6;6;5;3;4;4;1;2;1;1;2;1
2;1;2;1;1;1;1;2;3;2;1;3;1;3;3;4;2;4;1;2;2;5;3;3;1;2;5;1;1;1;1;2;3;3;3;3;7;6;3;1;-99;4;1;1;2;1;1
1;2;6;6;7;4;7;7;5;3;7;7;7;5;7;7;7;6;7;7;7;7;5;7;7;7;7;7;7;7;7;5;7;7;7;2;3;11;2;1;2;1;2;1
2;1;7;3;6;6;6;7;7;7;7;7;7;5;7;6;7;7;6;5;6;6;5;3;6;7;6;6;5;6;7;7;5;5;5;6;2;2;13;4;1;1;2;1;1
1;2;4;3;4;2;4;4;4;1;5;5;4;5;4;6;4;6;4;5;5;3;3;6;5;4;2;4;3;4;1;3;4;2;2;11;2;1;2;1;2;1
2;2;4;3;4;4;4;4;5;1;4;5;4;5;5;4;6;6;5;5;5;4;4;5;5;4;5;4;5;4;5;5;5;7;7;6;5;3;4;3;1;2;2;1;1
1;2;5;2;3;1;7;7;7;5;7;7;5;7;5;7;3;7;2;6;5;7;7;6;5;7;7;5;7;7;7;7;5;5;5;7;3;4;3;5;1;2;1;2;1
```

Fig. 3.3 The Corporate Reputation Data.csv file viewed in a text editor. (Source: authors' screenshot from R)

character, and the missing values are coded as −99. If you wish to import this file to the global environment, you can use the `read.csv()` function, specifying the arguments *file* = "Corporate Reputation Data.csv", *header* = TRUE, and *sep* = ";" and assigning the output to the `corp_rep_data` variable:

```
# Load the corporate reputation data
corp_rep_data <- read.csv(file = "Corporate Reputation Data.
csv", header = TRUE, sep = ";")
```

When clicking on the `corp_rep_data` object in the environment panel of RStudio, the source window opens at the top left of the screen (Fig. 3.4).

> **Important**
> Inspect the loaded data to ensure that the correct numbers of columns (indicators), rows (observations or cases), and column headers (indicator names) appear in the loaded data. Note that SEMinR uses the asterisk ("*") character when naming interaction terms as used in, for example, moderation analysis, so please ensure that asterisks are not present in the indicator names. Duplicate indicator names will also cause errors in SEMinR. Finally, **missing values** should be represented with a missing value indicator (such as −99, which is commonly used), so they can be appropriately identified and treated as missing values.

We encourage you to follow the above steps to download and read a dataset. Alternatively, you can also access that particular dataset directly from SEMinR. To help demonstrate its features, SEMinR comes bundled with two datasets, the corporate reputation dataset (Hair et al., 2022; `corp_rep_data`) and the European

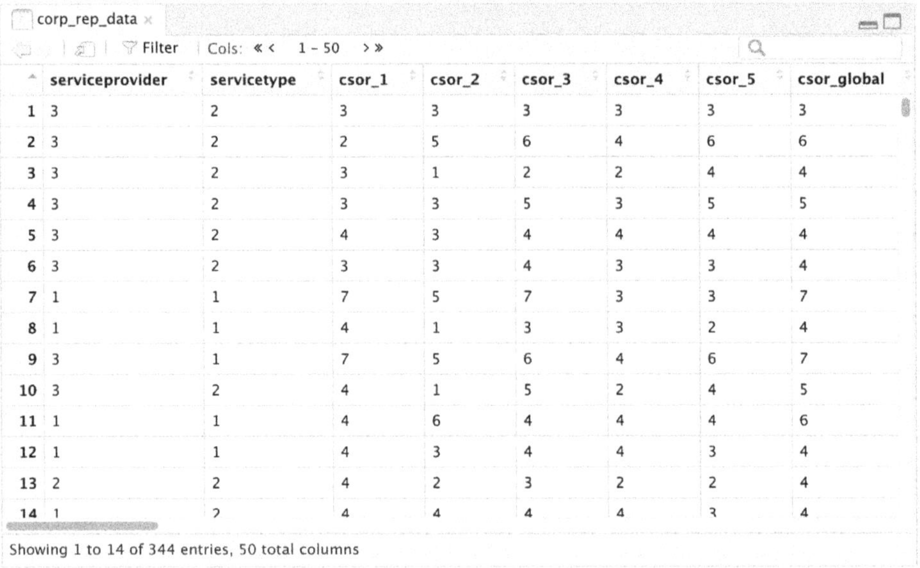

56   Chapter 3 · The SEMinR Package

serviceprovider	servicetype	csor_1	csor_2	csor_3	csor_4	csor_5	csor_global
1 3	2	3	3	3	3	3	3
2 3	2	2	5	6	4	6	6
3 3	2	3	1	2	2	4	4
4 3	2	3	3	5	3	5	5
5 3	2	4	3	4	4	4	4
6 3	2	3	3	4	3	3	4
7 1	1	7	5	7	3	3	7
8 1	1	4	1	3	3	2	4
9 3	1	7	5	6	4	6	7
10 3	2	4	1	5	2	4	5
11 1	1	4	6	4	4	4	6
12 1	1	4	3	4	4	3	4
13 2	2	4	2	3	2	2	4
14 1	2	4	4	4	4	3	4

Showing 1 to 14 of 344 entries, 50 total columns

■ **Fig. 3.4** Inspecting the `corp_rep_data` object. (Source: authors' screenshot from RStudio)

Customer Satisfaction Index (ECSI) dataset (Tenenhaus, Esposito Vinzi, Chatelin, & Lauro, 2005; `mobi`). When the SEMinR library has been loaded to the global environment (`library(seminr)`), the data are accessible by simply calling the object names (`corp_rep_data` or `mobi`).

Whichever way you have loaded the `corp_rep_data`, we can now inspect the dataset by using the `head()` function. `head()` is a useful function that outputs the first few fields of an object:

```
# Show the first several rows of the corporate reputation data
head(corp_rep_data)
```

It is clear from inspecting the head of the `corp_rep_data` object (■ Fig. 3.5) that the file has been loaded correctly and has the value "-99" set for the missing values. With the data loaded correctly, we now turn to the measurement model specification.

3.3 Specifying the Measurement Models

Path models are made up of two elements: (1) the measurement models (also called outer models in PLS-SEM), which describe the relationships between the latent variables and their measures (i.e., their indicators), and (2) the structural model (also called the inner model in PLS-SEM), which describes the relationships

3.3 · Specifying the Measurement Models

```
Console   Terminal ×   Jobs ×
~/seminr/
> # Show the first several rows of the corporate reputation data
> head(corp_rep_data)
  serviceprovider servicetype csor_1 csor_2 csor_3 csor_4 csor_5 csor_global attr_1
1               3           2      3      3      3      3           3      5
2               3           2      2      5      6      4           6      6
3               3           2      3      1      2      2           4      5
4               3           2      3      3      5      3           5      3
5               3           2      4      3      4      4           4      6
6               3           2      3      3      4      3           4      4
  attr_2 attr_3 attr_global perf_1 perf_2 perf_3 perf_4 perf_5 perf_global qual_1
1      1      3           5      5      4      2      5      6           6      5
2      6      6           6      6      6      6      6      6           6      6
3      6      5           6      4      4      2      5      4           5      3
4      7      5           7      5      5      5      3      6           6      5
5      6      6           6      5      6      7      6      5           7      6
6      1      5           5      6      6      4      5      6           6      5
  qual_2 qual_3 qual_4 qual_5 qual_6 qual_7 qual_8 qual_global like_1 like_2 like_3
1      6      4      2      4      4      2      5           6      3      1      2
2      6      6      6      5      6      6      5           6      6      6      6
3      4      3      4      3      5      4      4           5      5      5      5
4      6      6      7      5      4      5      6           7      6      5      6
5      5      7      7      6      6      6      7           7      6      6      7
6      5      5      6      5      6      3      4           6      6      7      7
  comp_1 comp_2 comp_3 cusl_1 cusl_2 cusl_3 cusa age education occupation nphh
1      4      5      5      5      3      3      5    2          3         11    5
2      6      7      6      7      7      7      7    6          3        -99    2
3      4      5      2      7      7      5      6    2          3         11    2
4      6      4      4      7      7      7      6    3          4         11    1
5      6      4      6      6      7      7      6    2          2         12    5
6      3      4      4      7      7      7      6    2          2         11    1
  sample_type mga_1 mga_2 mga_3 mga_4 switch_1 switch_2 switch_3 switch_4
1           1     2     1     1     1        3        1        3        2
2           1     2     1     1     1        5        5        4        4
3           1     2     1     1     1        4        3        2        3
4           1     2     1     1     1        3        4        4        2
5           1     2     1     1     1        5        5        5        4
```

◻ **Fig. 3.5** The head of the corporate reputation dataset. (Source: authors' screenshot from RStudio)

between the latent variables. We begin with describing how to specify the **measurement models**.

The basis for determining the relationships between constructs and their corresponding indicator variables is measurement theory. A sound measurement theory is a necessary condition to obtain useful results from any PLS-SEM analysis. Hypothesis tests involving the structural relationships among constructs will only be as reliable or valid as the construct measures.

SEMinR uses the `constructs()` function to specify the list of all construct measurement models. Within this list, we can then define various constructs:
- `composite()` specifies the measurement of individual constructs.
- `interaction_term()` specifies interaction terms.
- `higher_composite()` specifies hierarchical component models (higher-order constructs; Sarstedt et al., 2019).

Table 3.3 The arguments for the `composite()` function

Argument	Value
`construct_name`	The name of the construct to be created
`item_names`	A vector of the item names, usually created by the `multi_items()` or `single_item()` functions
`weights`	Defines the estimation mode for each measurement model. `Mode_A` or `correlation_weights` for reflectively specified measurement models and `mode_B` or `regression_weights` for formatively specified measurement models `Mode_A` is the default value if `weights` are not specified. ▶ Sect. 3.4 contains explanations of mode A and mode B

Source: authors' own table

The `constructs()` function compiles the list of constructs and their respective measurement model definitions. We must supply it with any number of individual `composite()`, `interaction_term()`, or `higher_composite()` constructs using their respective functions. Note that neither a dataset nor a structural model is specified in the measurement model stage, so we can reuse the measurement model object across different datasets and structural models.

The `composite()` function describes the measurement model of a single construct and takes the arguments shown in ◘ Table 3.3.

SEMinR strives to make specification of measurement items shorter and cleaner using `multi_items()`, which creates a vector of multiple measurement items with similar names or `single_item()` that describes a single measurement item. For example, we can use `composite()` for PLS path models to describe the reflectively measured *COMP* construct with its indicator variables *comp_1*, *comp_2*, and *comp_3*: `composite("COMP", multi_items("comp_", 1:3), weights = mode_A)`; ▶ Sect. 3.5 contains explanations of mode A and mode B. When no measurement weighting scheme is specified, the argument default is set to `mode_A`. Similarly, we can use `composite()` to define the single-item measurement model of *CUSA* as `composite("CUSA", single_item("cusa"))`. Combining the four measurement models within the `constructs()` function, we can define the measurement model for the simple model in ◘ Fig. 3.2. Note: If an error occurs, make sure you used the `library(seminr)` command in R to load the SEMinR package before executing the program code.

```
# Create measurement model
simple_mm <- constructs(
  composite("COMP", multi_items("comp_", 1:3)),
  composite("LIKE", multi_items("like_", 1:3)),
  composite("CUSA", single_item("cusa")),
  composite("CUSL", multi_items("cusl_", 1:3)))
```

The program code above facilitates the specification of standard measurement models. However, the `constructs()` function also allows specifying more complex models, such as interaction terms (Memon et al., 2019) and higher-order constructs (Sarstedt et al., 2019). We will discuss the `interaction_term()` function for specifying interactions in more detail in ▶ Chap. 8.

3.4 Specifying the Structural Model

With our measurement model specified, we now specify the **structural model**. When a structural model is being developed, two primary issues need to be considered: the sequence of the constructs and the relationships between them. Both issues are critical to the concept of modeling because they represent the hypotheses and their relationships to the theory being tested.

In most cases, researchers examine linear independent–dependent relationships between two or more constructs in the path model. Theory may suggest, however, that model relationships are more complex and involve mediation or moderation relationships. In the following section, we briefly introduce these different relationship types. In ▶ Chaps. 7 and 8, we explain how they can be estimated and interpreted using SEMinR.

SEMinR makes structural model specification more human readable, domain relevant, and explicit by using these functions:
- `relationships()` specifies all the structural relationships between all constructs.
- `paths()` specifies relationships between sets of antecedents and outcomes.

The simple model in ◘ Fig. 3.2 has five relationships. For example, to specify the relationships from *COMP* and *LIKE* to *CUSA* and *CUSL*, we use the `from` and `to` arguments in the path function: `paths(from = c("COMP", "LIKE"), to = c("CUSA", "CUSL"))`.

```
# Create structural model
simple_sm <- relationships(
   paths(from = c("COMP", "LIKE"), to = c("CUSA", "CUSL")),
   paths(from = c("CUSA"), to = c("CUSL")))
```

Note that neither a dataset nor a measurement model is specified in the structural model stage, so we can reuse the structural model object `simple_sm` across different datasets and measurement models.

3.5 Estimating the Model

After having specified the measurement and structural models, the next step is the **model estimation** using the **PLS-SEM algorithm**. For this task, the algorithm needs to determine the scores of the constructs that are used as input for (single and multiple) partial regression models within the path model. After the algorithm has calculated the construct scores, the scores are used to estimate each partial regression model in the path model. As a result, we obtain the estimates for all relationships in the measurement models (i.e., the indicator weights/loadings) and the structural model (i.e., the path coefficients).

The setup of the measurement models depends on whether the construct under consideration is modeled as reflective or formative. When a **reflective measurement model** is assumed for a construct, the indicator loadings are typically estimated through `mode A`. It estimates the relationship from the construct to each indicator based on a reflective measurement model that uses bivariate regressions (i.e., a single indicator variable represents the dependent variable, while the construct score represents the independent variable). As a result, we obtain correlations between the construct and each of its indicators (i.e., **correlation weights**), which become the **indicator loadings**. In contrast, when a **formative measurement model** is assumed for a construct, the indicator weights are typically estimated using multiple regression. More specifically, the measurement model estimation applies PLS-SEM's **mode B**, in which the construct represents a dependent variable and its associated indicator variables are the multiple independent variables. As a result, we obtain **regression weights** for the relationships from the indicators to the construct, which represent the **indicator weights**. While the use of mode A (i.e., correlation weights) for reflective measurement models and mode B (i.e., regression weights) for formative measurement models represents the standard approach to estimate the relationships between the constructs and their indicators in PLS-SEM, researchers may choose a different mode per type of measurement model in special situations (see also Hair et al., 2022; Rigdon, 2012).

Structural model calculations are executed as follows. The partial regressions for the structural model specify an endogenous construct as the dependent variable in a regression model. This endogenous construct's direct predecessors (i.e., latent variables with a direct relationship leading to the specific endogenous construct) are the independent variables in a regression used to estimate the **path coefficients**. Hence, there is a partial regression model for every endogenous construct to estimate all the path coefficients in the structural model.

All partial regression models are estimated by the PLS-SEM algorithm's iterative procedures, which comprise two stages. In the first stage, the construct scores are estimated. Then, in the second stage, the final estimates of the indicator weights and loadings are calculated, as well as the structural model's path coefficients and the resulting R^2 values of the endogenous latent variables. Appendix A of this textbook provides a detailed description of the PLS-SEM algorithm's stages (see also Lohmöller, 1989).

To estimate a PLS path model, algorithmic options and argument settings must be selected. The algorithmic options and argument settings include selecting the structural model path weighting scheme. SEMinR allows the user to apply two structural model **weighting schemes**: (1) the **factor weighting scheme** and (2) the **path weighting scheme**. While the results differ little across the alternative weighting schemes, path weighting is the most popular and recommended approach. This weighting scheme provides the highest R^2 value for endogenous latent variables

3.5 · Estimating the Model

Table 3.4 Arguments for the `estimate_pls()` function

Argument	Value
`data`	The dataset containing the indicator data
`measurement_model`	The measurement model described by the `constructs()` function
`structural_model`	The structural model described by the `paths()` function
`inner_weights`	The weighting scheme for path estimation. Use either `path_weighting` for path weighting (default) or `path_factorial` for factor weighting (see also Chin, 1998; Lohmöller, 1989)
`missing`	An argument declaring which missing value scheme should be used to replace the missing values. `mean_replacement` is used by default
`missing_value`	An argument declaring which value to be used to indicate missing values in the data. NA is used by default
`maxIt`	The maximum number of iterations to attempt when estimating the PLS path model. 300 is used by default
`stopCriterion`	The minimum change in the indicator weights/loadings between two consecutive iterations must be smaller than this threshold (or the maximum number of iterations is reached). 7 is used by default and represents 10^{-7} or 0.0000001

Source: authors' own table

and is generally applicable for all kinds of PLS path model specifications and estimations. Chin (1989) provides further details on the different weighting schemes available in PLS-SEM.

SEMinR uses the `estimate_pls()` function to estimate the PLS-SEM model. This function applies the arguments shown in ◘ Table 3.4. Please note that arguments with default values do not need to be specified but will revert to the default value when not specified.

We now estimate the PLS-SEM model by using the `estimate_pls()` function with arguments *data* = `corp_rep_data`, *measurement_model* = `simple_mm`, *structural_model* = `simple_sm`, *inner_weights* = `path_weighting`, *missing* = `mean_replacement`, and *missing_value* = "-99" and assign the output to `corp_rep_simple_model`.

```
# Estimate the model
corp_rep_simple_model <- estimate_pls(data = corp_rep_data,
  measurement_model = simple_mm,
  structural_model = simple_sm,
  inner_weights = path_weighting,
  missing = mean_replacement,
  missing_value = "-99")
```

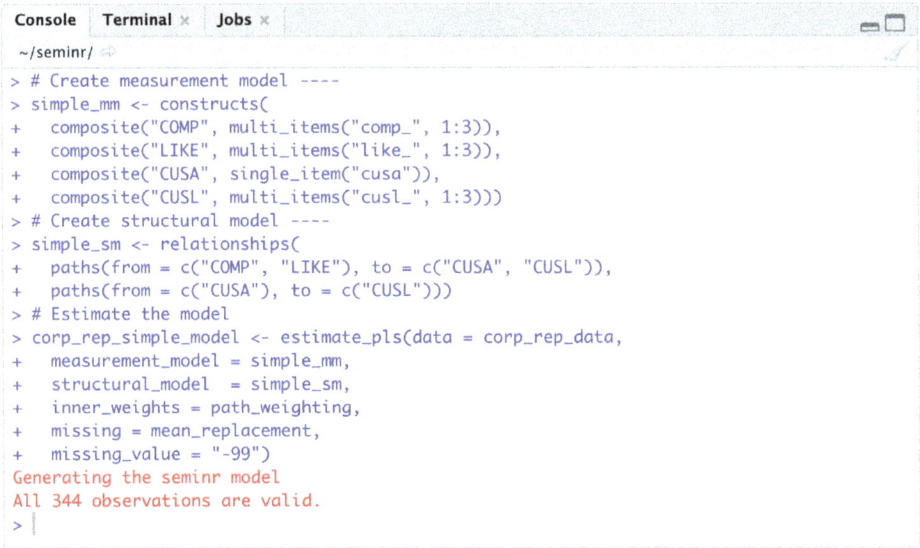

```
> # Create measurement model ----
> simple_mm <- constructs(
+   composite("COMP", multi_items("comp_", 1:3)),
+   composite("LIKE", multi_items("like_", 1:3)),
+   composite("CUSA", single_item("cusa")),
+   composite("CUSL", multi_items("cusl_", 1:3)))
> # Create structural model ----
> simple_sm <- relationships(
+   paths(from = c("COMP", "LIKE"), to = c("CUSA", "CUSL")),
+   paths(from = c("CUSA"), to = c("CUSL")))
> # Estimate the model
> corp_rep_simple_model <- estimate_pls(data = corp_rep_data,
+   measurement_model = simple_mm,
+   structural_model  = simple_sm,
+   inner_weights = path_weighting,
+   missing = mean_replacement,
+   missing_value = "-99")
Generating the seminr model
All 344 observations are valid.
>
```

Fig. 3.6 The estimated simple corporate reputation model. (Source: authors' screenshot from RStudio)

Note that the arguments for `inner_weights`, `missing`, and `missing_value` can be omitted if the default arguments are used. This is equivalent to the previous code block:

```
# Estimate the model with default settings
corp_rep_simple_model <- estimate_pls(data = corp_rep_data,
  measurement_model = simple_mm,
  structural_model = simple_sm,
  missing_value = "-99")
```

When the PLS-SEM algorithm has converged, the message "Generating the seminr model. All 344 observations are valid" will be shown in the console window (Fig. 3.6).

3.6 Summarizing the Model

Once the model has been estimated, we can summarize the model and generate a report of the results using the `summary()` function, which is used to extract the output and parameters of importance from an estimated model. SEMinR supports the use of `summary()` for the `estimate_pls()`, `bootstrap_model()`, and `predict_pls()` functions.

The `summary()` function applied to a SEMinR model object produces a `summary.seminr_model` class object, which can be stored in a variable and contains

3.6 · Summarizing the Model

Table 3.5 Elements of the `summary.seminr_model` object

Sub-object	Contains
`$meta`	The estimation function and version information
`$iterations`	The number of iterations for the PLS-SEM algorithm to converge
`$paths`	The model's path coefficients and (adjusted) R^2 values
`$total_effects`	The model's total effects
`$total_indirect_effects`	The model's total indirect effects
`$loadings`	The indicator loadings for all constructs
`$weights`	The indicator weights for all constructs
`$validity`	The metrics necessary to evaluate the construct measures' validity
`$reliability`	The metrics necessary to evaluate the construct measures' reliability
`$composite_scores`	The estimated scores for constructs
`$vif_antecedents`	The metrics used to evaluate structural model collinearity
`$fSquare`	The f^2 metric for all structural model relationships
`$descriptives`	The descriptive statistics of the indicator data
`$it_criteria`	The information theoretic model selection criteria for the estimated model

Source: authors' own table

the sub-objects shown in ◘ Table 3.5 that can be inspected using the `$` operator (e.g., `summary_simple_corp_rep$meta`). These sub-objects relate to model estimates, which serve as a basis for the assessment of the measurement and structural models (Hair, Risher, Sarstedt, & Ringle, 2019).

```
# Summarize the model results
summary_simple_corp_rep <- summary(corp_rep_simple_model)

# Inspect the model's path coefficients and the R^2 values
summary_simple_corp_rep$paths

# Inspect the construct reliability metrics
summary_simple_corp_rep$reliability
```

```
> # Summarize the model results
> summary_simple_corp_rep <- summary(corp_rep_simple_model)
> # Inspect the structural paths
> summary_simple_corp_rep$paths
         CUSA  CUSL
R^2     0.295 0.562
AdjR^2  0.290 0.558
COMP    0.162 0.009
LIKE    0.424 0.342
CUSA          . 0.504
> # Inspect the construct reliability metrics
> summary_simple_corp_rep$reliability
     alpha rhoC   AVE   rhoA
COMP 0.776 0.865 0.681 0.832
LIKE 0.831 0.899 0.747 0.836
CUSA 1.000 1.000 1.000 1.000
CUSL 0.831 0.899 0.748 0.839

Alpha, rhoC, and rhoA should exceed 0.7 while AVE should exceed 0.5
>
```

◘ **Fig. 3.7** Inspecting the summary report elements. (Source: authors' screenshot from RStudio)

◘ Figure 3.7 shows the results stored in the `summary_simple_corp_rep$paths` and `summary_simple_corp_rep$reliability` sub-objects.

3.7 Bootstrapping the Model

PLS-SEM is a nonparametric method – thus, we need to perform **bootstrapping** to estimate standard errors and compute confidence intervals. Bootstrapping will be discussed in more detail in ▶ Chaps. 5 and 6, but for now, we introduce the function and arguments.

SEMinR conducts high-performance bootstrapping using parallel processing, which utilizes the full performance of the central processing unit (CPU). The `bootstrap_model()` function is used to bootstrap a previously estimated SEMinR model. This function applies the arguments shown in ◘ Table 3.6.

In our example, we use the `bootstrap_model()` function and specify the arguments *seminr_model* = `corp_rep_simple_model`, *nboot* = 1000, *cores* = `NULL`, *seed* = 123. In this example, we use 1,000 bootstrap subsamples. However, the final result computations should draw on 10,000 subsamples (Streukens & Leroi-Werelds, 2016). These computations may take a short while (i.e., the R program remains idle). We first assign the output of the bootstrapping to the `boot_simple_corp_rep` variable. We then summarize this variable, assign-

3.7 · Bootstrapping the Model

Table 3.6 Arguments for the `bootstrap_model()` function

Argument	Value
`seminr_model`	A SEMinR model produced by `estimate_pls()`
`nboot`	The number of bootstrap subsamples to be generated. The number of subsamples must be at least equal to the number of valid observations in the dataset. Streukens and Leroi-Werelds (2016) suggest drawing at least 10,000 subsamples (see also Hair et al., 2022). For intermediary analyses, the number of subsamples can be considerably smaller (e.g., 1,000) to save computational time
`cores`	The number of CPU cores to use when performing parallel processing. Default is set to NULL which utilizes the max number of cores available on your computer
`seed`	The starting seed to use to make the random process replicable. Default is set to 123

Source: authors' own table

Table 3.7 Elements of the `summary.bootstrap_model` object

Sub-object	Contains
`$nboot`	The number of bootstrap subsamples generated during bootstrapping
`$bootstrapped_paths`	The bootstrap-estimated standard error, *t*-statistic, and confidence intervals for the path coefficients
`$bootstrapped_weights`	The bootstrap-estimated standard error, *t*-statistic, and confidence intervals for the indicator weights
`$bootstrapped_loadings`	The bootstrap-estimated standard error, *t*-statistic, and confidence intervals for the indicator loadings
`$bootstrapped_HTMT`	The bootstrap-estimated standard error, *t*-statistic, and confidence intervals for the HTMT values
`$bootstrapped_total_paths`	The bootstrap-estimated standard error, *t*-statistic, and confidence intervals for the model's total effects

Source: authors' own table

ing the output of `summary()` to the `sum_boot_simple_corp_rep` variable. The summarized bootstrap model object (i.e., `sum_boot_simple_corp_rep`) contains the elements shown in Table 3.7, which can be inspected using the `$` operator.

```
# Bootstrap the model
boot_simple_corp_rep <- bootstrap_model(seminr_model = corp_
rep_simple_model,
  nboot = 1000,
  cores = NULL,
  seed = 123)

# Store the summary of the bootstrapped model
sum_boot_simple_corp_rep <- summary(boot_simple_corp_rep)

# Inspect the bootstrapped structural paths
sum_boot_simple_corp_rep$bootstrapped_paths

# Inspect the bootstrapped indicator loadings
sum_boot_simple_corp_rep$bootstrapped_loadings
```

◘ Figure 3.8 shows the results of the bootstrap procedure for the path coefficients and indicator loadings. Note that bootstrapping is a random process, and your results might be slightly different from those presented here.

3.8 Plotting, Printing, and Exporting Results to Articles

When model estimation, evaluation, and analysis have been completed, it is often necessary to export the results generated in R to a report, such as an Apache OpenOffice writer document (.odt) or Microsoft PowerPoint presentation (.ppt or .pptx). Throughout this book, we provide screenshots for demonstrating the code outputs to the console in RStudio. However, we do not recommend this method to be used for copying and pasting results to research reports or articles. Instead, we recommend exporting tables and matrices to .csv files, which can be imported into documents or presentations, and that figures are exported to .pdf files to ensure the best print quality. In this section, we demonstrate how to best export results for high print quality and readability.

The **write.csv()** function takes an object from the global environment and writes it into a .csv file in the working directory of the project. This function applies two arguments: *x* is the name of the object to be written to file, and *file* is the name of the file to be created and written to. Thus, if we wish to report the bootstrapped paths from the previously discussed simple model, we would use the **write.csv()** function with argument *x* = **sum_boot_simple_corp_rep$bootstrapped_loadings** and *file* = "boot_loadings.csv".

3.8 · Plotting, Printing, and Exporting Results to Articles

```
Console   Terminal ×   Jobs ×
~/seminr/
> # Bootstrap the model
> boot_simple_corp_rep <- bootstrap_model(seminr_model = corp_rep_simple_model,
+    nboot = 1000,
+    cores = NULL,
+    seed = 123)
Bootstrapping model using seminr...
SEMinR Model successfully bootstrapped
> # Store the summary of the bootstrapped model
> sum_boot_simple_corp_rep <- summary(boot_simple_corp_rep)
> # Inspect the bootstrapped structural paths
> sum_boot_simple_corp_rep$bootstrapped_paths
             Original Est. Bootstrap Mean Bootstrap SD T Stat. 2.5% CI 97.5% CI
COMP -> CUSA        0.162          0.166       0.068   2.374    0.038    0.298
COMP -> CUSL        0.009          0.011       0.056   0.165   -0.098    0.126
LIKE -> CUSA        0.424          0.422       0.062   6.858    0.299    0.542
LIKE -> CUSL        0.342          0.340       0.056   6.059    0.227    0.450
CUSA -> CUSL        0.504          0.504       0.042  11.978    0.419    0.585
> # Inspect the bootstrapped indicator loadings
> sum_boot_simple_corp_rep$bootstrapped_loadings
            Original Est. Bootstrap Mean Bootstrap SD T Stat. 2.5% CI 97.5% CI
comp_1 -> COMP      0.858          0.858       0.021  41.366    0.813    0.895
comp_2 -> COMP      0.798          0.797       0.029  27.709    0.730    0.843
comp_3 -> COMP      0.818          0.814       0.031  26.246    0.746    0.866
like_1 -> LIKE      0.879          0.880       0.017  51.088    0.843    0.910
like_2 -> LIKE      0.870          0.869       0.018  47.428    0.830    0.900
like_3 -> LIKE      0.843          0.842       0.020  41.417    0.799    0.879
cusa   -> CUSA      1.000          1.000       0.000       .    1.000    1.000
cusl_1 -> CUSL      0.833          0.832       0.024  35.331    0.780    0.874
cusl_2 -> CUSL      0.917          0.917       0.010  88.874    0.894    0.935
cusl_3 -> CUSL      0.843          0.842       0.023  37.134    0.793    0.881
>
```

◘ **Fig. 3.8** Bootstrapped structural paths and indicator loadings. (Source: authors' screenshot from RStudio)

```
# Write the bootstrapped paths object to csv file
write.csv(x = sum_boot_simple_corp_rep$bootstrapped_loadings,
    file = "boot_loadings.csv")
```

Once the boot_loadings.csv file has been saved into the working directory, we can open it with Apache OpenOffice Calc, Microsoft Excel, or other spreadsheet software. These spreadsheet software applications enable formatting and editing the table to produce high-quality tables in reports. We followed this procedure to create ◘ Table 3.8 of bootstrapped indicator loadings for the simple corporate reputation model.

Next, we discuss how to generate high-quality figures from the SEMinR results. First, we generate a sample plot for export from RStudio. To do this, we use a sub-

◘ **Table 3.8** Export of bootstrapped indicator loadings from SEMinR

Paths	Original est.	Bootstrap mean	Bootstrap SD	T stat.	2.5% CI	97.5% CI
comp_1 -> COMP	0.858	0.858	0.021	41.366	0.813	0.895
comp_2 -> COMP	0.798	0.797	0.029	27.709	0.730	0.843
comp_3 -> COMP	0.818	0.814	0.031	26.246	0.746	0.866
like_1 -> LIKE	0.879	0.880	0.017	51.088	0.843	0.910
like_2 -> LIKE	0.870	0.869	0.018	47.428	0.830	0.900
like_3 -> LIKE	0.843	0.842	0.020	41.417	0.799	0.879
cusa -> CUSA	1	1	0	NA	1	1
cusl_1 -> CUSL	0.833	0.832	0.024	35.331	0.780	0.874
cusl_2 -> CUSL	0.917	0.917	0.010	88.874	0.894	0.935
cusl_3 -> CUSL	0.843	0.842	0.023	37.134	0.793	0.881

Source: authors' own table

object of `summary_simple_corp_rep` and plot the constructs' internal consistency reliabilities (i.e., Cronbach's alpha, rho_A, and rho_C) with `plot(summary_simple_corp_rep$reliability)`. Once this plot displays in the plots tab in RStudio (◘ Fig. 3.9), click the **Export** dropdown list and select **Save as PDF** to bring up the save plot as a .pdf window. Select the size and output name and save the document. Note that the size will affect the rendering of the plot and might need to be adjusted several times before the ideal format is found. These .pdf images can be imported directly into documents and reports at very high print quality. Alternatively, we can save the plot as an image file in .png, .jpeg, .eps, and many other formats. To do so, click the **Export** dropdown list in the **plots** tab and select **Save as Image**.

3.8 · Plotting, Printing, and Exporting Results to Articles

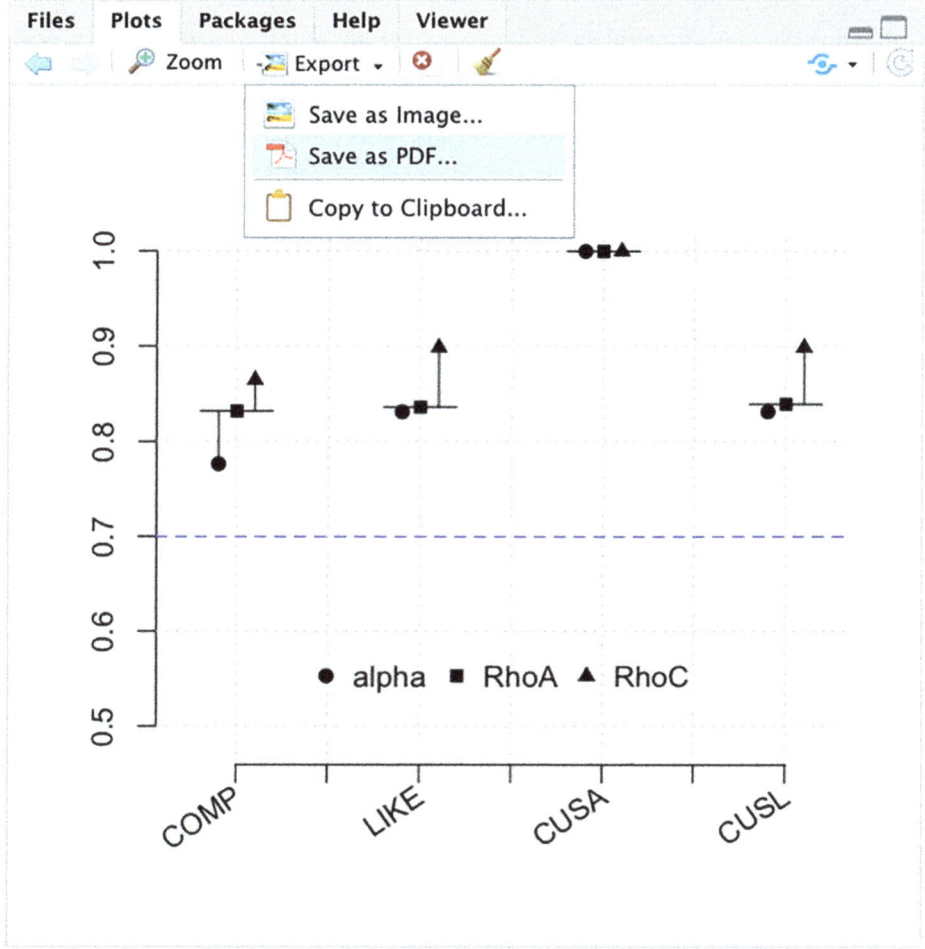

● **Fig. 3.9** Exporting the plot from RStudio using Save as PDF. (Source: authors' screenshot from RStudio)

Summary

In this chapter, we introduced the SEMinR syntax necessary for loading data, specifying and estimating a PLS path model, and reporting the results. Unlike popular graphical user interface software that uses menus and buttons, using a programming language, such as R, creates many opportunities for errors and bugs to be introduced. It is crucial that you are well versed in the SEMinR syntax, functions, and arguments before you proceed to the next few chapters. For this reason, we strongly recommend reviewing this chapter several times and attempting to complete the exercises before moving onto subsequent chapters. The upside of the programming approach is that every step and parameter of your analysis are explicitly defined for others to repeat or replicate. In addition, more experienced users can draw on a large number of supplementary R packages that extend the analyses supported by SEMinR.

The SEMinR syntax for PLS-SEM is broadly divided into four stages: (1) loading and cleaning the data, (2) specifying the measurement models, (3) specifying the structural model, and (4) estimating, bootstrapping, and summarizing the model. When loading data, it is important that the format of the file to be imported is well understood to prevent later errors. Special attention should be paid to the column headers, the separator and decimal characters used, and the missing value indicator. The raw data file can be inspected using a text editor prior to importing it into the RStudio environment. The imported data should also be compared to the raw data file to ensure no errors occurred in the process.

The measurement model is specified using the SEMinR functions `constructs()`, `composite()`, `interaction_term()`, and `multi_items()` or `single_item()`. The measurement model can be specified and reused across different datasets and structural model configurations. The structural model is specified using `relationships()`, `paths()`, and intuitive arguments *from* and *to* for specific paths. The PLS path model is estimated using the `estimate_pls()` function, which allows for specification of the inner model weighting scheme, as path weighting or factorial. The `bootstrap_model()` function is used to bootstrap a previously estimated SEMinR model. Reports are generated using the `summarize()`, `plot()`, and `print()` functions, and high-quality figures and tables can be exported to reports and presentations.

Exercise

The SEMinR package comes bundled with a model (i.e., the influencer model), which analyzes if consumers are likely to follow social media influencers' purchase recommendations and whether they feel connected with the influencer. Specifically, the model examines the impact of self-influencer connection (i.e., the level of own identification with the influencer presenting a specific product, SIC) on product liking (*PL*), perceived quality (*PQ*), and purchase intention (*PI*). That is, product liking and perceived quality act as potential mediators in the relationship between self-influencer connection and purchase intention. Finally, the model hypothesizes a direct effect from purchase intention to willingness to pay (*WTP*). Pick (2020) provides the theoretical background on a similar influencer model.

The data were collected as part of a larger study on social media influencer marketing (Pick, 2020) via an online survey between January and April 2019. The final dataset consists of $N = 222$ observations. The dataset is bundled with the SEMinR package and is named **influencer_data**. Participants saw either a "real" influencer called Franklin who presented a fitness shake ($N = 100$) or a "fake" influencer called Emma who presented a hand blender ($N = 122$) (indicator, *influencer_group*). After seeing the real or fake influencer, participants provided information about their self-

3.8 · Plotting, Printing, and Exporting Results to Articles

influencer connection on a 7-point Likert scale (1 = completely disagree, 7 = completely agree). Different from Pick (2020), we consider self-influencer connection as a formative measure using the set of items shown in ◘ Table 3.9. To assess the formative construct's convergent validity, a single item was included in the survey (indicator, *sic_global*), which serves as the criterion measure for a redundancy analysis.

In the next step, respondents stated their perceived influencer competence (used in ► Chap. 8), perceived quality, product liking, and purchase intention, all of which are measured reflectively on a 7-point Likert scale (1 = completely disagree, 7 = completely agree). Finally, willingness to pay is measured using a single question, asking respondents for their willingness to pay (in Euro) for the presented product. See ◘ Table 3.10 for a complete list of item wordings. The table also includes items for an additional construct (perceived influencer competence), which we will introduce in ► Chap. 8.

The influencer model is illustrated in ◘ Fig. 3.10. If you need help or hints, consult the SEMinR demo topic file for the influencer model:

```
# Access the demo file for the ECSI dataset
demo(topic = "seminr-pls-influencer", package = "seminr")
```

1. Reproduce the influencer measurement models in SEMinR syntax.
2. Reproduce the influencer structural model in SEMinR syntax.
3. Estimate the influencer model using the standard settings. Remember to specify the **influencer_data** dataset.

◘ **Table 3.9** Indicators for the formatively measured construct of the influencer model

Self-influencer connection (SIC)	
sic_1	The influencer reflects who I am
sic_2	I can identify with the influencer
sic_3	I feel a personal connection to the influencer
sic_4	I (can) use the influencer to communicate who I am to other people
sic_5	I think the influencer helps (could help) me become the type of person I want to be
sic_6	I consider the influencer to be "me"
sic_7	The influencer suits me well
sic_global	My personality and the personality of the influencer relate to one another

Source: authors' own table

Table 3.10 Indicators for the reflectively measured construct of the influencer model

Perceived Influencer Competence (PIC)	
pic_1	The influencer is qualified
pic_2	The influencer is competent
pic_3	The influencer is an expert
pic_4	The influencer is experienced
pic_5	The influencer is knowledgeable
Perceived Quality (PQ)	
pq_1	The product has excellent quality
pq_2	The product looks reliable and durable
pq_3	The product will have fewer problems
pq_4	The product has excellent quality features
Product Liking (PL)	
pl_1	I dislike the product
pl_2	The product is appealing to me
pl_3	The presented product raises a positive feeling in me
pl_4	The product is interesting to me
Purchase Intention (PI)	
pi_1	It is very likely that I will purchase this product
pi_2	I will purchase this product the next time I need it
pi_3	I would definitely try out the products
pi_4	I would recommend this product to my friends
pi_5	I am willing to purchase this product
Willingness to Pay (WTP)	
wtp	Please state your willingness to pay (in Euro) for the presented product

Source: authors' own table

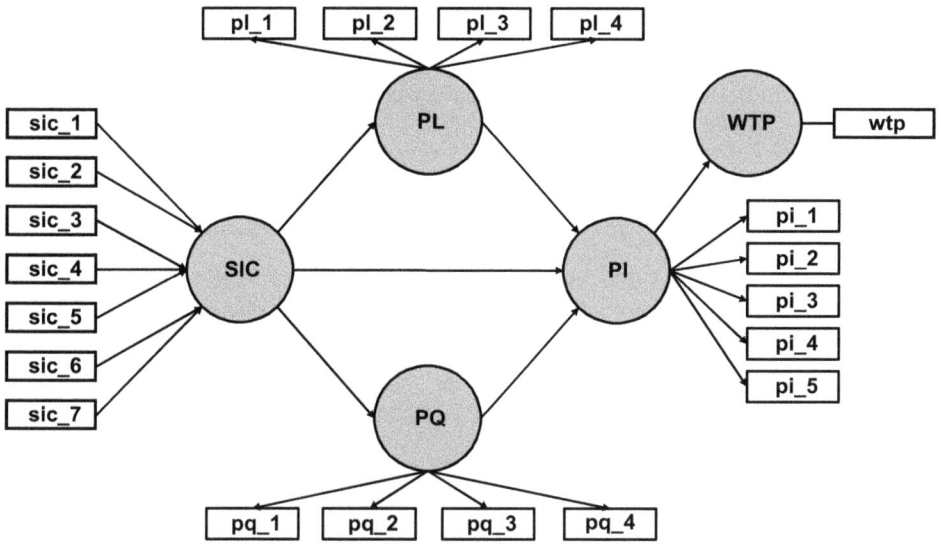

Fig. 3.10 Influencer model. (Source: authors' own figure)

References

Chin, W. W. (1998). The partial least squares approach to structural equation modeling. In G. A. Marcoulides (Ed.), *Modern methods for business research* (pp. 295–358). Mahwah, NJ: Erlbaum.

Eberl, M. (2010). An application of PLS in multi-group analysis: The need for differentiated corporate-level marketing in the mobile communications industry. In V. Esposito Vinzi, W. W. Chin, J. Henseler, & H. Wang (Eds.), *Handbook of partial least squares: Concepts, methods and applications in marketing and related fields (Springer Handbooks of Computational Statistics Series)* (Vol. II, pp. 487–514). Berlin: Springer.

Hair, J. F., Hult, G. T. M., Ringle, C. M., & Sarstedt, M. (2022). *A primer on partial least squares structural equation modeling (PLS-SEM)* (3rd ed.). Thousand Oaks, CA: Sage.

Hair, J. F., Risher, J. J., Sarstedt, M., & Ringle, C. M. (2019). When to use and how to report the results of PLS-SEM. *European Business Review, 31*(1), 2–24.

Helm, S., Eggert, A., & Garnefeld, I. (2010). Modelling the impact of corporate reputation on customer satisfaction and loyalty using PLS. In V. Esposito Vinzi, W. W. Chin, J. Henseler, & H. Wang (Eds.), *Handbook of partial least squares: Concepts, methods and applications in marketing and related fields (Springer Handbooks of Computational Statistics Series)* (Vol. II, pp. 515–534). Berlin: Springer.

Lohmöller, J.-B. (1989). *Latent variable path modeling with partial least squares*. Heidelberg: Physica.

Memon, M. A., Cheah, J.-H., Ramayah, T., Ting, H., Chuah, F., & Cham, T. H. (2019). Moderation analysis: Issues and guidelines. *Journal of Applied Structural Equation Modeling, 3*(1), i–ix.

Pick, M. (2020). Psychological ownership in social media influencer marketing. *European Business Review, 33*(1), 9–30.

R Core Team. (2021). *R: A language and environment for statistical computing [computer software]*. Vienna, Austria: R Foundation for Statistical Computing. Retrieved from https://www.R-project.org/

Rigdon, E. E. (2012). Rethinking partial least squares path modeling: In praise of simple methods. *Long Range Planning, 45*(5–6), 341–358.

Rosseel, Y. (2012). Lavaan: An R package for structural equation modeling and more. Version 0.5–12 (beta). *Journal of Statistical Software, 48*(2), 1–36.

Sarstedt, M., Wilczynski, P., & Melewar, T. C. (2013). Measuring reputation in global markets—A comparison of reputation measures' convergent and criterion validities. *Journal of World Business, 48*(3), 329–339.

Sarstedt, M., Hair, J. F., Cheah, J. H., Becker, J. M., & Ringle, C. M. (2019). How to specify, estimate, and validate higher-order constructs in PLS-SEM. *Australasian Marketing Journal, 27*(3), 197–211.

Streukens, S., & Leroi-Werelds, S. (2016). Bootstrapping and PLS-SEM: A step-by-step guide to get more out of your bootstrapping results. *European Management Journal, 34*(6), 618–632.

Tenenhaus, M., Esposito Vinzi, V., Chatelin, Y.-M., & Lauro, C. (2005). PLS path modeling. *Computational Statistics & Data Analysis, 48*(1), 159–205.

Suggested Reading

Chin, W. W. (1998). The partial least squares approach to structural equation modeling. In G. A. Marcoulides (Ed.), *Modern methods for business research* (pp. 295–358). Mahwah, NJ: Erlbaum.

Hair, J. F., Hult, G. T. M., Ringle, C. M., & Sarstedt, M. (2022). *A primer on partial least squares structural equation modeling (PLS-SEM)* (3rd ed.). Thousand Oaks, CA: Sage.

Hair, J. F., Risher, J. J., Sarstedt, M., & Ringle, C. M. (2019). When to use and how to report the results of PLS-SEM. *European Business Review, 31*(1), 2–24.

Ray, S., & Danks, N.P. (2020). SEMinR Vignette. Retrieved from: https://cran.r-project.org/web/packages/seminr/vignettes/SEMinR.html

Tenenhaus, M., Esposito Vinzi, V., Chatelin, Y.-M., & Lauro, C. (2005). PLS path modeling. *Computational Statistics & Data Analysis, 48*(1), 159–205.

Open Access This chapter is licensed under the terms of the Creative Commons Attribution 4.0 International License (http://creativecommons.org/licenses/by/4.0/), which permits use, sharing, adaptation, distribution and reproduction in any medium or format, as long as you give appropriate credit to the original author(s) and the source, provide a link to the Creative Commons license and indicate if changes were made.

The images or other third party material in this chapter are included in the chapter's Creative Commons license, unless indicated otherwise in a credit line to the material. If material is not included in the chapter's Creative Commons license and your intended use is not permitted by statutory regulation or exceeds the permitted use, you will need to obtain permission directly from the copyright holder.

Evaluation of Reflective Measurement Models

Contents

4.1 Introduction – 76

4.2 Indicator Reliability – 77

4.3 Internal Consistency Reliability – 77

4.4 Convergent Validity – 78

4.5 Discriminant Validity – 78

4.6 Case Study Illustration: Reflective Measurement Models – 80

References – 89

© The Author(s) 2021
J. F. Hair Jr. et al., *Partial Least Squares Structural Equation Modeling (PLS-SEM) Using R*, Classroom Companion: Business,
https://doi.org/10.1007/978-3-030-80519-7_4

Chapter 4 · Evaluation of Reflective Measurement Models

Learning Objectives
After reading this chapter, you should understand:
1. The concept of indicator reliability
2. The different metrics for assessing internal consistency reliability
3. How to interpret the average variance extracted (AVE) as a measure of convergent validity
4. How to evaluate discriminant validity using the HTMT criterion
5. How to use SEMinR to assess reflectively measured constructs in the corporate reputation example

4.1 Introduction

This chapter describes how to evaluate the quality of reflective measurement models estimated by PLS-SEM, both in in terms of reliability and validity. Assessing reflective measurement models includes evaluating the reliability of measures, on both an indicator level (indicator reliability) and a construct level (internal consistency reliability). Validity assessment focuses on each measure's convergent validity using the average variance extracted (AVE). Moreover, the heterotrait–monotrait (HTMT) ratio of correlations allows to assess a reflectively measured construct's discriminant validity in comparison with other construct measures in the same model. ◘ Figure 4.1 illustrates the reflective measurement model evaluation process. In the following sections, we address each criterion for the evaluation of reflective measurement models and offer rules of thumb for their use. In the second part of this chapter, we explain how to apply the metrics to our corporate reputation example using SEMinR.

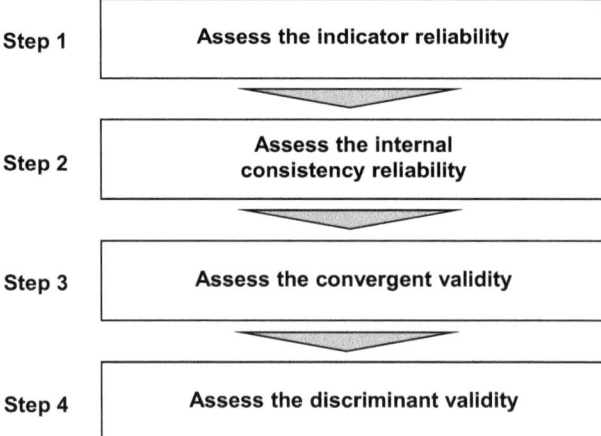

◘ Fig. 4.1 Reflective measurement model assessment procedure. (Source: authors' own figure)

4.2 Indicator Reliability

The first step in reflective measurement model assessment involves examining how much of each indicator's variance is explained by its construct, which is indicative of **indicator reliability**. To compute an indicator's explained variance, we need to square the indicator loading, which is the bivariate correlation between indicator and construct. As such, the indicator reliability indicates the **communality** of an indicator. **Indicator loadings** above 0.708 are recommended, since they indicate that the construct explains more than 50 percent of the indicator's variance, thus providing acceptable indicator reliability.

Researchers frequently obtain weaker indicator loadings (< 0.708) for their measurement models in social science studies, especially when newly developed scales are used (Hulland, 1999). Rather than automatically eliminating indicators when their loading is below 0.70, researchers should carefully examine the effects of indicator removal on other reliability and validity measures. Generally, indicators with loadings between 0.40 and 0.708 should be considered for removal only when deleting the indicator leads to an increase in the internal consistency reliability or convergent validity (discussed in the next sections) above the suggested threshold value. Another consideration in the decision of whether to delete an indicator is the extent to which its removal affects **content validity**, which refers to the extent to which a measure represents all facets of a given construct. As a consequence, indicators with weaker loadings are sometimes retained. Indicators with very low loadings (below 0.40) should, however, always be eliminated from the measurement model (Hair, Hult, Ringle, & Sarstedt, 2022).

4.3 Internal Consistency Reliability

The second step in reflective measurement model assessment involves examining **internal consistency reliability**. Internal consistency reliability is the extent to which indicators measuring the same construct are associated with each other. One of the primary measures used in PLS-SEM is Jöreskog's (1971) **composite reliability rho$_c$**. Higher values indicate higher levels of reliability. For example, reliability values between 0.60 and 0.70 are considered "acceptable in exploratory research," whereas values between 0.70 and 0.90 range from "satisfactory to good." Values above 0.90 (and definitely above 0.95) are problematic, since they indicate that the indicators are redundant, thereby reducing construct validity (Diamantopoulos, Sarstedt, Fuchs, Wilczynski, & Kaiser, 2012). Reliability values of 0.95 and above also suggest the possibility of undesirable response patterns (e.g., straight-lining), thereby triggering inflated correlations among the error terms of the indicators.

Cronbach's alpha is another measure of internal consistency reliability, which assumes the same thresholds as the composite reliability (rho$_c$). A major limitation of Cronbach's alpha, however, is that it assumes all indicator loadings are the same in the population (also referred to as tau-equivalence). The violation of this assumption manifests itself in lower reliability values than those produced by rho$_c$. Nevertheless, researchers have shown that even in the absence of tau-equivalence, Cronbach's alpha is an acceptable lower-bound approximation of the true internal consistency reliability (Trizano-Hermosilla & Alvarado, 2016).

While Cronbach's alpha is rather conservative, the composite reliability rho$_c$ may be too liberal, and the construct's true reliability is typically viewed as within these two extreme values. As an alternative and building on Dijkstra (2010), subsequent research has proposed the exact (or consistent) **reliability coefficient rho$_A$** (Dijkstra, 2014; Dijkstra & Henseler, 2015). The reliability coefficient rho$_A$ usually lies between the conservative Cronbach's alpha and the liberal composite reliability and is therefore considered and acceptable compromise between these two measures.

4.4 Convergent Validity

The third step is to assess (the) **convergent validity** of each construct. Convergent validity is the extent to which the construct converges in order to explain the variance of its indicators. The metric used for evaluating a construct's convergent validity is the **average variance extracted (AVE)** for all indicators on each construct. The AVE is defined as the grand mean value of the squared loadings of the indicators associated with the construct (i.e., the sum of the squared loadings divided by the number of indicators). Therefore, the AVE is equivalent to the **communality** of a construct. The minimum acceptable AVE is 0.50 – an AVE of 0.50 or higher indicates the construct explains 50 percent or more of the indicators' variance that make up the construct (Hair et al., 2022).

4.5 Discriminant Validity

The fourth step is to assess **discriminant validity**. This metric measures the extent to which a construct is empirically distinct from other constructs in the structural model. Fornell and Larcker (1981) proposed the traditional metric and suggested that each construct's AVE (squared variance within) should be compared to the squared inter-construct correlation (as a measure of shared variance between constructs) of that same construct and all other reflectively measured constructs in the structural model – the shared variance between all model constructs should not be larger than their AVEs. Recent research indicates, however, that this metric is not suitable for discriminant validity assessment. For example, Henseler, Ringle, and Sarstedt (2015) show that the Fornell–Larcker criterion (i.e., FL in SEMinR) does not perform well, particularly when the indicator loadings on a construct differ only slightly (e.g., all the indicator loadings are between 0.65 and 0.85). Hence, in empirical applications, the Fornell–Larcker criterion often fails to reliably identify discriminant validity problems (Radomir & Moisescu, 2019) and should therefore be avoided. Nonetheless, we include this criterion in our discussion, as many researchers are familiar with it.

4.5 · Discriminant Validity

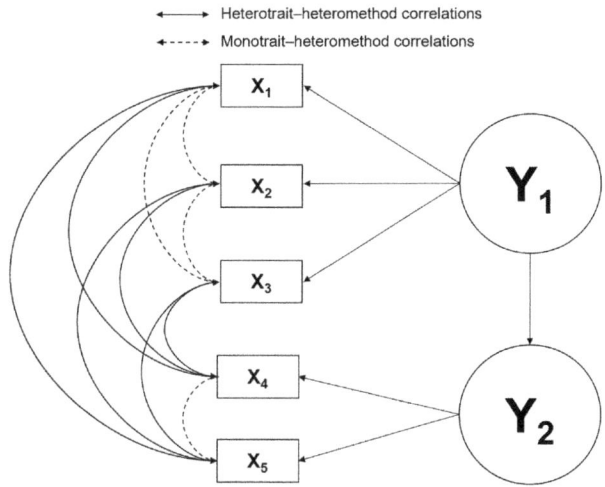

Fig. 4.2 Discriminant validity assessment using the HTMT. (Source: authors' own figure)

As a better alternative, we recommend the **heterotrait–monotrait ratio (HTMT)** of correlations (Henseler et al., 2015) to assess discriminant validity. The HTMT is defined as the mean value of the indicator correlations across constructs (i.e., the **heterotrait–heteromethod correlations**) relative to the (geometric) mean of the average correlations for the indicators measuring the same construct (i.e., the **monotrait–heteromethod correlations**). ◘ Figure 4.2 illustrates this concept. The arrows connecting indicators of different constructs represent the heterotrait–heteromethod correlations, which should be as small as possible. On the contrary, the monotrait–heteromethod correlations – represented by the dashed arrows – represent the correlations among indicators measuring the same concept, which should be as high as possible.

Discriminant validity problems are present when HTMT values are high. Henseler et al. (2015) propose a threshold value of 0.90 for structural models with constructs that are conceptually very similar, such as cognitive satisfaction, affective satisfaction, and loyalty. In such a setting, an HTMT value above 0.90 would suggest that discriminant validity is not present. But when constructs are conceptually more distinct, a lower, more conservative, threshold value is suggested, such as 0.85 (Henseler et al., 2015).

In addition, bootstrap confidence intervals can be used to test if the HTMT is significantly different from 1.0 (Henseler et al., 2015) or a lower threshold value, such as 0.9 or 0.85, which should be defined based on the study context (Franke & Sarstedt, 2019). To do so, we need to assess whether the upper bound of the 95% confidence interval (assuming a significance level of 5%) is lower than 0.90 or 0.85. Hence, we have to consider a 95% one-sided bootstrap confidence interval, whose upper boundary is identical to the one produced when computing a 90% two-sided bootstrap confidence interval. To obtain the bootstrap confidence intervals, in line with Aguirre-Urreta and Rönkkö (2018), researchers should generally use the percentile method. In addition, researchers should always use 10,000 bootstrap

Table 4.1 Summary of the criteria and rules of thumb for their use

Criterion	Metrics and thresholds
Reflective indicator loadings	≥ 0.708
Internal consistency reliability	Cronbach's alpha is the lower bound, and the composite reliability rho_c is the upper bound for internal consistency reliability. The reliability coefficient rho_A usually lies between these bounds and may serve as a good representation of a construct's internal consistency reliability Minimum 0.70 (or 0.60 in exploratory research) Maximum of 0.95 to avoid indicator redundancy, which would compromise content validity Recommended 0.80 to 0.90
Convergent validity	AVE ≥ 0.50
Discriminant validity	For conceptually similar constructs, HTMT <0.90 For conceptually different constructs, HTMT <0.85 Test if the HTMT is significantly lower than the threshold value

Source: authors' own table

samples (Streukens & Leroi-Werelds, 2016). See ► Chap. 5 for details on bootstrapping and confidence intervals.

◻ Table 4.1 summarizes all the metrics that need to be applied when assessing reflective measurement models.

4.6 Case Study Illustration: Reflective Measurement Models

We continue analyzing the simple corporate reputation PLS path model introduced in the previous chapter. In ► Chap. 3, we explained and demonstrated how to load the data, create the structural model and measurement model objects, and estimate the PLS path model using the SEMinR syntax. In the following, we discuss how to evaluate reflective measurement models, using the simple corporate reputation model (► Fig. 3.2 in ► Chap. 3) as an example.

Recall that to specify and estimate the model, we must first load the data and specify the measurement model and structural model. The model is then estimated by using the `estimate_pls()` command, and the output is assigned to an object. In our case study, we name this object `corp_rep_pls_model`. Once the PLS path model has been estimated, we can access the reports and analysis results by running the `summary()` function. To be able to view different parts of the analysis in greater detail, we suggest assigning the output to a newly created object that we call `summary_corp_rep` in our example (◻ Fig. 4.3).

4.6 · Case Study Illustration: Reflective Measurement Models

```
> # Load the SEMinR library
> library(seminr)
> # Load the data ----
> corp_rep_data <- corp_rep_data
> # Create measurement model ----
> corp_rep_mm <- constructs(
+   composite("COMP", multi_items("comp_", 1:3)),
+   composite("LIKE", multi_items("like_", 1:3)),
+   composite("CUSA", single_item("cusa")),
+   composite("CUSL", multi_items("cusl_", 1:3)))
> # Create structural model ----
> corp_rep_sm <- relationships(
+   paths(from = c("COMP", "LIKE"), to = c("CUSA", "CUSL")),
+   paths(from = c("CUSA"), to = c("CUSL")))
> # Estimate the model
> corp_rep_pls_model <- estimate_pls(
+   data = corp_rep_data,
+   measurement_model = corp_rep_mm,
+   structural_model  = corp_rep_sm,
+   missing = mean_replacement,
+   missing_value = "-99")
Generating the seminr model
All 344 observations are valid.
> # Summarize the model results
> summary_corp_rep <- summary(corp_rep_pls_model)
> # Inspect iterations
> summary_corp_rep$iterations
[1] 4
>
```

Fig. 4.3 Recap on loading data, specifying and summarizing the model, and inspecting iterations. (Source: authors' screenshot from RStudio)

```
# Load the SEMinR library
library(seminr)

# Load the data
corp_rep_data <- corp_rep_data

# Create measurement model
corp_rep_mm <- constructs(
  composite("COMP", multi_items("comp_", 1:3)),
  composite("LIKE", multi_items("like_", 1:3)),
  composite("CUSA", single_item("cusa")),
  composite("CUSL", multi_items("cusl_", 1:3)))

# Create structural model
corp_rep_sm <- relationships(
  paths(from = c("COMP", "LIKE"), to = c("CUSA", "CUSL")),
  paths(from = c("CUSA"), to = c("CUSL")))

# Estimating the model
corp_rep_pls_model <- estimate_pls(
```

```
    data = corp_rep_data,
    measurement_model = corp_rep_mm,
    structural_model = corp_rep_sm,
    missing = mean_replacement,
    missing_value = "-99")

# Summarize the model results
summary_corp_rep <- summary(corp_rep_pls_model)
```

Note that the results are not automatically shown but can be extracted as needed from the **summary_corp_rep** object. For a reminder on what is returned from the **summary()** function applied to a SEMinR model and stored in the **summary_corp_rep** object, refer to ▶ Table 3.5. Before analyzing the results, we advise to first check if the algorithm converged (i.e., the stop criterion of the algorithm was reached and not the maximum number of iterations – see ▶ Table 3.4 for setting these arguments in the **estimate_pls()** function). To do so, it is necessary to inspect the **iterations** element within the **summary_corp_rep** object by using the **$** operator.

```
# Iterations to converge
summary_corp_rep$iterations
```

The upper part of ◘ Fig. 4.3 shows the code for loading the model, estimating the object **corp_rep_pls_model**, and summarizing the model to the **summary_corp_rep** object. The lower part of the figure shows the number of **iterations** that the PLS-SEM algorithm needed to converge. This number should be lower than the maximum number of iterations (e.g., 300). The bottom of ◘ Fig. 4.3 indicates that the algorithm converged after iteration 4.

If the PLS-SEM algorithm does not converge in fewer than 300 iterations, which is the default setting in most PLS-SEM software, the algorithm could not find a stable solution. This kind of situation almost never occurs. But if it does occur, there are two possible causes: (1) The selected stop criterion is set at a very small level (e.g., 1.0E-10 as opposed to the standard of 1.0E-7), so that small changes in the coefficients of the measurement models prevent the PLS-SEM algorithm from stopping, or (2) there are problems with the data and it needs to be checked carefully. For example, data problems may occur if the sample size is too small or if the responses to an indicator include many identical values (i.e., the same data points, which results in insufficient variability, error message is singular matrix).

In the following, we inspect the **summary_corp_rep** object to obtain statistics relevant for assessing the construct measures' internal consistency reliability, convergent validity, and discriminant validity. The simple corporate reputation model contains three constructs with reflective measurement models (i.e., *COMP*, *CUSL*, and *LIKE*) as well as a single-item construct (*CUSA*). For the reflective measure-

4.6 · Case Study Illustration: Reflective Measurement Models

```
Console  Terminal ×  Jobs ×
~/seminr/
> # Inspect the outer loadings
> summary_corp_rep$loadings
        COMP  LIKE  CUSA  CUSL
comp_1 0.858 0.000 0.000 0.000
comp_2 0.798 0.000 0.000 0.000
comp_3 0.818 0.000 0.000 0.000
like_1 0.000 0.879 0.000 0.000
like_2 0.000 0.870 0.000 0.000
like_3 0.000 0.843 0.000 0.000
cusa   0.000 0.000 1.000 0.000
cusl_1 0.000 0.000 0.000 0.833
cusl_2 0.000 0.000 0.000 0.917
cusl_3 0.000 0.000 0.000 0.843
> # Inspect the indicator reliability
> summary_corp_rep$loadings^2
        COMP  LIKE  CUSA  CUSL
comp_1 0.736 0.000 0.000 0.000
comp_2 0.638 0.000 0.000 0.000
comp_3 0.669 0.000 0.000 0.000
like_1 0.000 0.773 0.000 0.000
like_2 0.000 0.757 0.000 0.000
like_3 0.000 0.711 0.000 0.000
cusa   0.000 0.000 1.000 0.000
cusl_1 0.000 0.000 0.000 0.694
cusl_2 0.000 0.000 0.000 0.841
cusl_3 0.000 0.000 0.000 0.710
>
```

Fig. 4.4 Indicator loadings and indicator reliability. (Source: authors' screenshot from RStudio)

ment model, we need to estimate the relationships between the reflectively measured constructs and their indicators (i.e., loadings). Figure 4.4 displays the results for the indicator loadings, which can be found by using the $ operator when inspecting the `summary_corp_rep` object. The calculation of indicator reliability (Fig. 4.4) can be automated by squaring the values in the indicator loading table by using the ^ operator to square all values (i.e., ^2):

```
# Inspect the indicator loadings
summary_corp_rep$loadings
# Inspect the indicator reliability
summary_corp_rep$loadings^2
```

All indicator loadings of the reflectively measured constructs *COMP*, *CUSL*, and *LIKE* are well above the threshold value of **0.708** (Hair, Risher, Sarstedt, & Ringle, 2019), which suggests sufficient levels of indicator reliability. The indicator *comp_2* (loading, **0.798**) has the smallest indicator-explained variance with a value of **0.638** (= 0.798^2), while the indicator *cusl_2* (loading, **0.917**) has the highest explained variance, with a value of **0.841** (= 0.917^2) – both values are well above the threshold value of **0.5**.

```
Console  Terminal ×  Jobs ×
~/seminr/
> # Inspect the internal consistency and reliability
> summary_corp_rep$reliability
     alpha  rhoC   AVE  rhoA
COMP 0.776 0.865 0.681 0.832
LIKE 0.831 0.899 0.747 0.836
CUSA 1.000 1.000 1.000 1.000
CUSL 0.831 0.899 0.748 0.839

Alpha, rhoC, and rhoA should exceed 0.7 while AVE should exceed 0.5
> # Plot the reliabilities of constructs
> plot(summary_corp_rep$reliability)
>
```

◘ **Fig. 4.5** Construct reliability and convergent validity table. (Source: authors' screenshot from RStudio)

To evaluate the composite reliability of the construct measures, once again inspect the `summary_corp_rep` object by using `$reliability`:

```
# Inspect the composite reliability
summary_corp_rep$reliability
```

The internal consistency reliability values are displayed in a matrix format (◘ Fig. 4.5). With rho_A values of **0.832** (*COMP*), **0.839** (*CUSL*), and **0.836** (*LIKE*), all three reflectively measured constructs have high levels of internal consistency reliability. Similarly, the results for Cronbach's alpha (**0.776** for *COMP*, **0.831** for *CUSL*, and **0.831** for *LIKE*) and the composite reliability rho_c (**0.865** for *COMP*, **0.899** for *CUSL*, and **0.899** for *LIKE*) are above the 0.70 threshold (Hair et al., 2019), indicating that all construct measures are reliable. Note that the internal consistency reliability values of *CUSA* (**1.000**) must not be interpreted as an indication of perfect reliability – since *CUSA* is measured with a single item and its internal consistency reliability is by definition 1.

The results can also be visualized using a bar chart, requested by the `plot()` function on the `summary_corp_rep$reliability` object. This plot visualizes the reliability in terms of Cronbach's alpha, rho_A, and rho_C for all constructs. Note that the plots will be outputted to the plots panel window in RStudio (◘ Fig. 4.6):

```
# Plot the reliabilities of constructs
plot(summary_corp_rep$reliability)
```

The horizontal dashed blue line indicates the common minimum threshold level for the three reliability measures (i.e., 0.70). As indicated in ◘ Fig. 4.6, all Cronbach's alpha, rho_A, and rho_C values exceed the threshold.

4.6 · Case Study Illustration: Reflective Measurement Models

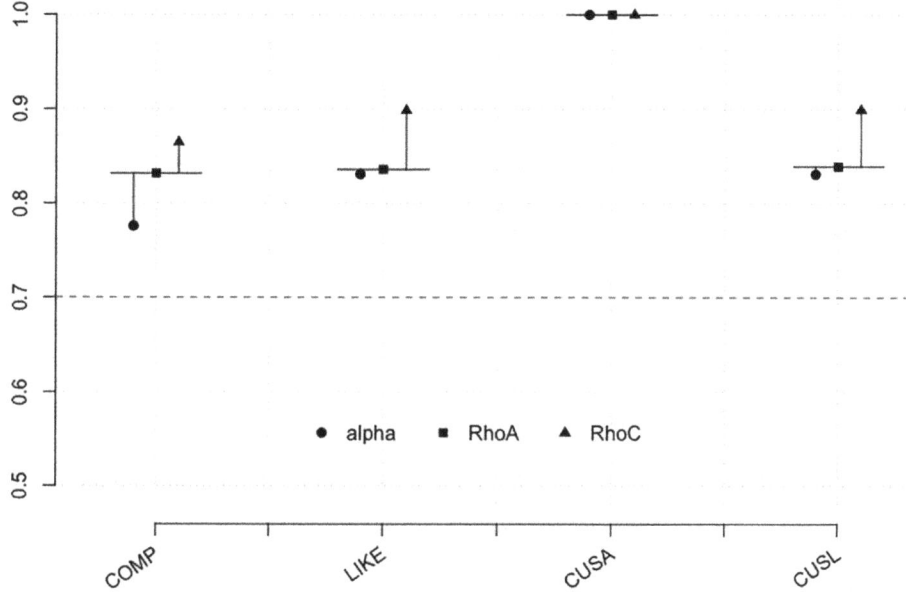

● **Fig. 4.6** Reliability charts. (Source: authors' screenshot from R)

Convergent validity assessment is based on the average variance extracted (AVE) values (Hair et al., 2019), which can also be accessed by **summary_corp_rep$reliability**. ● Figure 4.5 shows the AVE values along with the internal consistency reliability values. In this example, the AVE values of *COMP* (**0.681**), *CUSL* (**0.748**), and *LIKE* (**0.747**) are well above the required minimum level of 0.50 (Hair et al., 2019). Thus, the measures of the three reflectively measured constructs have high levels of convergent validity.

Finally, SEMinR offers several approaches to assess whether the construct measures empirically demonstrate discriminant validity. According to the Fornell–Larcker criterion (Fornell & Larcker, 1981), the square root of the AVE of each construct should be higher than the construct's highest correlation with any other construct in the model (this notion is identical to comparing the AVE with the squared correlations between the constructs). These results can be outputted by inspecting the **summary_corp_rep** object and **validity** element for the **fl_criteria**:

```
# Table of the FL criteria
summary_corp_rep$validity$fl_criteria
```

● Figure 4.7 shows the results of the Fornell–Larcker criterion assessment with the square root of the reflectively measured constructs' AVE on the diagonal and

```
Console   Terminal    Jobs
~/seminr/
> # Table of the FL criteria
> summary_corp_rep$validity$fl_criteria
      COMP  LIKE  CUSA  CUSL
COMP  0.825   .     .     .
LIKE  0.645 0.864   .     .
CUSA  0.436 0.528 1.000   .
CUSL  0.450 0.615 0.689 0.865

FL Criteria table reports square root of AVE on the diagonal and construct correlations on
the lower triangle.
>
```

■ **Fig. 4.7** Fornell–Larcker criterion table. (Source: authors' screenshot from RStudio)

```
Console   Terminal    Jobs
~/seminr/
> # HTMT Ratio
> summary_corp_rep$validity$htmt
      COMP  LIKE  CUSA CUSL
COMP    .     .     .    .
LIKE  0.780   .     .    .
CUSA  0.465 0.577   .    .
CUSL  0.532 0.737 0.755  .
>
```

■ **Fig. 4.8** HTMT result table. (Source: authors' screenshot from RStudio)

the correlations between the constructs in the off-diagonal position. For example, the reflectively measured construct $COMP$ has a value of **0.825** for the square root of its AVE, which needs to be compared with all correlation values in the column of $COMP$ (i.e., **0.645**, **0.436**, and **0.450**). Note that for CUSA, the comparison makes no sense, as the AVE of a single-item construct is **1.000** by design. Overall, the square roots of the AVEs for the reflectively measured constructs $COMP$ (**0.825**), $CUSL$ (**0.865**), and $LIKE$ (**0.864**) are all higher than the correlations of these constructs with other latent variables in the PLS path model.

Note that while frequently used in the past, the Fornell–Larcker criterion does not allow for reliably detecting discriminant validity issues. Specifically, in light of the Fornell–Larcker criterion's poor performance in detecting discriminant validity problems (Franke & Sarstedt, 2019; Henseler et al., 2015), any violation indicated by the criterion should be considered a severe issue. The primary criterion for discriminant validity assessment is the HTMT criterion, which can be accessed by inspecting the `summary_corp_rep()` object and `validity` element for the `$htmt`.

```
# HTMT criterion
summary_corp_rep$validity$htmt
```

4.6 · Case Study Illustration: Reflective Measurement Models

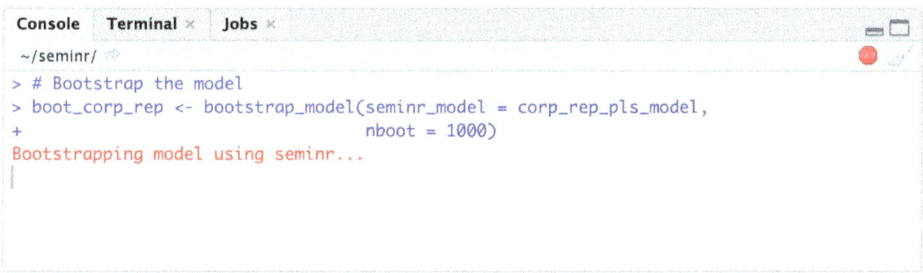

Fig. 4.9 Bootstrapping processing. (Source: authors' screenshot from RStudio)

Figure 4.8 shows the HTMT values for all pairs of constructs in a matrix format. As can be seen, all HTMT values are clearly lower than the more conservative threshold value of 0.85 (Henseler et al., 2015), even for *CUSA* and *CUSL*, which, from a conceptual viewpoint, are very similar. Recall that the threshold value for conceptually similar constructs, such as *CUSA* and *CUSL* or *COMP* and *LIKE*, is 0.90.

In addition to examining the HTMT values, researchers should test whether the HTMT values are significantly different from 1 or a lower threshold, such as 0.9 or even 0.85. This analysis requires computing bootstrap confidence intervals obtained by running the bootstrapping procedure. To do so, use the `bootstrap_model()` function and assign the output to an object, such as `boot_corp_rep`. Then, run the `summary()` function on the `boot_corp_rep` object and assign it to another object, such as `sum_boot_corp_rep`. In doing so, we need to set the significance level from 0.05 (default setting) to 0.10 using the ***alpha*** argument. In this way, we obtain 90% two-sided bootstrap confidence intervals for the HTMT values, which is equivalent to running a one-tailed test at 5%.

```
# Bootstrap the model
boot_corp_rep <- bootstrap_model(seminr_model = corp_rep_pls_
model, nboot = 1000)
sum_boot_corp_rep <- summary(boot_corp_rep, alpha = 0.10)
```

▶ Chapter 5 includes a more detailed introduction to the bootstrapping procedure and the argument settings. Bootstrapping should take a few seconds, since it is a processing-intensive operation. As the bootstrap computation is being performed, a red **STOP** indicator should show in the top-right corner of the console (Fig. 4.9). This indicator will automatically disappear when computation is complete, and the console will display "`SEMinR Model successfully bootstrapped.`"

```
Console   Terminal ×   Jobs ×
~/seminr/
> # Store the summary of the bootstrapped model
> sum_boot_corp_rep <- summary(boot_corp_rep, alpha = 0.10)
> # Extract the bootstrapped HTMT
> sum_boot_corp_rep$bootstrapped_HTMT
                Original Est. Bootstrap Mean Bootstrap SD T Stat.  5% CI 95% CI
COMP  ->  LIKE         0.780          0.779        0.040  19.278  0.706  0.843
COMP  ->  CUSA         0.465          0.467        0.056   8.338  0.366  0.554
COMP  ->  CUSL         0.532          0.533        0.059   9.046  0.433  0.627
LIKE  ->  CUSA         0.577          0.577        0.042  13.813  0.508  0.647
LIKE  ->  CUSL         0.737          0.736        0.042  17.721  0.667  0.801
CUSA  ->  CUSL         0.755          0.753        0.033  22.948  0.696  0.803
>
```

Fig. 4.10 Bootstrapped results and confidence intervals for HTMT. (Source: authors' screenshot from RStudio)

After running bootstrapping, access the bootstrapping confidence intervals of the HTMT by inspecting the `$bootstrapped_HTMT` of the `sum_boot_corp_rep` variable:

```
# Extract the bootstrapped HTMT
sum_boot_corp_rep$bootstrapped_HTMT
```

The output in Fig. 4.10 displays the original ratio estimates (column: **Original Est.**), bootstrapped mean ratio estimates (column: **Bootstrap Mean**), bootstrap standard deviation (column: **Bootstrap SD**), bootstrap *t*- statistic (column: **T Stat.**), and 90% confidence interval (columns: **5% CI** and **95% CI**, respectively) as produced by the percentile method. Note that the results in Fig. 4.10 might differ slightly from your results due to the random nature of the bootstrapping procedure. The differences in the overall bootstrapping results should be marginal if you use a sufficiently large number of bootstrap subsamples (e.g., 10,000). The columns labeled **5% CI** and **95% CI** show the lower and upper boundaries of the 90% confidence interval (percentile method). As can be seen, the confidence intervals' upper boundaries, in our example, are always lower than the threshold value of 0.90. For example, the lower and upper boundaries of the confidence interval of HTMT for the relationship between $COMP$ and $CUSA$ are **0.366** and **0.554**, respectively (again, your values might look slightly different because bootstrapping is a random process). To summarize, the bootstrap confidence interval results of the HTMT criterion clearly demonstrate the discriminant validity of the constructs and should be favored above the inferior Fornell–Larcker criterion.

Summary

The goal of reflective measurement model assessment is to ensure the reliability and validity of the construct measures and therefore provides support for the suitability of their inclusion in the path model. The key criteria include indicator reliability, internal consistency reliability (Cronbach's alpha, reliability rho_A, and composite reliability rho_C), convergent validity, and discriminant validity. Convergent validity implies that a construct includes more than 50% of the indicator's variance and is being evaluated using the AVE statistic. Another fundamental element of validity assessment concerns establishing discriminant validity, which ensures that each construct is empirically unique and captures a phenomenon not represented by other constructs in a statistical model. While the Fornell–Larcker criterion has long been the primary criterion for discriminant validity assessment, more recent research highlights that the HTMT criterion should be the preferred choice. Researchers using the HTMT should use bootstrapping to derive confidence intervals that allow assessing whether the values significantly differ from a specific threshold. Reflective measurement models are appropriate for further PLS-SEM analyses if they meet all these requirements.

Exercise

In this exercise, we once again call upon the influencer model and dataset described in the exercise section of ▶ Chap. 3. The data is called **influencer_data** and consists of 222 observations of 28 variables. The influencer model is illustrated in ▶ Fig. 3.10, and the indicators are described in ▶ Tables 3.9 and 3.10.
1. Load the influencer data, reproduce the influencer model in SEMinR syntax, and estimate the model.
2. Focus your attention on the three reflectively measured constructs product liking (*PL*), perceived quality (*PQ*), and purchase intention (*PI*). Evaluate the construct measures' reliability and validity as follows:
    (a) Do all three constructs meet the criteria for indicator reliability?
    (b) Do all three constructs meet the criteria for internal consistency reliability?
    (c) Do these three constructs display sufficient convergent validity?
    (d) Do these three constructs display sufficient discriminant validity?

References

Aguirre-Urreta, M. I., & Rönkkö, M. (2018). Statistical inference with PLSc using bootstrap confidence intervals. *MIS Quarterly, 42*(3), 1001–1020.

Diamantopoulos, A., Sarstedt, M., Fuchs, C., Wilczynski, P., & Kaiser, S. (2012). Guidelines for choosing between multi-item and single-item scales for construct measurement: A predictive validity perspective. *Journal of the Academy of Marketing Science, 40*(3), 434–449.

Dijkstra, T. K. (2010). Latent variables and indices: Herman Wold's basic design and partial least squares. In V. Esposito Vinzi, W. W. Chin, J. Henseler, & H. Wang (Eds.), *Handbook of partial least squares: Concepts, methods and applications Springer Handbooks of Computational Statistics Series* (Vol. II, pp. 23–46). Berlin: Springer.

Dijkstra, T. K. (2014). PLS' Janus face–response to professor Rigdon's 'rethinking partial least squares modeling: In praise of simple methods. *Long Range Planning, 47*(3), 146–153.

Dijkstra, T. K., & Henseler, J. (2015). Consistent partial least squares path modeling. *MIS Quarterly, 39*(2), 297–316.

Fornell, C., & Larcker, D. F. (1981). Evaluating structural equation models with unobservable variables and measurement error. *Journal of Marketing Research, 18*(1), 39–50.

Franke, G., & Sarstedt, M. (2019). Heuristics versus statistics in discriminant validity testing: A comparison of four procedures. *Internet Research, 29*(3), 430–447.

Hair, J. F., Hult, T., Ringle, C. M., & Sarstedt, M. (2022). *A primer on partial least squares structural equation modeling (PLS-SEM)* (3rd ed.). Thousand Oaks: Sage.

Henseler, J., Ringle, C. M., & Sarstedt, M. (2015). A new criterion for assessing discriminant validity in variance-based structural equation modeling. *Journal of the Academy of Marketing Science, 43*(1), 115–135.

Hair, J. F., Risher, J. J., Sarstedt, M., & Ringle, C. M. (2019). When to use and how to report the results of PLS-SEM. *European Business Review, 31*(1), 2–24.

Hulland, J. (1999). Use of partial least squares (PLS) in strategic management research: A review of four recent studies. *Strategic Management Journal, 20*(2), 195–204.

Jöreskog, K. G. (1971). Simultaneous factor analysis in several populations. *Psychometrika, 36*(4), 409–426.

Radomir, L., & Moisescu, O. I. (2019). Discriminant validity of the customer-based corporate reputation scale: Some causes for concern. *Journal of Product & Brand Management, 29*(4), 457–469.

Streukens, S., & Leroi-Werelds, S. (2016). Bootstrapping and PLS-SEM: A step-by-step guide to get more out of your bootstrapping results. *European Management Journal, 34*(6), 618–632.

Trizano-Hermosilla, I., & Alvarado, J. M. (2016). Best alternatives to Cronbach's alpha reliability in realistic conditions: Congeneric and asymmetrical measurements. *Frontiers in Psychology, 7*, 769.

Suggested Reading

Hair, J. F., Hult, T., Ringle, C. M., & Sarstedt, M. (2022). *A primer on partial least squares structural equation modeling (PLS-SEM)* (3rd ed.). Thousand Oaks: Sage.

Hair, J. F., Risher, J. J., Sarstedt, M., & Ringle, C. M. (2019). When to use and how to report the results of PLS-SEM. *European Business Review, 31*(1), 2–24.

Hair, J. F., Sarstedt, M., & Ringle, C. M. (2019). Rethinking some of the rethinking of partial least squares. *European Journal of Marketing, 53*(4), 566–584.

Sarstedt, M., Hair, J. F., & Ringle, C. M. (2021). Partial least squares structural equation modeling. In C. Homburg, M. Klarmann, & A. Vomberg (Eds.), *Handbook of Market Research*. Cham: Springer.

Open Access This chapter is licensed under the terms of the Creative Commons Attribution 4.0 International License (http://creativecommons.org/licenses/by/4.0/), which permits use, sharing, adaptation, distribution and reproduction in any medium or format, as long as you give appropriate credit to the original author(s) and the source, provide a link to the Creative Commons license and indicate if changes were made.

The images or other third party material in this chapter are included in the chapter's Creative Commons license, unless indicated otherwise in a credit line to the material. If material is not included in the chapter's Creative Commons license and your intended use is not permitted by statutory regulation or exceeds the permitted use, you will need to obtain permission directly from the copyright holder.

Evaluation of Formative Measurement Models

Contents

5.1 Convergent Validity – 92

5.2 Indicator Collinearity – 93

5.3 Statistical Significance and Relevance of the Indicator Weights – 93

5.4 Case Study Illustration: Formative Measurement Models – 97
5.4.1 Model Setup and Estimation – 97
5.4.2 Reflective Measurement Model Evaluation – 102
5.4.3 Formative Measurement Model Evaluation – 102

References – 111

© The Author(s) 2021
J. F. Hair Jr. et al., *Partial Least Squares Structural Equation Modeling (PLS-SEM) Using R*, Classroom Companion: Business, https://doi.org/10.1007/978-3-030-80519-7_5

Learning Objectives
After reading this chapter, you should understand:
1. The concept of redundancy analysis and how to apply it to evaluate convergent validity
2. Collinearity, its implications, and how to assess it
3. Significance testing using bootstrapping and bootstrap confidence intervals
4. How to assess formative measurement models using SEMinR

PLS-SEM is the preferred approach when formatively specified constructs are included in the PLS path model (Hair, Risher, Sarstedt, & Ringle, 2019). In this chapter, we discuss the key steps for evaluating **formative measurement models** (◘ Fig. 5.1). Relevant criteria include the assessment of (1) convergent validity, (2) indicator collinearity, and (3) statistical significance and relevance of the indicator weights. In the following, we introduce key criteria and their thresholds and illustrate their use with an extended version of the corporate reputation model.

5.1 Convergent Validity

In formative measurement model evaluation, **convergent validity** refers to the degree to which the formatively specified construct correlates with an alternative reflectively measured variable(s) of the same concept. Originally proposed by Chin (1998), the procedure is referred to as **redundancy analysis**. To execute this procedure for determining convergent validity, researchers must plan ahead in the research design stage by including an alternative measure of the formatively measured construct in their questionnaire. Cheah, Sarstedt, Ringle, Ramayah, and Ting (2018) show that a global single item, which captures the essence of the construct under consideration, is generally sufficient as an alternative measure – despite limitations with regard to criterion validity (Diamantopoulos, Sarstedt, Fuchs, Wilczynski, & Kaiser, 2012; Sarstedt, Diamantopoulos, Salzberger, & Baumgartner, 2016). When the model is based on secondary data, a variable measuring a similar

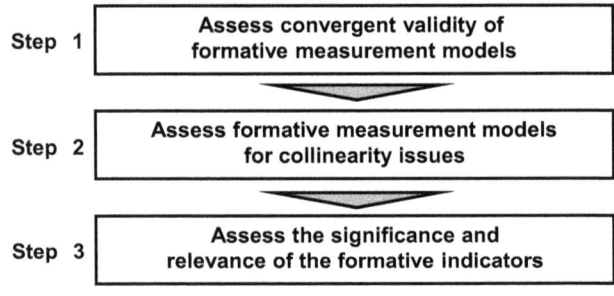

◘ Fig. 5.1 Formative measurement model assessment procedure. (Source: Hair, Hult, Ringle, & Sarstedt, 2022, Chap. 5; used with permission by Sage)

concept would be used (Houston, 2004). Hair et al. (2022) suggest the correlation of the formatively measured construct with the reflectively measured item(s) should be 0.708 or higher, which implies that the construct explains (more than) 50% of the alternative measure's variance.

5.2 Indicator Collinearity

Collinearity occurs when two or more indicators in a formative measurement model are highly correlated. High correlation increases the **standard error** of the indicator weights, thereby triggering type II errors (i.e., false negatives). More pronounced levels of collinearity can even trigger sign changes in the indicator weights, which leads to interpretational confounding. For example, a collinearity-induced sign change might lead to a negative weight in an indicator measuring an aspect of corporate performance such as "[the company] is a very well-managed company." Such a sign change would imply the better the respondents' assessment of the company's management, the lower its perceived performance. This type of result is inconsistent with a priori assumptions and is particularly counterintuitive when the correlation between the construct and the indicator is in fact positive. The standard metric for assessing indicator collinearity is the **variance inflation factor (VIF)**. When **VIF** values are higher, the level of collinearity is greater. **VIF** values of 5 or above indicate collinearity problems. In this case, researchers should take adequate measures to reduce the collinearity level, for example, by eliminating or merging indicators or establishing a **higher-order construct** – see Hair et al. (2022, Chap. 5). However, collinearity issues can also occur at lower **VIF** values of 3 (Becker, Ringle, Sarstedt, & Völckner, 2015; Mason & Perreault, 1991). Hence, when the analysis produces unexpected sign changes in the indicator weights, the initial step is to compare the sign of the relationship using bivariate correlation. If the relationship sign differs from the correlation sign, researchers should revise the model setup, also by eliminating or merging indicators or establishing a higher-order construct.

5.3 Statistical Significance and Relevance of the Indicator Weights

The third step in assessing formatively measured constructs is examining the statistical significance and relevance (i.e., size) of the indicator weights. The **indicator weights** result from regressing each formatively measured construct on its associated indicators. As such, they represent each indicator's relative importance for forming the construct. **Significance testing** of the indicator weights relies on the bootstrapping procedure, which facilitates deriving standard errors from the data without relying on any distributional assumptions (Hair, Sarstedt, Hopkins, & Kuppelwieser, 2014).

> **Excurse**
>
> In **bootstrapping**, a large number of samples (i.e., **bootstrap samples**) are drawn from the original sample, with replacement (Davison & Hinkley, 1997). The number of bootstrap samples should be high but must be at least equal to the number of valid observations in the dataset. Reviewing prior research on bootstrapping implementations, Streukens and Leroi-Werelds (2016) recommend that PLS-SEM applications should be based on at least 10,000 bootstrap samples. The bootstrap samples are used to estimate the PLS path model 10,000 times. The resulting parameter estimates, such as the indicator weights or path coefficients, form a bootstrap distribution that can be viewed as an approximation of the sampling distribution. Based on this distribution, it is possible to calculate the standard error, which is the standard deviation of the estimated coefficients across bootstrap samples. Using the standard error as input, we can evaluate the statistical significance of the model parameters.

The bootstrapping procedure yields t-values for the indicator weights (and other model parameters). We need to compare these t-values with the **critical values** from the standard normal distribution to decide whether the coefficients are significantly different from zero. Assuming a significance level of 5%, a t-value above 1.96 (two-tailed test) suggests that the indicator weight is statistically significant. The critical values for significance levels of 1% ($\alpha = 0.01$) and 10% ($\alpha = 0.10$) probability of error are 2.576 and 1.645 (two tailed), respectively.

Confidence intervals are an alternative way to test for the significance of indicator weights. They represent the range within which the population parameter will fall assuming a certain level of confidence (e.g., 95%). In the PLS-SEM context, we also refer to **bootstrap confidence intervals** because the construction of the confidence interval is inferred from the estimates generated by the bootstrapping process (Henseler, Ringle, & Sinkovics, 2009). Several types of confidence intervals have been proposed in the context of PLS-SEM – see Hair et al. (2022, Chap. 5) for an overview. Results from Aguirre-Urreta and Rönkkö (2018) indicate the **percentile method** is preferred, as it exceeds other methods in terms of coverage and balance, producing comparably narrow confidence intervals. If a confidence interval does not include the value zero, the weight can be considered statistically significant, and the indicator can be retained. On the contrary, if the confidence interval of an indicator weight includes zero, this indicates the weight is not statistically significant (assuming the given significance level, e.g., 5%). In such a situation, the indicator should be considered for removal from the measurement model.

However, if an indicator weight is not significant, it is not necessarily interpreted as evidence of poor measurement model quality. We recommend you also consider the **absolute contribution** of a formative indicator to the construct (Cenfetelli & Bassellier, 2009), which is determined by the formative indicator's loading. At a minimum, a formative indicator's loading should be statistically significant. Indicator loadings of 0.5 and higher suggest the indicator makes a sufficient absolute contribution to forming the construct, even if it lacks a significant **relative contribution**. ◘ Figure 5.2 shows the decision-making process for testing formative indicator weights.

5.3 · Statistical Significance and Relevance of the Indicator Weights

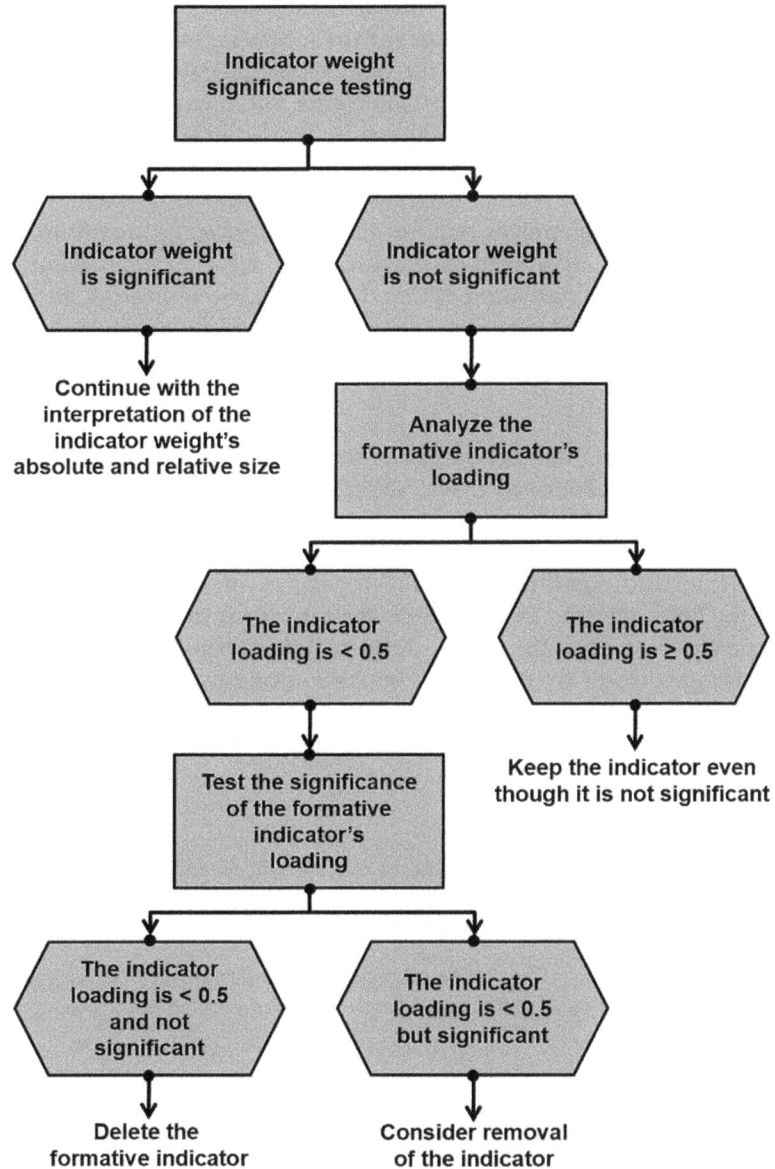

Fig. 5.2 Decision-making process for keeping or deleting formative indicators. (Source: Hair et al., 2022, Chap. 5; used with permission by Sage)

When deciding whether to delete formative indicators based on statistical outcomes, researchers need to be cautious for the following reasons. First, formative indicator weights are a function of the number of indicators used to measure a construct. The greater the number of indicators, the lower their average weight. Formative measurement models are inherently limited in the number of indicator weights that can be statistically significant (e.g., Cenfetelli & Bassellier, 2009). Second, indicators should seldom be removed from formative measurement models since formative measurement requires the indicators to fully capture the entire domain of a construct, as defined by the researcher in the conceptualization stage. In contrast to reflective measurement models, formative indicators are not interchangeable, and removing even one indicator can therefore reduce the measurement model's content validity (Bollen & Diamantopoulos, 2017).

> **Important**
> Formative indicators with nonsignificant weights should not automatically be removed from the measurement model, since this step may compromise the content validity of the construct.

After the statistical significance of the formative indicator weights has been assessed, the final step is to examine each indicator's relevance. With regard to relevance, indicator weights are standardized to values between −1 and +1. Thus, indicator weights closer to +1 (or −1) indicate strong positive (or negative) relationships, and weights closer to 0 indicate relatively weak relationships. ◘ Table 5.1 summarizes the rules of thumb for formative measurement model assessment.

◘ Table 5.1 Rules of thumb for formative measurement model assessment

Criterion	Metrics and thresholds
Convergent validity (redundancy analysis)	≥ 0.708 correlation between the formative construct and a reflective (or single-item) measurement of the same concept
Collinearity	Critical collinearity issues likely occur if **VIF** ≥ 5 Collinearity issues are usually uncritical if **VIF** = 3–5 Collinearity is not a problematic issue if **VIF** < 3
Statistical significance of indicator weights	t-values are greater than 2.576 ($\alpha = 0.01$), 1.960 ($\alpha = 0.05$), or 1.645 ($\alpha = 0.10$), respectively (two tailed) The 95% percentile confidence interval ($\alpha = 0.05$) does not include zero
Relevance of indicators with a significant weight	Larger significant indicator weights indicate a higher relative contribution of the indicator to the construct
Relevance of indicators with nonsignificant weights	Indicators with loadings of ≥0.50 that are statistically significant are considered relevant

Source: authors' own table

5.4 Case Study Illustration: Formative Measurement Models

5.4.1 Model Setup and Estimation

The simple corporate reputation model introduced in ▶ Chap. 3 (▶ Fig. 3.2) and evaluated in ▶ Chap. 4 describes the relationships between the two dimensions of corporate reputation (i.e., competence and likeability) as well as the two key target constructs (i.e., customer satisfaction and loyalty). While the simple model is useful to explain how corporate reputation affects customer satisfaction and customer loyalty, it does not indicate how companies can effectively manage (i.e., improve) their corporate reputation. Schwaiger (2004) identified four driver constructs of corporate reputation that companies can manage by means of corporate-level marketing activities. ◘ Table 5.2 lists and defines the four driver constructs of corporate reputation.

All four driver constructs are (positively) related to the competence and likeability dimensions of corporate reputation in the path model. ◘ Figure 5.3 shows

◘ **Table 5.2** The driver constructs of corporate reputation

Construct name	Construct definition
QUAL	The quality of a company's products and services as well as its quality of customer orientation
PERF	The company's economic and managerial performance
CSOR	The company's corporate social responsibility
ATTR	The company's attractiveness as an employer

Source: authors' own table

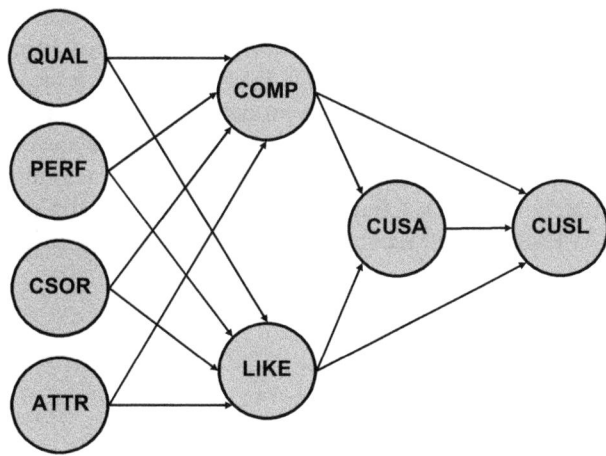

◘ **Fig. 5.3** The extended corporate reputation model. (Source: Hair et al., 2022, Chap. 5; used with permission by Sage)

the constructs and their relationships, which represent the extended structural model for our PLS-SEM example in the remaining chapters of the book. To summarize, the extended corporate reputation model has three main conceptual/theoretical components:
1. The target constructs of interest (*CUSA* and *CUSL*)
2. The two corporate reputation dimensions, *COMP* and *LIKE*, that represent key determinants of the target constructs
3. The four exogenous driver constructs (i.e., *ATTR*, *CSOR*, *PERF*, and *QUAL*) of the two corporate reputation dimensions

The endogenous constructs on the right-hand side in ◘ Fig. 5.3 include a single-item construct (i.e., *CUSA*) and three reflectively measured constructs (i.e., *COMP*, *CUSL*, and *LIKE*). In contrast, the four new driver constructs (i.e., exogenous latent variables) on the left-hand side of ◘ Fig. 5.3 (i.e., *ATTR*, *CSOR*, *PERF*, and *QUAL*) have formative measurement models in accordance with their role in the reputation model (Schwaiger, 2004). Specifically, the four new constructs are measured by a total of 21 formative indicators (detailed in ◘ Table 5.3) that have been derived from literature, qualitative studies, and quantitative pretests (for more details, see Schwaiger, 2004). ◘ Table 5.3 also lists the single-item reflective global measures for validating the formative driver constructs when executing the redundancy analysis.

We continue to use the `corp_rep_data` dataset with 344 observations introduced in ▶ Chap. 3 for our PLS-SEM analyses. Unlike in the simple model that was used in the previous chapter, we now also have to consider the formative measurement models when deciding on the minimum sample size required to estimate the model. The maximum number of arrowheads pointing at a particular construct occurs in the measurement model of *QUAL*. All other formatively measured constructs have fewer indicators. Similarly, there are fewer arrows pointing at each of the endogenous constructs in the structural model. Therefore, when building on the 10-time rule of thumb, we would need 8 · 10 = 80 observations. Alternatively, following Cohen's (1992) recommendations for multiple ordinary least squares regression analysis or running a power analysis using the G*Power program (Faul, Erdfelder, Buchner, & Lang, 2009), we would need only 54 observations to detect R^2 values of around 0.25, assuming a significance level of 5% and a statistical power of 80%. When considering the more conservative approach suggested by Kock and Hadaya (2018), we obtain a higher minimum sample size. Considering prior research on the corporate reputation model, we expect a minimum path coefficient of 0.15 in the structural model. Assuming a significance level of 5% and statistical power of 80%, the inverse square root method yields a minimum sample size of approximately 155 (see ▶ Chap. 1 for a discussion of sample size and power considerations).

The corporate reputation data can be accessed by the object name `corp_rep_data`:

```
# Load the SEMinR library
library(seminr)
# Load the corporate reputation data
corp_rep_data <- corp_rep_data
```

5.4 · Case Study Illustration: Formative Measurement Models

Table 5.3 The indicators of the formatively measured constructs

Quality (*QUAL*)

qual_1	The products/services offered by [the company] are of high quality
qual_2	[The company] is an innovator, rather than an imitator with respect to [industry]
qual_3	[The company]'s products/services offer good value for money
qual_4	The products/services offered by [the company] are good
qual_5	Customer concerns are held in high regard at [the company]
qual_6	[The company] is a reliable partner for customers
qual_7	[The company] is a trustworthy company
qual_8	I have a lot of respect for [the company]

Performance (*PERF*)

perf_1	[The company] is a very well-managed company
perf_2	[The company] is an economically stable company
perf_3	The business risk for [the company] is modest compared to its competitors
perf_4	[The company] has growth potential
perf_5	[The company] has a clear vision about the future of the company

Corporate social responsibility (*CSOR*)

csor_1	[The company] behaves in a socially conscious way
csor_2	[The company] is forthright in giving information to the public
csor_3	[The company] has a fair attitude toward competitors
csor_4	[The company] is concerned about the preservation of the environment
csor_5	[The company] is not only concerned about profits

Attractiveness (*ATTR*)

attr_1	[The company] is successful in attracting high-quality employees
attr_2	I could see myself working at [the company]
attr_3	I like the physical appearance of [the company] (company, buildings, shops, etc.)

Single-item measures of *QUAL*, *PERF*, *CSOR*, and *ATTR* for the redundancy analysis

qual_global	Please assess the overall quality of [the company's] activities
perf_global	Please assess [the company's] overall performance
csor_global	Please assess the extent to which [the company] acts in socially conscious ways
attr_global	[The company] has a high overall attractiveness

Source: Hair et al., 2022, Chap. 5; used with permission by Sage

> **Excurse**
>
> The corporate reputation data file and project are also bundled with SEMinR. Once the SEMinR library has been loaded, we can access the demonstration code for ► Chap. 5 by using the `demo()` function on the object "`seminr-primer-chap5`".

The extended corporate reputation model's structural and measurement models will have to be specified using the SEMinR syntax. Remember that the four drivers are formative constructs, estimated with `mode_B`, while *COMP*, *CUSL* and *LIKE* are reflective constructs, estimated with `mode_A`. The `weights` parameter of the `composite()` function is set by default to `mode_A`. Thus, when no weights are specified, the construct is estimated as being reflective. Alternatively, we can explicitly specify the `mode_A` setting for reflectively measured constructs or the `mode_B` setting for formatively measured constructs. Once the model is set up, we use the `estimate_pls()` function to estimate the model, this time specifying the *measurement_model* and *structural_model* parameters to the extended corporate reputation model objects (`corp_rep_mm_ext`, `corp_rep_sm_ext`). Finally, we apply the `summary()` function to the estimated SEMinR model object `corp_rep_pls_model_ext` and store the output in the `summary_corp_rep_ext` object:

```
# Create measurement model
corp_rep_mm_ext <- constructs(
  composite("QUAL", multi_items("qual_", 1:8), weights =
mode_B),
  composite("PERF", multi_items("perf_", 1:5), weights =
mode_B),
  composite("CSOR", multi_items("csor_", 1:5), weights =
mode_B),
  composite("ATTR", multi_items("attr_", 1:3), weights =
mode_B),
  composite("COMP", multi_items("comp_", 1:3)),
  composite("LIKE", multi_items("like_", 1:3)),
  composite("CUSA", single_item("cusa")),
  composite("CUSL", multi_items("cusl_", 1:3))
)
# Create structural model
corp_rep_sm_ext <- relationships(
  paths(from = c("QUAL", "PERF", "CSOR", "ATTR"), to =
c("COMP", "LIKE")),
  paths(from = c("COMP", "LIKE"), to = c("CUSA", "CUSL")),
  paths(from = c("CUSA"), to = c("CUSL"))
)
# Estimate the model
corp_rep_pls_model_ext <- estimate_pls(
  data = corp_rep_data,
  measurement_model = corp_rep_mm_ext,
  structural_model = corp_rep_sm_ext,
```

5.4 · Case Study Illustration: Formative Measurement Models

```
    missing = mean_replacement,
    missing_value = "-99")
# Summarize the model results
summary_corp_rep_ext <- summary(corp_rep_pls_model_ext)
```

Just like the indicator data that we used in previous chapters, the `corp_rep_data` dataset has very few missing values. The number of missing observations is reported in the descriptive statistic object nested within the summary return object. This report can be accessed by inspecting the `summary_corp_rep_ext$descriptives$statistics` object. Only the indicators *cusl_1* (three missing values, 0.87% of all responses on this indicator), *cusl_2* (four missing values, 1.16% of all responses on this indicator), *cusl_3* (three missing values, 0.87% of all responses on this indicator), and *cusa* (one missing value, 0.29% of all responses on this indicator) include missing values. Since the number of missing values is relatively small (i.e., less than 5% missing values per indicator; Hair et al., 2022, Chap. 2), we use mean value replacement to deal with missing data when running the PLS-SEM algorithm (see also Grimm & Wagner, 2020).

When the PLS-SEM algorithm stops running, check whether the algorithm converged (Hair et al., 2022, Chap. 3). For this example, the PLS-SEM algorithm will stop when the maximum number of 300 iterations or the stop criterion of 1.0E-7 (i.e., 0.0000001) is reached. To do so, it is necessary to inspect the `corp_rep_pls_model` object by using the `$` operator:

```
# Iterations to converge
summary_corp_rep_ext$iterations
```

The results show that the model estimation converged after eight iterations. Next, the model must be bootstrapped to assess the indicator weights' significance. For now, we run a simple bootstrap as conducted in ▶ Chap. 4. But in this chapter, we discuss the bootstrap function in further detail when assessing the formative indicator weights' significance. To run the bootstrapping procedure in SEMinR, we use the `bootstrap_model()` function and assign the output to a variable; we call our variable `boot_corp_rep_ext`. Then, we run the `summary()` function on the `boot_corp_rep` object and assign it to another variable, such as `sum_boot_corp_rep_ext`.

```
# Bootstrap the model
boot_corp_rep_ext <- bootstrap_model(
seminr_model = corp_rep_pls_model_ext, nboot = 1000)
# Store the summary of the bootstrapped model
sum_boot_corp_rep_ext <- summary(boot_corp_rep_ext,
alpha = 0.10)
```

5.4.2 Reflective Measurement Model Evaluation

An important characteristic of PLS-SEM is that the model estimates will change when any of the model relationships or variables are changed. We thus need to reassess the reflective measurement models to ensure that this portion of the model remains valid and reliable before continuing to evaluate the four new exogenous formative constructs. We then follow the reflective measurement model assessment procedure in ▶ Fig. 4.1 (for a refresher on this topic, return to ▶ Chap. 4). The reflectively measured constructs meet all criteria as discussed in ▶ Chap. 4 – for a detailed discussion of the assessment of reflectively measured constructs for this model, see Appendix B.

5.4.3 Formative Measurement Model Evaluation

To evaluate the formatively measured constructs of the extended corporate reputation model, we follow the formative measurement model assessment procedure (◘ Fig. 5.1). First, we need to examine whether the formatively measured constructs exhibit convergent validity. To do so, we need to carry out a separate redundancy analysis for each construct. The original survey contained global single-item measures with generic assessments of the four concepts – attractiveness, corporate social responsibility, performance, and quality – that we can use as measures of the dependent construct in the redundancy analyses (*attr_global*, *csor_global*, *perf_global*, and *qual_global*) (◘ Table 5.3). Note that when designing a research study that includes formatively measured constructs, you need to include this type of global measure in the survey. ◘ Figure 5.4 shows the model set-ups for the redundancy analyses of the four formatively measured constructs in the extended corporate reputation model.

```
# Redundancy analysis
# ATTR
# Create measurement model
ATTR_redundancy_mm <- constructs(
  composite("ATTR_F", multi_items("attr_", 1:3), weights = 
mode_B),
  composite("ATTR_G", single_item("attr_global"))
)
# Create structural model
ATTR_redundancy_sm <- relationships(
  paths(from = c("ATTR_F"), to = c("ATTR_G"))
)
# Estimate the model
ATTR_redundancy_pls_model <- estimate_pls(
  data = corp_rep_data,
  measurement_model = ATTR_redundancy_mm,
  structural_model = ATTR_redundancy_sm,
  missing = mean_replacement,
  missing_value = "-99")
# Summarize the model
sum_ATTR_red_model <- summary(ATTR_redundancy_pls_model)
# CSOR
```

5.4 · Case Study Illustration: Formative Measurement Models

```
# Create measurement model
CSOR_redundancy_mm <- constructs(
  composite("CSOR_F", multi_items("csor_", 1:5), weights = mode_B),
  composite("CSOR_G", single_item("csor_global"))
)
# Create structural model
CSOR_redundancy_sm <- relationships(
  paths(from = c("CSOR_F"), to = c("CSOR_G"))
)
# Estimate the model
CSOR_redundancy_pls_model <- estimate_pls(
  data = corp_rep_data,
  measurement_model = CSOR_redundancy_mm,
  structural_model = CSOR_redundancy_sm,
  missing = mean_replacement,
  missing_value = "-99")
# Summarize the model
sum_CSOR_red_model <- summary(CSOR_redundancy_pls_model)
# PERF
# Create measurement model
PERF_redundancy_mm <- constructs(
  composite("PERF_F", multi_items("perf_", 1:5), weights = mode_B),
  composite("PERF_G", single_item("perf_global"))
)
# Create structural model
PERF_redundancy_sm <- relationships(
  paths(from = c("PERF_F"), to = c("PERF_G"))
)
# Estimate the model
PERF_redundancy_pls_model <- estimate_pls(
  data = corp_rep_data,
  measurement_model = PERF_redundancy_mm,
  structural_model  = PERF_redundancy_sm,
  missing = mean_replacement,
  missing_value = "-99")
# Summarize the model
sum_PERF_red_model <- summary(PERF_redundancy_pls_model)

# QUAL
# Create measurement model
QUAL_redundancy_mm <- constructs(
  composite("QUAL_F", multi_items("qual_", 1:8), weights = mode_B),
  composite("QUAL_G", single_item("qual_global"))
)
# Create structural model
QUAL_redundancy_sm <- relationships(
  paths(from = c("QUAL_F"), to = c("QUAL_G"))
)
# Estimate the model
QUAL_redundancy_pls_model <- estimate_pls(
```

```
    data = corp_rep_data,
    measurement_model = QUAL_redundancy_mm,
    structural_model  = QUAL_redundancy_sm,
    missing = mean_replacement,
    missing_value = "-99")
# Summarize the model
sum_QUAL_red_model <- summary(QUAL_redundancy_pls_model)
# Check the path coefficients for convergent validity
sum_ATTR_red_model$paths
sum_CSOR_red_model$paths
sum_PERF_red_model$paths
sum_QUAL_red_model$paths
```

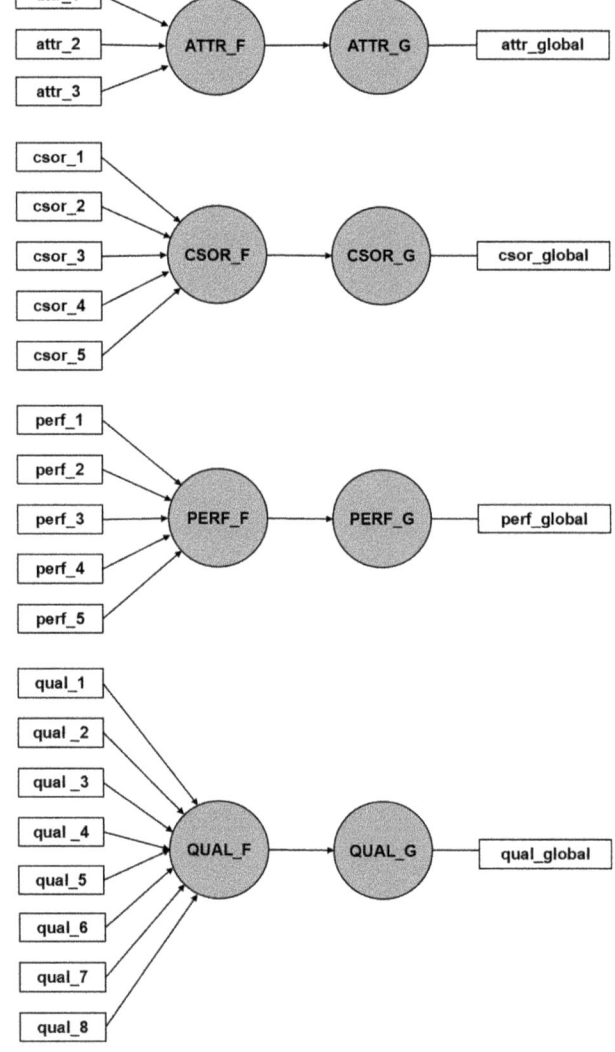

Fig. 5.4 Redundancy analysis of formatively measured constructs. (Source: authors' own figure)

5.4 · Case Study Illustration: Formative Measurement Models

In order to run the redundancy analysis for a formatively measured construct, it must be linked with an alternative measure of the same concept. When considering the formatively measured construct *ATTR*, the measurement model for the redundancy analysis consists of two constructs: (1) *ATTR_F*, which is measured by three formative indicators *attr_1*, *attr_2*, and *attr_3*, and (2) *ATTR_G*, which is measured by the single item *attr_global*. The structural model consists of a single path from *ATTR_F* to *ATTR_G*. We then estimate this model using the `corp_rep_data` dataset and assign the output to the `ATTR_redundancy_pls_model` object. Finally, to identify the path between the two constructs, we need to inspect the `sum_ATTR_red_model$paths`.

> Each redundancy analysis model is included in the SEMinR demo file accessible at `demo ("seminr-primer-chap5")`, so that the code can easily be replicated. Alternatively, we can create these four models for the convergent validity assessment manually using the code outlined above. Following the steps described in previous chapters, a new structural and measurement model must be created using the SEMinR syntax for each redundancy analysis, and the subsequently estimated model object needs to be inspected for the path coefficients.

> Figure 5.5 shows the results for the redundancy analysis of the four formatively measured constructs. For the *ATTR* construct, this analysis yields a path coefficient of 0.874, which is above the recommended threshold of 0.708 (Table 5.1),

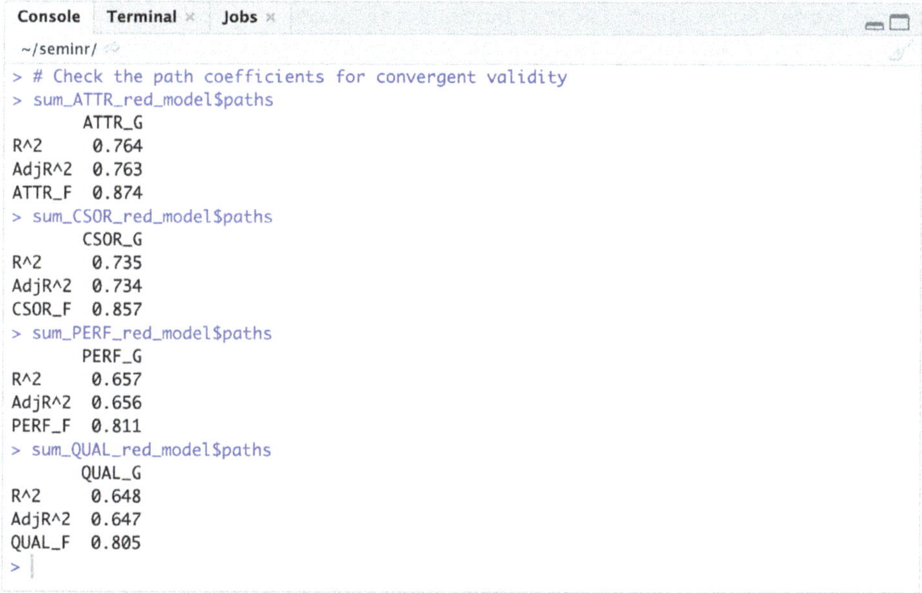

```
Console   Terminal    Jobs
~/seminr/
> # Check the path coefficients for convergent validity
> sum_ATTR_red_model$paths
         ATTR_G
R^2      0.764
AdjR^2   0.763
ATTR_F   0.874
> sum_CSOR_red_model$paths
         CSOR_G
R^2      0.735
AdjR^2   0.734
CSOR_F   0.857
> sum_PERF_red_model$paths
         PERF_G
R^2      0.657
AdjR^2   0.656
PERF_F   0.811
> sum_QUAL_red_model$paths
         QUAL_G
R^2      0.648
AdjR^2   0.647
QUAL_F   0.805
>
```

Fig. 5.5 Output of the redundancy analysis for formative measurement models. (Source: authors' screenshot from R)

thus providing support for the formatively measured construct's convergent validity. The redundancy analyses of *CSOR*, *PERF*, and *QUAL* yield estimates of 0.857, 0.811, and 0.805, respectively. Thus, all formatively measured constructs exhibit convergent validity.

In the second step of the assessment procedure (◘ Fig. 5.1), we check the formative measurement models for collinearity by looking at the formative indicators' **VIF** values. The **summary_corp_rep_ext** object can be inspected for the indicator **VIF** values by considering the **validity** element for **vif_items**; **summary_corp_rep_ext$validity$vif_items**.

```
# Collinearity analysis
summary_corp_rep_ext$validity$vif_items
```

Note that SEMinR also provides **VIF** values for reflective indicators. However, since we expect high correlations among reflective indicators, we do not interpret these results but focus on the formative indicators' **VIF** values.

According to the results in ◘ Fig. 5.6, *qual_3* has the highest **VIF** value (2.269). Hence, all **VIF** values are uniformly below the conservative threshold value of 3 (◘ Table 5.1). We therefore conclude that collinearity does not reach critical levels in any of the formative measurement models and is not an issue for the estimation of the extended corporate reputation model.

Next, we need to analyze the indicator weights for their significance and relevance (◘ Fig. 5.1). We first consider the significance of the indicator weights by means of bootstrapping. To run the bootstrapping procedure, we use the **bootstrap_model()** function. The first parameter (i.e., *seminr_model*) allows specifying the model on which we apply bootstrapping. The second parameter *nboot* allows us to select the number of bootstrap samples to use. Per default, we should use 10,000 bootstrap samples (Streukens & Leroi-Werelds, 2016). Since using such a great number of samples requires much computational time, we may choose a smaller number of samples (e.g., 1,000) for the initial model estimation. For the final result reporting, however, we should use the recommended number of 10,000 bootstrap samples.

The *cores* parameter enables us to use multiple cores of your computer's central processing unit (CPU). We recommend using this option since it makes bootstrapping much faster. As you might not know the number of cores in your device, we recommend using the **parallel::detectCores()** function to automatically detect the number of cores and use the maximum cores available. By default, *cores* will be set to the maximum value and as such, if you do not specify this parameter, your bootstrap will default to using the maximum computing power of your CPU. Finally, *seed* allows reproducing the results of a specific bootstrap run while maintaining the random nature of the process. Assign the output of the **bootstrap_model()** function to the **boot_corp_rep_ext** object. Finally, we need to run the **summary()** function on the **boot_corp_rep_ext** object and set the *alpha* parameter. The *alpha* parameter allows selecting the significance level (the default

5.4 · Case Study Illustration: Formative Measurement Models

```
Console   Terminal   Jobs
~/seminr/
> # Collinearity analysis ----
> summary_corp_rep_ext$validity$vif_items
QUAL :
qual_1 qual_2 qual_3 qual_4 qual_5 qual_6 qual_7 qual_8
 1.806  1.632  2.269  1.957  2.201  2.008  1.623  1.362

PERF :
perf_1 perf_2 perf_3 perf_4 perf_5
 1.560  1.506  1.229  1.316  1.331

CSOR :
csor_1 csor_2 csor_3 csor_4 csor_5
 1.560  1.487  1.735  1.556  1.712

ATTR :
attr_1 attr_2 attr_3
 1.275  1.129  1.264

COMP :
comp_1 comp_2 comp_3
 1.397  1.787  1.888

LIKE :
like_1 like_2 like_3
 1.945  2.000  1.811

CUSA :
cusa
   1

CUSL :
cusl_1 cusl_2 cusl_3
 1.802  2.564  1.933

>
```

■ **Fig. 5.6** VIF values. (Source: authors' screenshot from R)

is 0.05) for two-tailed testing. When testing indicator weights, we follow general convention and apply two-tailed testing at a significance level of 5%.

```
# Bootstrap the model
# seminr_model is the SEMinR model to be bootstrapped
# nboot is the number of bootstrap iterations to run
# cores is the number of cpu cores to use
# in multicore bootstrapping
# parallel::detectCores() allows for using
# the maximum cores on your device
# seed is the seed to be used for making bootstrap replicable
```

```
boot_corp_rep_ext <- bootstrap_model(
  seminr_model = corp_rep_pls_model_ext,
  nboot = 1000,
  cores = parallel::detectCores(),
  seed = 123)
# Summarize the results of the bootstrap
# alpha sets the specified level for significance, i.e. 0.05
sum_boot_corp_rep_ext <- summary(boot_corp_rep_ext, alpha =
0.05)
# Inspect the bootstrapping results for indicator weights
sum_boot_corp_rep_ext$bootstrapped_weights
```

At this point in the analysis, we are only interested in the significance of the indicator weights and therefore consider only the measurement model. We thus inspect the **sum_boot_corp_rep_ext$bootstrapped_weights** object to obtain the results in ◘ Fig. 5.7.

◘ Figure 5.7 shows *t*-values for the measurement model relationships produced by the bootstrapping procedure. Note that bootstrapped values are generated for all measurement model weights, but we only consider the indicators of the formative constructs. The original estimate of an indicator weight (shown in the second column, **Original Est.**; ◘ Fig. 5.7) divided by the bootstrap standard error, which equals the bootstrap standard deviation (column: **Bootstrap SD**), for that indicator weight results in its empirical *t*-value as displayed in the third-to-last column in ◘ Fig. 5.7 (column: **T Stat.**). Recall that the critical values for significance levels of 1% ($\alpha = 0.01$), 5% ($\alpha = 0.05$), and 10% ($\alpha = 0.10$) probability of error are 2.576, 1.960, and 1.645 (two tailed), respectively.

> **Attention**
> The bootstrapping results shown in ◘ Fig. 5.7 will differ from your results. A **seed** is used in random computational processes to make the random process reproducible. However, note that for the same seed, different hardware and software combinations will generate different results. The important feature of the seed is that it ensures that the results are replicable on your computer or on computers with a similar hardware and software setup. Recall that bootstrapping builds on randomly drawn samples, so each time you run the bootstrapping routine with a different seed, different samples will be drawn. The differences become very small, however, if the number of bootstrapping samples is sufficiently large (e.g., 10,000).

The bootstrapping result report also provides bootstrap confidence intervals using the percentile method (Hair et al., 2022; Chap. 5). The lower boundary of the 95% confidence interval (**2.5% CI**) is displayed in the second-to-last column, whereas the upper boundary of the confidence interval (**97.5% CI**) is shown in the last column. We can readily use these confidence intervals for significance testing. Specifically, a null hypothesis H_0 that a certain parameter, such as an indicator weight w_1, equals zero (i.e., $H_0: w_1 = 0$) in the population is rejected at a given level

5.4 · Case Study Illustration: Formative Measurement Models

```
> # Inspect the bootstrapping results for outer weights
> sum_boot_corp_rep_ext$bootstrapped_weights
              Original Est. Bootstrap Mean Bootstrap SD T Stat. 2.5% CI 97.5% CI
qual_1  -> QUAL       0.202          0.207        0.061   3.338   0.093    0.321
qual_2  -> QUAL       0.041          0.040        0.051   0.808  -0.063    0.135
qual_3  -> QUAL       0.106          0.104        0.065   1.629  -0.027    0.221
qual_4  -> QUAL      -0.005         -0.004        0.054  -0.085  -0.103    0.103
qual_5  -> QUAL       0.160          0.160        0.059   2.714   0.044    0.268
qual_6  -> QUAL       0.398          0.394        0.064   6.224   0.259    0.512
qual_7  -> QUAL       0.229          0.224        0.057   4.006   0.109    0.333
qual_8  -> QUAL       0.190          0.190        0.061   3.099   0.070    0.312
perf_1  -> PERF       0.468          0.465        0.068   6.887   0.326    0.594
perf_2  -> PERF       0.177          0.180        0.068   2.584   0.050    0.314
perf_3  -> PERF       0.194          0.189        0.054   3.603   0.089    0.304
perf_4  -> PERF       0.340          0.339        0.072   4.746   0.201    0.485
perf_5  -> PERF       0.199          0.197        0.062   3.184   0.075    0.323
csor_1  -> CSOR       0.306          0.300        0.083   3.671   0.139    0.467
csor_2  -> CSOR       0.037          0.035        0.069   0.536  -0.097    0.173
csor_3  -> CSOR       0.406          0.406        0.083   4.863   0.241    0.563
csor_4  -> CSOR       0.080          0.079        0.076   1.058  -0.076    0.220
csor_5  -> CSOR       0.416          0.416        0.089   4.662   0.245    0.607
attr_1  -> ATTR       0.414          0.415        0.071   5.848   0.273    0.544
attr_2  -> ATTR       0.201          0.196        0.063   3.165   0.074    0.322
attr_3  -> ATTR       0.658          0.655        0.062  10.549   0.537    0.770
comp_1  -> COMP       0.469          0.468        0.021  22.413   0.429    0.512
comp_2  -> COMP       0.365          0.366        0.017  21.421   0.335    0.400
comp_3  -> COMP       0.372          0.373        0.014  26.068   0.346    0.401
like_1  -> LIKE       0.419          0.420        0.014  29.343   0.393    0.448
like_2  -> LIKE       0.374          0.374        0.013  28.576   0.351    0.401
like_3  -> LIKE       0.363          0.363        0.014  26.477   0.337    0.390
cusa    -> CUSA       1.000          1.000        0.000       .   1.000    1.000
cusl_1  -> CUSL       0.369          0.369        0.016  23.494   0.338    0.401
cusl_2  -> CUSL       0.420          0.421        0.015  28.972   0.395    0.452
cusl_3  -> CUSL       0.365          0.365        0.015  24.427   0.335    0.393
>
```

Fig. 5.7 Bootstrapped indicator weights. (Source: authors' screenshot from R)

α, if the corresponding $(1 - \alpha)\%$ bootstrap confidence interval does *not* include zero. In other words, if a confidence interval for an estimated coefficient, such as an indicator weight w_1, does not include zero, the hypothesis that w_1 equals zero is rejected, and we assume a significant effect.

Looking at the significance levels, we find that all formative indicators are significant at a 5% level, except *csor_2*, *csor_4*, *qual_2*, *qual_3*, and *qual_4*. For these indicators, the 95% confidence intervals include the value zero. For example, for *csor_2*, our analysis produced a lower boundary of **−0.097** and an upper boundary of **0.173**. Similarly, these indicators' *t*-values are clearly lower than 1.960, providing support for their lack of statistical significance.

To assess these indicators' absolute importance, we examine the indicator loadings by running `sum_boot_corp_rep_ext$bootstrapped_loadings`. The output in ■ Fig. 5.8 (column: **Original Est.**) shows that the lowest indicator loading of these five formative indicators occurs for *qual_2* (**0.570**). Furthermore,

```
> # Inspect the bootstrapping results for the outer loadings
> sum_boot_corp_rep_ext$bootstrapped_loadings
              Original Est. Bootstrap Mean Bootstrap SD T Stat. 2.5% CI 97.5% CI
qual_1  -> QUAL      0.741          0.738        0.045  16.619   0.640    0.819
qual_2  -> QUAL      0.570          0.568        0.054  10.636   0.454    0.668
qual_3  -> QUAL      0.749          0.744        0.039  19.281   0.663    0.815
qual_4  -> QUAL      0.664          0.658        0.045  14.606   0.567    0.738
qual_5  -> QUAL      0.787          0.780        0.034  23.222   0.711    0.842
qual_6  -> QUAL      0.856          0.848        0.031  27.547   0.781    0.901
qual_7  -> QUAL      0.722          0.713        0.042  17.090   0.626    0.790
qual_8  -> QUAL      0.627          0.622        0.049  12.706   0.520    0.711
perf_1  -> PERF      0.846          0.839        0.035  24.055   0.766    0.902
perf_2  -> PERF      0.690          0.686        0.047  14.665   0.587    0.775
perf_3  -> PERF      0.573          0.568        0.051  11.156   0.466    0.664
perf_4  -> PERF      0.717          0.715        0.050  14.249   0.614    0.815
perf_5  -> PERF      0.638          0.634        0.059  10.760   0.507    0.739
csor_1  -> CSOR      0.771          0.761        0.050  15.397   0.652    0.852
csor_2  -> CSOR      0.571          0.562        0.060   9.432   0.437    0.671
csor_3  -> CSOR      0.838          0.830        0.043  19.467   0.737    0.904
csor_4  -> CSOR      0.617          0.610        0.057  10.745   0.492    0.716
csor_5  -> CSOR      0.848          0.841        0.043  19.726   0.749    0.917
attr_1  -> ATTR      0.754          0.753        0.051  14.919   0.645    0.841
attr_2  -> ATTR      0.506          0.501        0.066   7.609   0.362    0.626
attr_3  -> ATTR      0.891          0.887        0.033  26.678   0.816    0.946
comp_1  -> COMP      0.824          0.822        0.021  39.717   0.778    0.858
comp_2  -> COMP      0.821          0.821        0.020  40.457   0.781    0.856
comp_3  -> COMP      0.844          0.843        0.019  43.658   0.804    0.878
like_1  -> LIKE      0.880          0.880        0.016  55.828   0.847    0.907
like_2  -> LIKE      0.869          0.867        0.017  50.469   0.832    0.899
like_3  -> LIKE      0.844          0.844        0.019  44.828   0.803    0.879
cusa    -> CUSA      1.000          1.000        0.000      .    1.000    1.000
cusl_1  -> CUSL      0.833          0.832        0.024  35.285   0.780    0.874
cusl_2  -> CUSL      0.917          0.917        0.010  89.030   0.894    0.935
cusl_3  -> CUSL      0.843          0.842        0.023  37.177   0.793    0.881
>
```

Fig. 5.8 Bootstrapped indicator loadings. (Source: authors' screenshot from R)

results from bootstrapping show that the *t*-values of the five indicator loadings (i.e., *csor_2*, *csor_4*, *qual_2*, *qual_3*, and *qual_4*) are clearly above 2.576, suggesting that all indicator loadings are significant at a level of 1% (◘ Fig. 5.8). Moreover, prior research and theory also provide support for the relevance of these indicators for capturing the corporate social responsibility and quality dimensions of corporate reputation (Eberl, 2010; Sarstedt, Wilczynski, & Melewar, 2013; Schwaiger, 2004; Schwaiger, Sarstedt, & Taylor, 2010). Thus, we retain all indicators in the formatively measured constructs, even though not every indicator weight is significant.

The analysis of indicator weights concludes the evaluation of the formative measurement models. Considering the results from ▶ Chaps. 4 and 5 jointly, all reflective and formative constructs exhibit satisfactory levels of measurement quality. Thus, we can now proceed with the evaluation of the structural model (▶ Chap. 6).

Summary

The evaluation of formative measurement models starts with convergent validity to ensure that the entire domain of the construct and all of its relevant facets have been covered by the indicators. In the next step, researchers assess whether pronounced levels of collinearity among indicators exist, which would inflate standard errors and potentially lead to sign changes in the indicator weights. The final step involves examining each indicator's relative contribution to forming the construct. Hence, the significance and relevance of the indicator weights must be assessed. It is valuable to also report the bootstrap confidence interval that provides additional information on the stability of the coefficient estimates. Nonsignificant indicator weights should not automatically be interpreted as indicating poor measurement model quality. Rather, researchers should also consider a formative indicator's absolute contribution to its construct (i.e., its loading). Only if both indicator weights and loadings are low or even nonsignificant should researchers consider deleting a formative indicator.

Exercise

We continue with the analysis of the influencer model as introduced in ▶ Chaps. 3 and 4. The dataset is called **influencer_data** and consists of 222 observations of 28 variables. ▶ Figure 3.10 illustrates the PLS path model; ▶ Tables 3.9 and 3.10 describe the indicators. Note that the indicator *sic_global* serves as global single item in the redundancy analysis of the *SIC* construct.

Load the influencer data, reproduce the influencer model in the SEMinR syntax, and estimate the PLS path model. As we have already assessed the reliability and validity of the reflective measures, we focus on the analysis of the *SIC* construct as follows:
1. Does the *SIC* construct display convergent validity?
2. Do the construct indicators suffer from collinearity issues?
3. Are all indicator weights statistically significant and relevant?
4. If not, based on the indicator loadings and their significance, would you consider deleting one or more of the indicators?

References

Aguirre-Urreta, M. I., & Rönkkö, M. (2018). Statistical inference with PLSc using bootstrap confidence intervals. *MIS Quarterly, 42*(3), 1001–1020.

Becker, J.-M., Ringle, C. M., Sarstedt, M., & Völckner, F. (2015). How collinearity affects mixture regression results. *Marketing Letters, 26*(4), 643–659.

Bollen, K. A., & Diamantopoulos, A. (2017). In defense of causal-formative indicators: A minority report. *Psychological Methods, 22*(3), 581–596.

Cenfetelli, R. T., & Bassellier, G. (2009). Interpretation of formative measurement in information systems research. *MIS Quarterly, 33*(4), 689–708.

Cheah, J. H., Sarstedt, M., Ringle, C. M., Ramayah, T., & Ting, H. (2018). Convergent validity assessment of formatively measured constructs in PLS-SEM. *International Journal of Contemporary Hospitality Management, 30*(11), 3192–3210.

Chin, W. W. (1998). The partial least squares approach to structural equation modeling. *Modern Methods for Business Research, 295*(2), 295–336.

Cohen, J. (1992). A power primer. *Psychological Bulletin, 112*(1), 155–159.

Davison, A. C., & Hinkley, D. V. (1997). *Bootstrap Methods and Their Application.* Cambridge, MA: Cambridge University Press.

Diamantopoulos, A., Sarstedt, M., Fuchs, C., Wilczynski, P., & Kaiser, S. (2012). Guidelines for choosing between multi-item and single-item scales for construct measurement: A predictive validity perspective. *Journal of the Academy of Marketing Science, 40*(3), 434–449.

Eberl, M. (2010). An application of PLS in multi-group analysis: The need for differentiated corporate-level marketing in the mobile communications industry. In V. Esposito Vinzi, W. W. Chin, J. Henseler, & H. Wang (Eds.), *Handbook of Partial Least Squares: Concepts, Methods and Applications.* (Springer handbooks of computational statistics series, vol. II) (pp. 487–514). Berlin: Springer.

Faul, F., Erdfelder, E., Buchner, A., & Lang, A.-G. (2009). Statistical power analyses using G*Power 3.1: Tests for correlation and regression analyses. *Behavior Research Methods, 41*(4), 1149–1160.

Grimm, M. S., & Wagner, R. (2020). The impact of missing values on PLS, ML and FIML model fit. *Archives of Data Science, Series A, 6*(1), 04.

Hair, J. F., Hult, T., Ringle, C. M., & Sarstedt, M. (2022). *A primer on partial least squares structural equation modeling (PLS-SEM)* (3rd ed.). Thousand Oaks, CA: Sage.

Hair, J. F., Risher, J. J., Sarstedt, M., & Ringle, C. M. (2019). When to use and how to report the results of PLS-SEM. *European Business Review, 31*(1), 2–24.

Hair, J. F., Sarstedt, M., Hopkins, L., & Kuppelwieser, V. G. (2014). Partial least squares structural equation modeling (PLS-SEM): An emerging tool in business research. *European Business Review, 26*(2), 106–121.

Henseler, J., Ringle, C. M., & Sinkovics, R. R. (2009). The use of partial least squares path modeling in international marketing. *Advances in International Marketing, 20*, 277–320.

Houston, M. B. (2004). Assessing the validity of secondary data proxies for marketing constructs. *Journal of Business Research, 57*(2), 154–161.

Kock, N., & Hadaya, P. (2018). Minimum sample size estimation in PLS-SEM: The inverse square root and gamma-exponential methods. *Information Systems Journal, 28*(1), 227–261.

Mason, C. H., & Perreault, W. D. (1991). Collinearity, power, and interpretation of multiple regression analysis. *Journal of Marketing Research, 28*(3), 268–280.

Sarstedt, M., Diamantopoulos, A., Salzberger, T., & Baumgartner, P. (2016). Selecting single items to measure doubly-concrete constructs: A cautionary tale. *Journal of Business Research, 69*(8), 3159–3167.

Sarstedt, M., Wilczynski, P., & Melewar, T. (2013). Measuring reputation in global markets: A comparison of reputation measures' convergent and criterion validities. *Journal of World Business, 48*(3), 329–339.

Schwaiger, M. (2004). Components and parameters of corporate reputation: An empirical study. *Schmalenbach Business Review, 56*(1), 46–71.

Schwaiger, M., Sarstedt, M., & Taylor, C. R. (2010). Art for the sake of the corporation: Audi, BMW Group, DaimlerChrysler, Montblanc, Siemens, and Volkswagen help explore the effect of sponsorship on corporate reputations. *Journal of Advertising Research, 50*(1), 77–90.

Streukens, S., & Leroi-Werelds, S. (2016). Bootstrapping and PLS-SEM: A step-by-step guide to get more out of your bootstrap results. *European Management Journal, 34*(6), 618–632.

Suggested Reading

Cenfetelli, R. T., & Bassellier, G. (2009). Interpretation of formative measurement in information systems research. *MIS Quarterly, 33*(4), 689–708.

Hair, J. F., Hult, T., Ringle, C. M., & Sarstedt, M. (2022). *A primer on partial least squares structural equation modeling (PLS-SEM)* (3rd ed.). Thousand Oaks, CA: Sage.

Sarstedt, M., Hair, J. F., Ringle, C. M., Thiele, K. O., & Gudergan, S. P. (2016). Estimation issues with PLS and CBSEM: Where the bias lies! *Journal of Business Research, 69*(10), 3998–4010.

Suggested Reading

Open Access This chapter is licensed under the terms of the Creative Commons Attribution 4.0 International License (http://creativecommons.org/licenses/by/4.0/), which permits use, sharing, adaptation, distribution and reproduction in any medium or format, as long as you give appropriate credit to the original author(s) and the source, provide a link to the Creative Commons license and indicate if changes were made.

The images or other third party material in this chapter are included in the chapter's Creative Commons license, unless indicated otherwise in a credit line to the material. If material is not included in the chapter's Creative Commons license and your intended use is not permitted by statutory regulation or exceeds the permitted use, you will need to obtain permission directly from the copyright holder.

Evaluation of the Structural Model

Contents

6.1 Assess Collinearity Issues of the Structural Model – 117

6.2 Assess the Significance and Relevance of the Structural Model Relationships – 117

6.3 Assess the Model's Explanatory Power – 118

6.4 Assess the Model's Predictive Power – 119

6.5 Model Comparisons – 121

6.6 Case Study Illustration: Structural Model Evaluation – 123

References – 136

© The Author(s) 2021
J. F. Hair Jr. et al., *Partial Least Squares Structural Equation Modeling (PLS-SEM) Using R*, Classroom Companion: Business, https://doi.org/10.1007/978-3-030-80519-7_6

Chapter 6 · Evaluation of the Structural Model

> **Learning Objectives**
> After reading this chapter, you should understand:
> 1. The steps involved in structural model assessment
> 2. The concept of explanatory power and how to evaluate it
> 3. How to use $PLS_{predict}$ to assess a model's predictive power
> 4. The concept of model comparison and metrics for selecting the best model
> 5. How to assess structural models using SEMinR

Once you have confirmed that the measurement of constructs is reliable and valid, the next step addresses the assessment of the structural model results. ◘ Figure 6.1 shows a systematic approach to the structural model assessment. In the first step, you need to examine the structural model for potential collinearity issues. The reason is that the estimation of path coefficients in the structural models is based on ordinary least squares (OLS) regressions of each endogenous construct on its corresponding predictor constructs. Just as in an OLS regression, the path coefficients might be biased if the estimation involves high levels of collinearity among predictor constructs. Once you have ensured that collinearity is not a problem, you will evaluate the significance and relevance of the structural model relationships (i.e., the path coefficients). Steps 3 and 4 of the procedure involve examining the model's explanatory power and predictive power. In addition, some research situations involve the computation and comparison of alternative models, which can emerge from different theories or contexts. PLS-SEM facilitates the comparison of alternative models using established criteria, which are well known from the regression literature. As model comparisons are not relevant for every PLS-SEM analysis, Step 5 should be considered optional.

◘ **Fig. 6.1** Structural model assessment procedure. (Source: Hair, Hult, Ringle, & Sarstedt, 2022, Chap. 6; used with permission by Sage)

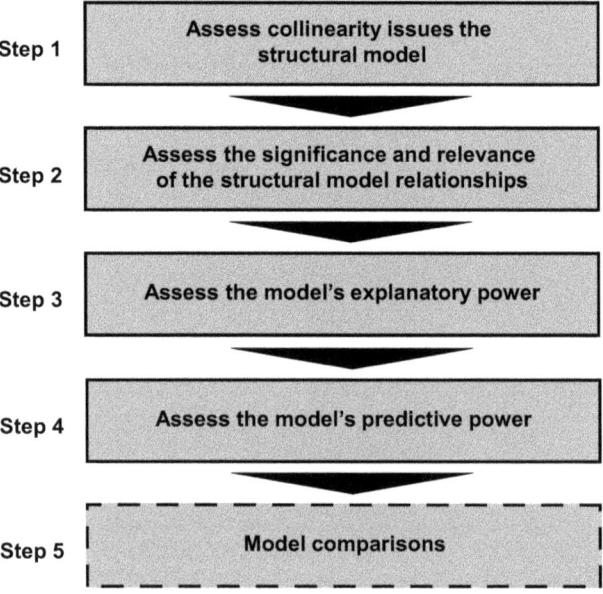

> **Excurse**
>
> Model fit indices enable judging how well a hypothesized model structure fits the empirical data and are an integral part of any CB-SEM analysis. However, the notion of model fit as known from CB-SEM is not transferrable to PLS-SEM as the method follows a different aim when estimating model parameters (i.e., with the aim of maximizing the explained variance instead of minimizing the divergence between covariance matrices) – see Hair, Sarstedt, and Ringle (2019). Nevertheless, research has brought forward several PLS-SEM-based model fit measures such as SRMR, RMS_{theta}, and the exact fit test (Henseler et al., 2014; Lohmöller, 1989, Chap. 2), which, however, have proven ineffective in detecting model misspecifications in settings commonly encountered in applied research. Instead, structural model assessment in PLS-SEM focuses on evaluating the model's explanatory and predictive power. For a detailed discussion of model fit in PLS-SEM, see Chap. 6 in Hair et al. (2022).

6.1 Assess Collinearity Issues of the Structural Model

Structural model coefficients for the relationships between constructs are derived from estimating a series of regression equations. As the point estimates and standard errors can be biased by strong correlations of each set of predictor constructs (Sarstedt & Mooi, 2019; Chap. 7), the structural model regressions must be examined for potential **collinearity** issues. This process is similar to assessing formative measurement models, but in this case, the construct scores of the predictor constructs in each regression in the structural model are used to calculate the **variance inflation factor (VIF)** values. VIF values above 5 are indicative of probable collinearity issues among predictor constructs, but collinearity can also occur at lower VIF values of 3–5 (Becker, Ringle, Sarstedt, & Völckner, 2015; Mason & Perreault, 1991). If collinearity is a problem, a frequently used option is to create higher-order constructs (Hair, Risher, Sarstedt, & Ringle, 2019; Hair, Sarstedt, Ringle, & Gudergan, 2018; Chap. 2; Sarstedt et al., 2019).

6.2 Assess the Significance and Relevance of the Structural Model Relationships

In the next step, the **significance of the path coefficients** and **relevance of the path coefficients** are evaluated. Analogous to the assessment of formative indicator weights (▶ Chap. 5), the significance assessment builds on bootstrapping standard errors as a basis for calculating *t*-values of path coefficients or alternatively confidence intervals (Streukens & Leroi-Werelds, 2016). A path coefficient is significant at the 5% level if the value zero does not fall into the 95% confidence interval. In general, the percentile method should be used to construct the confidence intervals (Aguirre-Urreta & Rönkkö, 2018). For a recap on bootstrapping, return to ▶ Chap. 5.

In terms of relevance, path coefficients are usually between −1 and +1, with coefficients closer to −1 representing strong negative relationships and those closer to +1 indicating strong positive relationships. Note that values below −1 and above +1 may technically occur, for instance, when collinearity is at very high levels. Path coefficients larger than +/−1 are not acceptable, and multicollinearity reduction methods must be implemented. As PLS-SEM processes standardized data, the path coefficients indicate the changes in an endogenous construct's values that are associated with standard deviation unit changes in a certain predictor construct, holding all other predictor constructs constant. For example, a path coefficient of 0.505 indicates that when the predictor construct increases by one standard deviation unit, the endogenous construct will increase by 0.505 standard deviation units.

The research context is important when determining whether the size of a path coefficient is meaningful. Thus, when examining structural model results, researchers should also interpret total effects, defined as the sum of the direct effect (if any) and all indirect effects linking one construct to another in the model. The examination of total effects between constructs, including all their indirect effects, provides a more comprehensive picture of the structural model relationships (Nitzl, Roldán, & Cepeda Carrión, 2016).

6.3 Assess the Model's Explanatory Power

The next step involves examining the **coefficient of determination** (R^2) of the endogenous construct(s). The R^2 represents the variance explained in each of the endogenous constructs and is a measure of the model's **explanatory power** (Shmueli & Koppius, 2011), also referred to as **in-sample predictive power** (Rigdon, 2012). The R^2 ranges from 0 to 1, with higher values indicating a greater explanatory power. As a general guideline, R^2 values of 0.75, 0.50, and 0.25 can be considered substantial, moderate, and weak, respectively, in many social science disciplines (Hair, Ringle, & Sarstedt, 2011). But acceptable R^2 values are based on the research context, and in some disciplines, an R^2 value as low as 0.10 is considered satisfactory, as for example, in predicting stock returns (e.g., Raithel, Sarstedt, Scharf, & Schwaiger, 2012).

Researchers should also be aware that R^2 is a function of the number of predictor constructs – the greater the number of predictor constructs, the higher the R^2. Therefore, the R^2 should always be interpreted relative to the context of the study, based on the R^2 values from related studies as well as models of similar complexity. R^2 values can also be too high when the model overfits the data. In case of model overfit, the (partial regression) model is too complex, which results in fitting the random noise inherent in the sample rather than reflecting the overall population. The same model would likely not fit on another sample drawn from the same population (Sharma, Sarstedt, Shmueli, Kim, & Thiele, 2019). When measuring a concept that is inherently predictable, such as physical processes, R^2 values of (up to) 0.90 might be plausible. However, similar R^2 value levels in a model that predicts human attitudes, perceptions, and intentions would likely indicate model overfit (Hair, Risher, et al., 2019). A limitation of R^2 is that the metric will tend to increase as more explanatory variables are introduced to a model. The adjusted R^2 metric accounts for this by adjusting the R^2 value based upon the number of explanatory variables in relation to the data size and is seen as a more conservative estimate of R^2 (Theil, 1961). But because of the correction factor introduced to account for data and model size, the adjusted R^2 is not a precise indication of an endogenous construct's explained variance (Sarstedt & Mooi, 2019; Chap. 7).

Researchers can also assess how the removal of a selected predictor construct affects an endogenous construct's R^2 value. This metric is the f^2 **effect size** and is similar to the size of the path coefficients. More precisely, the rank order of the relevance of the predictor constructs in explaining a dependent construct in the structural model is often the same when comparing the size of the path coefficients and the f^2 effect sizes. In such situations, the f^2 effect size is typically only reported if requested by editors or reviewers. Otherwise (i.e., if the rank order of constructs' relevance in explaining a dependent construct in the structural model differs when comparing the size of the path coefficients and the f^2 effect sizes), the researcher may report the f^2 effect size to offer an alternative perspective on the results. In addition, some other research settings call for the reporting of effect sizes, such as in moderation analysis (Memon et al., 2019; see Chap. 7).

6.4 Assess the Model's Predictive Power

Many researchers interpret the R^2 statistic as a measure of their model's predictive power (Sarstedt & Danks, 2021; Shmueli & Koppius, 2011). This interpretation is not entirely correct, however, since the R^2 only indicates the model's in-sample explanatory power – it says nothing about the model's **predictive power** (Chin et al., 2020; Hair & Sarstedt, 2021), also referred to as **out-of-sample predictive power**, which indicates a model's ability to predict new or future observations. Addressing this concern, Shmueli, Ray, Estrada, and Chatla (2016) introduced $PLS_{predict}$, a procedure for out-of-sample prediction. Execution of $PLS_{predict}$ involves estimating the model on a **training sample** and evaluating its predictive performance on a **holdout sample** (Shmueli et al., 2019). Note that the holdout sample is separated from the total sample before executing the initial analysis on the training sample data, so it includes data that were not used in the model estimation.

> **Important**
> The R^2 is a measure of a model's explanatory power. It does not, however, indicate a model's out-of-sample predictive power.

$PLS_{predict}$ executes ***k*-fold cross-validation**. A fold is a subgroup of the total sample, while *k* is the number of subgroups. That is, the total dataset is randomly split into *k* equally sized subsets of data. For example, a cross-validation based on *k* = 5 folds splits the sample into five equally sized data subsets (i.e., groups of data). $PLS_{predict}$

Fig. 6.2 *k*-fold cross-validation procedure. (Source: authors' own figure)

Fold 1	Fold 2	Fold 3	Fold 4	Fold 5
Holdout 1	Training	Training	Training	Training
Training	Holdout 2	Training	Training	Training
Training	Training	Holdout 3	Training	Training
Training	Training	Training	Holdout 4	Training
Training	Training	Training	Training	Holdout 5

then combines *k*-1 subsets (i.e., four groups of data) into a single training sample that is used to predict the remaining fifth subset. The fifth subset is the holdout sample for the first cross-validation run. This cross-validation process is then repeated *k* times (i.e., five times), with each of the five subsets used once as the holdout sample and the remaining cases being combined into the training sample. Thus, each case in every holdout sample has a predicted value estimated with the respective training sample in which that case was not used to estimate the model parameters. Leave-one-out cross-validation (LOOCV) is a subset of *k*-fold cross-validation where only one observation is included in the holdout sample. ◘ Figure 6.2 visualizes the cross-validation process. Shmueli et al. (2019) recommend setting *k* = 10, but researchers need to make sure that the training sample for each fold meets minimum sample size guidelines (e.g., by following the inverse square root method, see also ► Chap. 1).

The generation of the *k* subsets of data is a random process and can therefore result in extreme partitions that potentially lead to abnormal solutions. To avoid such abnormal solutions, researchers should run $PLS_{predict}$ multiple times. Shmueli et al. (2019) generally recommend running the procedure ten times. However, when the aim is to mimic how the PLS model will eventually be used to predict a new observation using a single model (estimated from the entire dataset), $PLS_{predict}$ should be run only once (i.e., without repetitions).

To assess a model's predictive power, researchers can draw on several **prediction statistics** that quantify the amount of **prediction error** in the indicators of a particular endogenous construct. When analyzing the prediction errors, the focus should be on the model's key endogenous construct – and not on examining the prediction errors for the indicators of all endogenous constructs. The most popular metric to quantify the degree of prediction error is the **root-mean-square error (RMSE)**. This metric is the square root of the average of the squared differences between the predictions and the actual observations. Note that the RMSE squares the errors before averaging, so the statistic assigns a greater weight to larger errors, which makes it particularly useful when large errors are undesirable – as it is common in predictive analyses. Another popular metric is the **mean absolute error (MAE)**. This metric measures the average magnitude of the errors in a set of predictions without considering their direction (over- or underestimation). The MAE thus is the average absolute difference between the predictions and the actual observations, with all the individual differences having equal weight.

In most instances, researchers should use the RMSE to examine a model's predictive power. But if the prediction error distribution is highly nonsymmetric, as evidenced in a long left or right tail in the distribution of prediction errors (Danks & Ray, 2018), the MAE is the more appropriate prediction statistic (Shmueli et al., 2019). These prediction statistics depend on the indicators' measurement scales, so the absolute size of their raw values does not have much meaning.

To interpret these metrics, researchers need to compare each indicator's RMSE (or MAE) values with a naïve **linear regression model (LM) benchmark**. The LM benchmark values are obtained by running a linear regression of each of the dependent construct's indicators on the indicators of the exogenous constructs in the PLS path model (Danks & Ray, 2018). In comparing the RMSE (or MAE) values with the LM values, the following guidelines apply (Shmueli et al., 2019):
1. If *all* indicators in the PLS-SEM analysis have lower RMSE (or MAE) values compared to the naïve LM benchmark, the model has high predictive power.
2. If the *majority* (or the same number) of indicators in the PLS-SEM analysis yields smaller prediction errors compared to the LM, this indicates a medium predictive power.
3. If a *minority* of the dependent construct's indicators produce lower PLS-SEM prediction errors compared to the naïve LM benchmark, this indicates the model has low predictive power.
4. If the PLS-SEM analysis (compared to the LM) yields lower prediction errors in terms of the RMSE (or the MAE) for *none* of the indicators, this indicates the model lacks predictive power.

An important decision when using $PLS_{predict}$ is how to generate the predictions when the PLS path model includes a mediator construct (mediation is discussed further in ▶ Chap. 7), which is both a predictor to the outcome and itself the outcome of an antecedent. SEMinR offers two alternatives to generate predictions in such a model setup (Shmueli et al., 2016). Researchers can choose to generate predictions using either the direct antecedents (DAs) or the earliest antecedents (EAs). In the DA approach, $PLS_{predict}$ would consider both the antecedent and the mediator as predictors of outcome constructs, whereas in the EA approach, the mediator would be excluded from the analysis. Danks (2021) presents simulation evidence that the DA approach generates predictions with the highest accuracy. We therefore recommend using this approach.

6.5 Model Comparisons

In a final, optional step, researchers may be interested in conducting **model comparisons**. Models are compared across different model configurations resulting from different theories or research contexts and are evaluated for predictive power.

Sharma et al. (2019, 2021) recently compared the efficacy of various metrics for model comparison tasks and found that Schwarz's (1978) **Bayesian information criterion (BIC)** and **Geweke and Meese's** (1981) **criterion (GM)** achieve a sound trade-off between model fit and predictive power in the estimation of PLS path models. These (information theoretic) model selection criteria facilitate the comparison of models in terms of model fit and predictive power without having to use a holdout sample, which is particularly useful for PLS-SEM analyses that often draw on small sample sizes. In applying these metrics, researchers should estimate each model separately and select the model that minimizes the value in BIC or GM for a certain target construct. That is, the model that produces the lowest value in BIC or GM is to be selected. While BIC and GM exhibit practically the same performance in model selection tasks, BIC is considerably easier to compute. Hence, our illustrations will focus on this criterion.

> **Important**
> When comparing different models, researchers should select the one that minimizes the BIC value for a certain target construct.

One issue in the application of the BIC is that – in its simple form (i.e., raw values) – the criterion does not offer any insights regarding the relative weights of evidence in favor of models under consideration (Burnham & Anderson, 2004; Chap. 2.9). More precisely, while the differences in BIC and GM values are useful in ranking and selecting models, such differences can often be small in practice, leading to model selection uncertainty. To resolve this issue, researchers can use the BIC (and GM) values to compute **Akaike weights**. These weights determine a model's relative likelihood of being the data generation model, given the data and a set of competing models (Danks, Sharma, & Sarstedt, 2020) – see Wagenmakers and Farrell (2004) for a sample application. The higher the Akaike weights, the more likely that the selected model better represents the data generation model.

> **Excurse**
>
> A further development of the prediction-oriented model comparisons in PLS-SEM is the **cross-validated predictive ability test** (**CVPAT**; Liengaard et al., 2021). This approach offers a statistical test to decide whether an alternative model offers significantly higher out-of-sample predictive power than an established model. A statistical test is particularly advantageous if the differences in BIC values for deciding for one or the other model are relatively small. In addition, the test statistic of the CVPAT is suitable for prediction-oriented model comparison in the context of the development and validation of theories. As such, CVPAT offers researchers an important tool for selecting a model on which they can base, for example, strategic management and policy decisions. Future extensions of CVPAT will also support a test for the predictive power assessment of a single model (Hair, 2021).

6.6 · Case Study Illustration: Structural Model Evaluation

Table 6.1 Rules of thumb for structural model assessment (Source: authors' own table)

Criterion	Metrics and thresholds
Collinearity	Critical collinearity issues likely occur if VIF ≥ 5 Collinearity issues are usually uncritical if VIF = 3–5 Collinearity is not a problematic issue if VIF < 3
Significance and relevance of the path coefficients	Apply bootstrapping to assess the significance of the path coefficients on the ground of t-values or confidence intervals Assess the magnitude of path coefficients Assess the f^2 values for each path and check that they follow the same rank order as the path coefficient magnitude
R^2 value	R^2 values of 0.75, 0.50, and 0.25 are considered substantial, moderate, and weak. However, R^2 values have to be interpreted in the context of the model and its complexity. Excessive R^2 values indicate that the model overfits the data
$PLS_{predict}$	Focus on one key target construct in the analysis Set $k = 10$, assuming each subgroup meets the minimum required sample size Use ten repetitions Compare the RMSE (or the MAE) values produced by PLS-SEM with those produced by the LM for each indicator. Check if the PLS-SEM analysis (compared to the LM) yields lower prediction errors in terms of RMSE (or MAE) for all (high predictive power), the majority or the same number (medium predictive power), the minority (low predictive power), or none of the indicators (no predictive power) Use the DA approach to generate predictions in mediation models
Model comparisons	Select the model that minimizes the value in BIC or GM compared to other models in the set Compute Akaike weights for additional evidence for a model's relative likelihood

▪ Table 6.1 summarizes the metrics that need to be applied when evaluating the structural model.

6.6 Case Study Illustration: Structural Model Evaluation

We continue evaluating the extended corporate reputation model introduced in ► Chap. 5. In the prior chapters, we focused on the evaluation of the measurement models. We now turn our attention to the structural model, which describes the relationships between constructs.

```
# Load the SEMinR library
library(seminr)
# Load the data
corp_rep_data <- corp_rep_data
# Create measurement model
```

```
corp_rep_mm_ext <- constructs(
  composite("QUAL", multi_items("qual_", 1:8), weights = mode_B),
  composite("PERF", multi_items("perf_", 1:5), weights = mode_B),
  composite("CSOR", multi_items("csor_", 1:5), weights = mode_B),
  composite("ATTR", multi_items("attr_", 1:3), weights = mode_B),
  composite("COMP", multi_items("comp_", 1:3)),
  composite("LIKE", multi_items("like_", 1:3)),
  composite("CUSA", single_item("cusa")),
  composite("CUSL", multi_items("cusl_", 1:3))
)
# Create structural model
corp_rep_sm_ext <- relationships(
  paths(from = c("QUAL", "PERF", "CSOR", "ATTR"), to = c("COMP", "LIKE")),
  paths(from = c("COMP", "LIKE"), to = c("CUSA", "CUSL")),
  paths(from = c("CUSA"), to = c("CUSL"))
)
# Estimate the model
corp_rep_pls_model_ext <- estimate_pls(
  data = corp_rep_data,
  measurement_model = corp_rep_mm_ext,
  structural_model = corp_rep_sm_ext,
  missing = mean_replacement,
  missing_value = "-99")
# Summarize the results of the model estimation
summary_corp_rep_ext <- summary(corp_rep_pls_model_ext)
# Bootstrap the model
boot_corp_rep_ext <- bootstrap_model(
  seminr_model = corp_rep_pls_model_ext,
  nboot = 1000,
  cores = parallel::detectCores(),
  seed = 123)
# Summarize the results of the bootstrap
summary_boot_corp_rep_ext <- summary(boot_corp_rep_ext,
                                     alpha = 0.05)
```

We follow the structural model assessment procedure (Step 1 in ◘ Fig. 6.1) and begin with an evaluation of the collinearity of predictor constructs in relation to each endogenous construct. The corporate reputation model has four endogenous constructs (◘ Fig. 6.3), namely, *COMP*, *LIKE*, *CUSA*, and *CUSL*. We examine the VIF values for the predictor constructs by inspecting the **vif_antecedents** element within the **summary_corp_rep_ext** object:

```
# Inspect the structural model collinearity VIF
summary_corp_rep_ext$vif_antecedents
```

As can be seen in ◘ Fig. 6.4, all VIF values are clearly below the threshold of 5. However, *QUAL's* VIF value (**3.487**) is above 3, suggesting the possibility of

6.6 · Case Study Illustration: Structural Model Evaluation

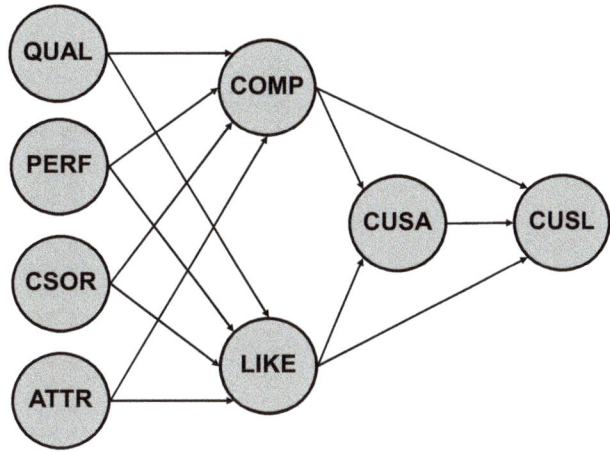

Fig. 6.3 The extended corporate reputation model. (Source: Hair et al., 2022, Chap. 5; used with permission by Sage)

Fig. 6.4 VIF values for structural model. (Source: authors' screenshot from RStudio)

collinearity problems. Since the one exception is close to 3, we can conclude that collinearity among predictor constructs is likely not a critical issue in the structural model, and we can continue examining the result report.

Next, in the structural model assessment procedure (Step 2 in **Fig. 6.1**), we need to evaluate the relevance and significance of the structural paths. The results of the bootstrapping of structural paths can be accessed by inspecting the **bootstrapped_paths** element nested in the **summary_boot_corp_ext** object (**Fig. 6.5**).

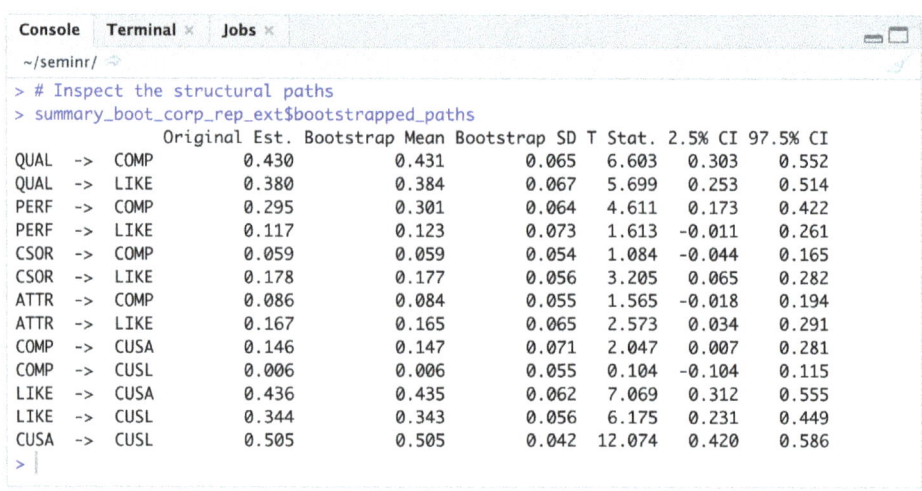

○ **Fig. 6.5** Path coefficient estimates, significance, and confidence intervals. (Source: authors' screenshot from RStudio)

```
# Inspect the structural paths
summary_boot_corp_rep_ext$bootstrapped_paths
# Inspect the total effects
summary_boot_corp_rep_ext$bootstrapped_total_paths
# Inspect the model RSquares
summary_corp_rep_ext$paths
# Inspect the effect sizes
summary_corp_rep_ext$fSquare
```

First, let's consider the original path coefficient estimates (column: **Original Est.**, ○ Fig. 6.5) for the exogenous driver constructs. For example, we find that $QUAL$ has a strong positive impact on both $COMP$ (**0.430**) and $LIKE$ (**0.380**). A similar pattern of relationships emerges for $PERF$, but with lower effect sizes. On the contrary, $CSOR$ exerts a much lower impact on these two constructs as evidenced in path coefficient estimates of **0.059** for $COMP$ and **0.178** for $LIKE$. Similarly, $ATTR$ has only a low impact on $COMP$ and $LIKE$. Further analyzing the path coefficient estimates, we find that $LIKE$ is the primary driver of both $CUSA$ (**0.436**) and $CUSL$ (**0.344**), as demonstrated by the larger path coefficients compared with those of $COMP$.

Let's now review the results for statistical significance. Assuming a 5% significance level (as specified with the parameter `alpha = 0.05` in the `bootstrap_model()` function), the t-values (**T Stat.** column, ○ Fig. 6.5) estimated from the bootstrapping should exceed the value of 1.960. We find that several relationships are significant, including five of the exogenous driver construct relationships ($QUAL \rightarrow COMP$, $t =$ **6.603**; $QUAL \rightarrow LIKE$, $t =$ **5.699**; $PERF \rightarrow COMP$, $t =$ **4.611**; $CSOR \rightarrow LIKE$, $t =$ **3.205**; $ATTR \rightarrow LIKE$, $t =$ **2.573**). At the same time, however, three of the exogenous driver relationships are not statistically significant ($PERF \rightarrow LIKE$,

6.6 · Case Study Illustration: Structural Model Evaluation

$t = 1.613$; $CSOR \rightarrow COMP$, $t = 1.084$; $ATTR \rightarrow COMP$, $t = 1.565$). Reviewing the statistical significance of the path coefficients for the endogenous construct relationships, we see that four of the five paths are statistically significant. The one path that is not significant is from $COMP$ to $CUSL$ ($t = 0.104$). These results suggest that companies should concentrate their marketing efforts on enhancing their likeability (by strengthening customers' quality perceptions) rather than their perceived competence to maximize customer loyalty. This is not surprising, considering that customers rated mobile network operators. Since their services (provision of network capabilities) are intangible, affective judgments play a much more important role than cognitive judgments for establishing customer loyalty.

> Note that, although a seed is set, the random results generated might differ across software and hardware combinations. Hence, your results will likely look slightly different from those in ◘ Fig. 6.5.

It is also important to consider the total effects to gain an idea of the impact of the four exogenous driver constructs on the outcome constructs $CUSA$ and $CUSL$. To evaluate the total effects, we need to inspect the **bootstrapped_total_paths** element of **summary_boot_corp_rep_ext** (◘ Fig. 6.6).

Of the four driver constructs, $QUAL$ has the strongest total effect on $CUSL$ (**0.248**), followed by $CSOR$ (**0.105**), $ATTR$ (**0.101**), and $PERF$ (**0.089**). Therefore,

```
Console    Terminal ×    Jobs ×
~/seminr/
> # Inspect the total effects
> summary_boot_corp_rep_ext$bootstrapped_total_paths
              Original Est. Bootstrap Mean Bootstrap SD T Stat. 2.5% CI 97.5% CI
QUAL -> COMP         0.430          0.431        0.065   6.603    0.303    0.552
QUAL -> LIKE         0.380          0.384        0.067   5.699    0.253    0.514
QUAL -> CUSA         0.228          0.230        0.039   5.923    0.154    0.310
QUAL -> CUSL         0.248          0.251        0.044   5.679    0.165    0.337
PERF -> COMP         0.295          0.301        0.064   4.611    0.173    0.422
PERF -> LIKE         0.117          0.123        0.073   1.613   -0.011    0.261
PERF -> CUSA         0.094          0.098        0.040   2.373    0.024    0.179
PERF -> CUSL         0.089          0.094        0.045   1.968    0.009    0.180
CSOR -> COMP         0.059          0.059        0.054   1.084   -0.044    0.165
CSOR -> LIKE         0.178          0.177        0.056   3.205    0.065    0.282
CSOR -> CUSA         0.086          0.086        0.028   3.133    0.031    0.138
CSOR -> CUSL         0.105          0.105        0.033   3.166    0.038    0.172
ATTR -> COMP         0.086          0.084        0.055   1.565   -0.018    0.194
ATTR -> LIKE         0.167          0.165        0.065   2.573    0.034    0.291
ATTR -> CUSA         0.085          0.084        0.031   2.731    0.026    0.147
ATTR -> CUSL         0.101          0.100        0.038   2.652    0.028    0.178
COMP -> CUSA         0.146          0.147        0.071   2.047    0.007    0.281
COMP -> CUSL         0.079          0.081        0.069   1.155   -0.052    0.213
LIKE -> CUSA         0.436          0.435        0.062   7.069    0.312    0.555
LIKE -> CUSL         0.564          0.563        0.061   9.219    0.444    0.676
CUSA -> CUSL         0.505          0.505        0.042  12.074    0.420    0.586
>
```

◘ **Fig. 6.6** Total effect estimates, significance, and confidence intervals. (Source: authors' screenshot from RStudio)

it is advisable for companies to focus on marketing activities that positively influence the customers' perception of the quality of their products and services (*QUAL*). As can be seen, all of *QUAL*'s total effects are significant at a 5% level.

In Step 3 of the structural model assessment procedure (◘ Fig. 6.1), we need to consider the model's explanatory power by analyzing the R^2 of the endogenous constructs and the f^2 effect size of the predictor constructs. To start with, we need to examine the R^2 values of the endogenous constructs. The R^2 values of *COMP* (**0.631**), *CUSL* (**0.562**), and *LIKE* (**0.558**) can be considered moderate, whereas the R^2 value of *CUSA* (**0.292**) is weak (◘ Fig. 6.7). The weak R^2 value of *CUSA* may be the result of this construct being measured as a single item. We recommend customer satisfaction always be measured as a multi-item construct.

◘ Figure 6.8 shows the f^2 values for all combinations of endogenous constructs (represented by the columns) and corresponding exogenous (i.e., predictor) constructs (represented by the rows). For example, *LIKE* has a medium effect size of **0.159** on *CUSA* and of **0.138** on *CUSL*. On the contrary, *COMP* has no effect

```
Console   Terminal ×   Jobs ×
~/seminr/
> # Inspect the model RSquares
> summary_corp_rep_ext$paths
        COMP  LIKE  CUSA  CUSL
R^2    0.631 0.558 0.292 0.562
AdjR^2 0.627 0.552 0.288 0.558
QUAL   0.430 0.380     .     .
PERF   0.295 0.117     .     .
CSOR   0.059 0.178     .     .
ATTR   0.086 0.167     .     .
COMP       .     . 0.146 0.006
LIKE       .     . 0.436 0.344
CUSA       .     .     . 0.505
>
```

◘ **Fig. 6.7** Path coefficient estimates, R^2, and adjusted R^2 values. (Source: authors' screenshot from RStudio)

```
Console   Terminal ×   Jobs ×
~/seminr/
> # Inspect the effect sizes
> summary_corp_rep_ext$fSquare
      QUAL  PERF  CSOR  ATTR  COMP  LIKE  CUSA  CUSL
QUAL 0.000 0.000 0.000 0.000 0.144 0.094 0.000 0.000
PERF 0.000 0.000 0.000 0.000 0.076 0.011 0.000 0.000
CSOR 0.000 0.000 0.000 0.000 0.005 0.034 0.000 0.000
ATTR 0.000 0.000 0.000 0.000 0.009 0.030 0.000 0.000
COMP 0.000 0.000 0.000 0.000 0.000 0.000 0.018 0.000
LIKE 0.000 0.000 0.000 0.000 0.000 0.000 0.159 0.138
CUSA 0.000 0.000 0.000 0.000 0.000 0.000 0.000 0.403
CUSL 0.000 0.000 0.000 0.000 0.000 0.000 0.000 0.000
>
```

◘ **Fig. 6.8** f^2 effect sizes. (Source: authors' screenshot from RStudio)

6.6 · Case Study Illustration: Structural Model Evaluation

Table 6.2 A list of arguments for the `predict_pls()` function

Argument	Value
`model`	The PLS model, which contains the structural and measurement models used to generate predictions
`technique`	The `predict_DA` option for direct antecedent (DA) approach or `predict_EA` for the earliest antecedent (EA) approach (`predict_DA` is set as default)
`noFolds`	Number of folds to employ in the k-fold process, `NULL` is default whereby leave-one-out cross-validation (LOOCV) is performed
`reps`	Number of replications to run (`NULL` is default whereby the k-fold cross-validation is performed once)
`cores`	The number of cores to use for parallel processing

Source: authors' own table

on *CUSA* (**0.018**) or *CUSL* (**0.000**). The rank order of effect sizes is identical to the rank order on the grounds of the path coefficients.

Step 4 in the structural model assessment procedure (◘ Fig. 6.1) is the evaluation of the model's predictive power. To do so, we first have to generate the predictions using the `predict_pls()` function. ◘ Table 6.2 lists this function's arguments.

We run the $PLS_{predict}$ procedure with $k = 10$ folds and ten repetitions and thus set `noFolds = 10`, and `reps = 10`. In addition, we use the `predict_DA` approach. Finally, we summarize the $PLS_{predict}$ model and assign the output to the `sum_predict_corp_rep_ext` object:

```
# Generate the model predictions
predict_corp_rep_ext <- predict_pls(
  model = corp_rep_pls_model_ext,
  technique = predict_DA,
  noFolds = 10,
  reps = 10)
# Summarize the prediction results
sum_predict_corp_rep_ext <- summary(predict_corp_rep_ext)
```

The distributions of the prediction errors need to be assessed to decide the best metric for evaluating predictive power. If the prediction error is highly skewed, the MAE is a more appropriate metric than the RMSE. In order to assess the distribution of predictive error, we use the `plot()` function on the object `sum_predict_corp_rep_ext` and specify the *indicator* argument to the indicators of interest. We should focus on the key outcome construct *CUSL* and evaluate the indicators *cusl_1*, *cusl_2*, and *cusl_3*. First, we set the number of plots to display in the output to three plots arranged horizontally using the `par(mfrow=c(1,3))` command. Remember to set `par(mfrow=c(1,1))` after outputting the plots; otherwise, all future plots will be arranged horizontally in a sequence of three:

```
# Analyze the distribution of prediction error
par(mfrow=c(1,3))
plot(sum_predict_corp_rep_ext,
   indicator = "cusl_1")
plot(sum_predict_corp_rep_ext,
   indicator = "cusl_2")
plot(sum_predict_corp_rep_ext,
   indicator = "cusl_3")
par(mfrow=c(1,1))
```

The results in ◘ Fig. 6.9 show that while all three plots have a left tail and are mildly skewed to the right, the prediction error distributions are rather symmetric. We should therefore use the RMSE for our assessment of prediction errors.

We can investigate the RMSE and MAE values by calling the `sum_predict_corp_rep_ext` object.

```
# Compute the prediction statistics
sum_predict_corp_rep_ext
```

Analyzing the *CUSL* construct's indicators (◘ Fig. 6.10), we find that the PLS path model has lower out-of-sample predictive error (RMSE) compared to the naïve LM model benchmark for all three indicators (sections: **PLS out-of-sample metrics** and **LM out-of-sample metrics**): *cusl_1* (PLS, **1.192**; LM, **1.228**), *cusl_2* (PLS, **1.239**; LM, **1.312**), and *cusl_3* (PLS, **1.312**; LM, **1.380**). Accordingly, we conclude that the model has a high predictive power.

In Step 5 of the structural model assessment procedure (◘ Fig. 6.1), we will perform model comparisons. First, we set up three theoretically justifiable competing models (Model 1, Model 2, and Model 3, shown in ◘ Fig. 6.11). Specifically, we compare the original model that serves as the basis for our prior analyses (Model 1), with two more complex versions, in which the four driver constructs also relate to *CUSA* (Model 2) and *CUSL* (Model 3). As the models share the same measurement models, we need to specify them only once. Since each model has a unique structural model, we must specify three structural models according to ◘ Fig. 6.11. To begin, we assign the outputs to `structural_model1`, `structural_model2`, and `structural_model3`. We can then estimate three separate PLS path models and summarize the results.

6.6 · Case Study Illustration: Structural Model Evaluation

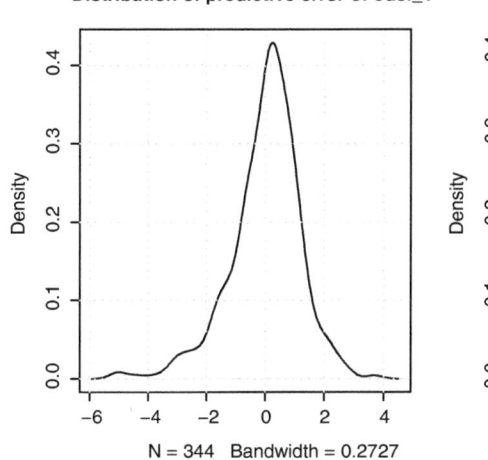

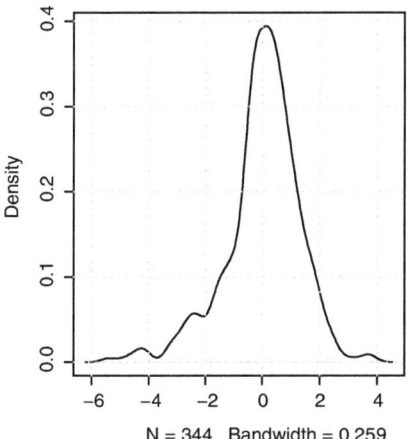

◘ **Fig. 6.9** Distribution of prediction error for indicators *cusl_1*, *cusl_2*, and *cusl_3*. (Source: authors' screenshot from RStudio)

```
# Estimate alternative models
# Create measurement model
measurement_model <- constructs(
  composite("QUAL", multi_items("qual_", 1:8), weights = mode_B),
  composite("PERF", multi_items("perf_", 1:5), weights = mode_B),
  composite("CSOR", multi_items("csor_", 1:5), weights = mode_B),
  composite("ATTR", multi_items("attr_", 1:3), weights = mode_B),
  composite("COMP", multi_items("comp_", 1:3)),
  composite("LIKE", multi_items("like_", 1:3)),
  composite("CUSA", single_item("cusa")),
  composite("CUSL", multi_items("cusl_", 1:3))
)
```

```
# Create structural models
# Model 1
structural_model1 <- relationships(
  paths(from = c("QUAL","PERF","CSOR","ATTR"), to = c("COMP",
"LIKE")),
  paths(from = c("COMP","LIKE"),  to = c("CUSA", "CUSL")),
  paths(from = "CUSA", to = c("CUSL"))
)
# Model 2
structural_model2 <- relationships(
  paths(from = c("QUAL","PERF","CSOR","ATTR"), to = c("COMP",
"LIKE", "CUSA")),
  paths(from = c("COMP","LIKE"),  to = c("CUSA", "CUSL")),
  paths(from = "CUSA", to = c("CUSL"))
)
# Model 3
structural_model3 <- relationships(
  paths(from = c("QUAL","PERF","CSOR","ATTR"),
        to = c("COMP", "LIKE", "CUSA", "CUSL")),
  paths(from = c("COMP","LIKE"),  to = c("CUSA", "CUSL")),
  paths(from = "CUSA", to = c("CUSL"))
)

# Estimate and summarize the models
pls_model1 <- estimate_pls(
  data = corp_rep_data,
  measurement_model = measurement_model,
  structural_model  = structural_model1,
  missing_value = "-99"
)
sum_model1 <- summary(pls_model1)

pls_model2 <- estimate_pls(
  data = corp_rep_data,
  measurement_model = measurement_model,
  structural_model  = structural_model2,
  missing_value = "-99"
)
sum_model2 <- summary(pls_model2)

pls_model3 <- estimate_pls(
  data = corp_rep_data,
  measurement_model = measurement_model,
  structural_model  = structural_model3,
  missing_value = "-99"
)
sum_model3 <- summary(pls_model3)
```

6.6 · Case Study Illustration: Structural Model Evaluation

```
> # Generate the model predictions
> predict_corp_rep_ext <- predict_pls(
+     model = corp_rep_pls_model_ext,
+     technique = predict_DA,
+     noFolds = 10,
+     reps = 10)
> # Summarize the prediction results
> sum_predict_corp_rep_ext <- summary(predict_corp_rep_ext)
> # Analyze the distribution of prediction error
> par(mfrow=c(1,3))
> plot(sum_predict_corp_rep_ext, indicator = "cusl_1")
> plot(sum_predict_corp_rep_ext, indicator = "cusl_2")
> plot(sum_predict_corp_rep_ext, indicator = "cusl_3")
> par(mfrow=c(1,1))
> # Inspect the results of PLSpredict
> sum_predict_corp_rep_ext

PLS in-sample metrics:
      comp_1 comp_2 comp_3 like_1 like_2 like_3  cusa cusl_1 cusl_2 cusl_3
RMSE   1.022  1.081  1.112  1.101  1.452  1.478 0.985  1.181  1.225  1.300
MAE    0.784  0.868  0.881  0.837  1.127  1.146 0.769  0.874  0.909  0.948

PLS out-of-sample metrics:
      comp_1 comp_2 comp_3 like_1 like_2 like_3  cusa cusl_1 cusl_2 cusl_3
RMSE   1.046  1.101  1.134  1.136  1.489  1.512 1.000  1.192  1.239  1.312
MAE    0.799  0.882  0.895  0.861  1.155  1.175 0.778  0.883  0.919  0.959

LM in-sample metrics:
      comp_1 comp_2 comp_3 like_1 like_2 like_3  cusa cusl_1 cusl_2 cusl_3
RMSE   0.938  1.011  1.011  0.968  1.315  1.346 0.770  1.086  1.161  1.222
MAE    0.717  0.799  0.788  0.744  1.020  1.050 0.609  0.794  0.873  0.911

LM out-of-sample metrics:
      comp_1 comp_2 comp_3 like_1 like_2 like_3  cusa cusl_1 cusl_2 cusl_3
RMSE   1.064  1.142  1.134  1.121  1.520  1.555 0.886  1.228  1.312  1.380
MAE    0.805  0.898  0.877  0.849  1.154  1.196 0.690  0.889  0.977  1.029
>
```

Fig. 6.10 Prediction metrics for outcome construct items. (Source: authors' screenshot from RStudio)

We focus our analysis on the *CUSA* construct as the immediate consequence of the two dimensions of corporate reputation (*LIKE* and *COMP*). In order to compare the models, we must first inspect each model for the estimated BIC value for the outcome construct of interest (i.e., *CUSA*). The matrix of the model's information criteria can be accessed by inspecting the `it_criteria` element in the `sum_model1` object, `sum_model1$it_criteria`. This matrix reports the BIC value for each outcome construct along with the Akaike information criterion (AIC), which is known to favor too complex models (Sharma et al., 2019, 2021). We can subset this matrix to return only the BIC row of the *CUSA* column by entering `sum_model1$it_criteria["BIC", "CUSA"]`. To compare the BIC for the

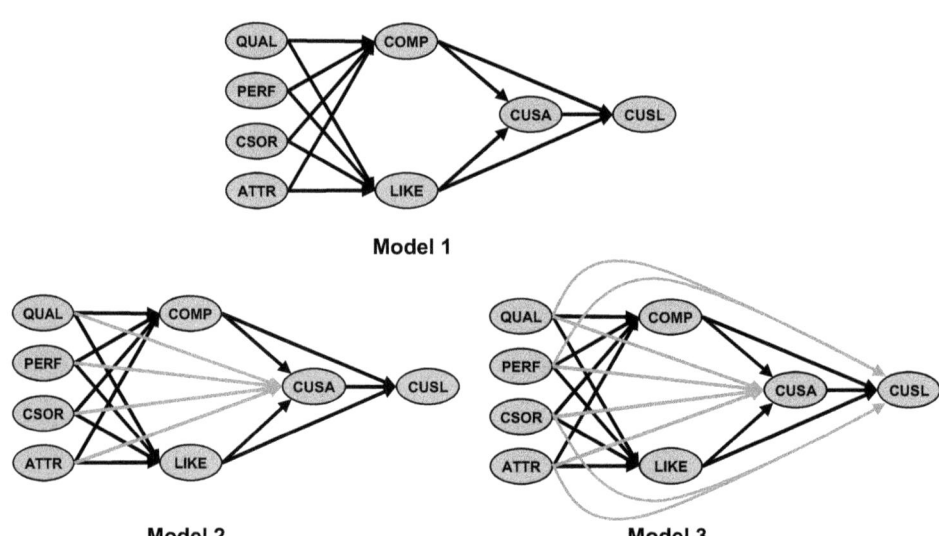

☐ **Fig. 6.11** Three competing models for predictive model comparison. (Source: Hair et al., 2022, Chap. 6; used with permission by Sage)

three models, we need to assign the BIC for *CUSA* for each model to a vector. We then name the vector using the **names()** function and inspect the **itcriteria_ vector**. In a final step, we request the BIC Akaike weights for the three models under consideration using the **compute_it_criteria_weights()** function.

```
# Inspect the IT Criteria matrix of Model1
sum_model1$it_criteria
# Subset the matrix to only return the BIC row and CUSL column
sum_model1$it_criteria["BIC", "CUSA"]
# Collect the vector of BIC values for CUSL
itcriteria_vector <- c(sum_model1$it_criteria["BIC","CUSA"],
                       sum_model2$it_criteria["BIC","CUSA"],
                       sum_model3$it_criteria["BIC","CUSA"])
# Assign the model names to IT Criteria vector
names(itcriteria_vector) <- c("Model1", "Model2", "Model3")
# Inspect the IT Criteria vector for competing models
itcriteria_vector
# Calculate the model BIC Akaike weights
compute_itcriteria_weights(itcriteria_vector)
```

We can now compare the BIC values (☐ Fig. 6.12) of Model 1 (**-102.206**), Model 2 (**-93.965**), and Model 3 (**-97.401**). The results suggest that Model 1 is superior in terms of model fit. To learn about the models' relative likelihoods, we can consult the BIC-based Akaike weights for Model 1 (**0.904**), Model 2 (**0.015**), and Model 3 (**0.082**). It is clear that Model 1 has a very strong weighting, so we conclude the model comparison indicates Model 1 is the superior model.

6.6 · Case Study Illustration: Structural Model Evaluation

```
Console  Terminal ×  Jobs ×
~/seminr/
> # Inspect the IT Criteria matrix of Model1
> sum_model1$it_criteria
        COMP     LIKE     CUSA     CUSL
AIC -333.825 -271.581 -113.728 -276.964
BIC -314.622 -252.378 -102.206 -261.602
> # Subset the matrix to only return the BIC row and CUSL column
> sum_model1$it_criteria["BIC", "CUSA"]
[1] -102.2062
> # Collect the vector of BIC values for CUSL
> itcriteria_vector <- c(sum_model1$it_criteria["BIC","CUSA"],
+                        sum_model2$it_criteria["BIC","CUSA"],
+                        sum_model3$it_criteria["BIC","CUSA"])
> # Assign the model names to IT Criteria vector
> names(itcriteria_vector) <- c("Model1", "Model2", "Model3")
> # Inspect the IT Criteria vector for competing models.
> itcriteria_vector
   Model1     Model2     Model3
-102.20623  -93.96473  -97.40109
> # Calculate the model BIC Akaike Weights
> compute_itcriteria_weights(itcriteria_vector)
   Model1     Model2     Model3
0.90357310 0.01466713 0.08175977
>
```

Fig. 6.12 BIC values and BIC Akaike weights for $CUSA$. (Source: authors' screenshot from RStudio)

Summary

The structural model assessment in PLS-SEM starts with the evaluation of potential collinearity among predictor constructs in structural model regressions, followed by the evaluation of the path coefficients' significance and relevance and concluding with the analysis of the model's explanatory and predictive power. After ensuring the model estimates are not affected by high levels of collinearity by examining VIF values, we need to test the path coefficients' significance by applying the bootstrapping routine and examining t-values or bootstrapping confidence intervals. To assess a model's explanatory power, researchers rely on the coefficient of determination (R^2). Predictive power assessment builds on $PLS_{predict}$, a holdout sample-based procedure that applies k-fold cross-validation to estimate the model parameters. Some research situations call for the comparison of alternative models. To compare different model configurations and select the best model, the BIC criterion should be used. The model, which yields the smallest BIC value, is considered the best model in the set. BIC-based Akaike weights offer further evidence for the relative likelihood of a model compared to alternative models in the set.

Exercise

We continue evaluating the influencer model introduced in the exercise section of ▶ Chap. 3 (▶ Fig. 3.10; ▶ Tables 3.9 and 3.10) and subsequently evaluated in the follow-up chapters. To start the exercise, load the influencer data, reproduce the influencer model in the SEMinR syntax, and estimate the model. We have evaluated both reflectively and formatively measured constructs in ▶ Chaps. 4 and 5, so we can now turn our attention to the structural model evaluation as follows:

1. Do any predictor constructs suffer from collinearity issues?
2. Are all structural paths significant and relevant? Which paths are of low or weak relevance?
3. Now focus on the key target construct *PI* as follows:
   (a) Does the model have satisfactory explanatory power in terms of this construct?
   (b) Does the model have satisfactory predictive power in terms of this construct?
   (c) Construct a theoretically justified competing model and conduct a model comparison in order to detect if the original influencer model is supported by the BIC statistic. Can you generate a model with a higher BIC-based Akaike weight than the original influencer model?

References

Aguirre-Urreta, M. I., & Rönkkö, M. (2018). Statistical inference with PLSc using bootstrap confidence intervals. *MIS Quarterly, 42*(3), 1001–1020.

Becker, J.-M., Ringle, C. M., Sarstedt, M., & Völckner, F. (2015). How collinearity affects mixture regression results. *Marketing Letters, 26*(4), 643–659.

Burnham, K. P., & Anderson, D. R. (2004). Multimodel inference: Understanding AIC and BIC in model selection. *Sociological Research Methods, 33*(2), 261–304.

Chin, W. W., Cheah, J.-H., Liu, Y., Ting, H., Lim, X.-J., & Cham, T. H. (2020). Demystifying the role of causal-predictive modeling using partial least squares structural equation modeling in information systems research. *Industrial Management & Data Systems, 120*(12), 2161–2209.

Danks, N. P., & Ray, S. (2018). Predictions from partial least squares models. In F. Ali, S. M. Rasoolimanesh, & C. Cobanoglu (Eds.), *Applying partial least squares in tourism and hospitality research* (pp. 35–52). Bingley: Emerald.

Danks, N. P., Sharma, P. N., & Sarstedt, M. (2020). Model selection uncertainty and multimodel inference in partial least squares structural equation modeling (PLS-SEM). *Journal of Business Research, 113*, 13–24.

Danks, N.P. (2021). The piggy in the middle: The role of mediators in PLS-SEM-based prediction. *The Data Base for Advances in Information Systems*, forthcoming.

Geweke, J., & Meese, R. (1981). Estimating regression models of finite but unknown order. *International Economic Review, 22*(1), 55–70.

Hair, J. F. (2021). Next generation prediction metrics for composite-based PLS-SEM. *Industrial Management & Data Systems, 121*(1), 5–11.

Hair, J. F., Ringle, C. M., & Sarstedt, M. (2011). PLS-SEM: Indeed a silver bullet. *Journal of Marketing Theory and Practice, 19*(2), 139–151.

Hair, J. F., Risher, J. J., Sarstedt, M., & Ringle, C. M. (2019). When to use and how to report the results of PLS-SEM. *European Business Review, 31*(1), 2–24.

References

Hair, J. F., & Sarstedt, M. (2021). Explanation plus prediction – The logical focus of project management research. *Project Management Journal, 52*(4), 319–322.

Hair, J. F., Sarstedt, M., & Ringle, C. M. (2019). Rethinking some of the rethinking of partial least squares. *European Journal of Marketing, 53*(4), 566–584.

Hair, J. F., Sarstedt, M., Ringle, C. M., & Gudergan, S. P. (2018). *Advanced issues in partial least squares structural equation modeling (PLS-SEM)*. Thousand Oaks, CA: Sage.

Henseler, J., Dijkstra, T. K., Sarstedt, M., Ringle, C. M., Diamantopoulos, A., Straub, D. W., et al. (2014). Common beliefs and reality about partial least squares: Comments on Rönkkö & Evermann (2013). *Organizational Research Methods, 17*(1), 182–209.

Liengaard, B., Sharma, P. N., Hult, G. T. M., Jensen, M. B., Sarstedt, M., Hair, J. F., & Ringle, C. M. (2021). Prediction: Coveted, yet forsaken? Introducing a cross-validated predictive ability test in partial least squares path modeling. *Decision Sciences, 52*(2), 362–392.

Lohmöller, J.-B. (1989). *Latent variable path modeling with partial least squares*. Heidelberg: Physica.

Mason, C. H., & Perreault, W. D. (1991). Collinearity, power, and interpretation of multiple regression analysis. *Journal of Marketing Research, 28*(3), 268–280.

Memon, M. A., Cheah, J. H., Ramayah, T., Ting, H., Chuah, F., & Cham, T. H. (2019). Moderation analysis: Issues and guidelines. *Journal of Applied Structural Equation Modeling, 3*(1), i–xi.

Nitzl, C., Roldán, J. L., & Cepeda Carrión, G. (2016). Mediation analysis in partial least squares path modeling. *Industrial Management & Data Systems, 119*(9), 1849–1864.

Raithel, S., Sarstedt, M., Scharf, S., & Schwaiger, M. (2012). On the value relevance of customer satisfaction. Multiple drivers and multiple markets. *Journal of the Academy of Marketing Science, 40*(4), 509–525.

Rigdon, E. E. (2012). Rethinking partial least squares path modeling: In praise of simple methods. *Long Range Planning, 45*(5–6), 341–358.

Sarstedt, M. & Danks, N. P. (2021). Prediction in HRM research—A gap between rhetoric and reality. *Human Resource Management Journal*, forthcoming.

Sarstedt, M., Hair, J. F., Cheah, J.-H., Becker, J.-M., & Ringle, C. M. (2019). How to specify, estimate, and validate higher-order models. *Australasian Marketing Journal, 27*(3), 197–211.

Sarstedt, M., & Mooi, E. (2019). *A concise guide to market research. The process, data, and methods using IBM SPSS statistics* (3rd ed.). Berlin: Springer.

Schwarz, G. (1978). Estimating the dimension of a model. *The Annals of Statistics, 6*(2), 461–464.

Sharma, P. N., Sarstedt, M., Shmueli, G., Kim, K. H., & Thiele, K. O. (2019). PLS-based model selection: The role of alternative explanations in Information Systems research. *Journal of the Association for Information Systems, 40*(4), 346–397.

Sharma, P. N., Shmueli G., Sarstedt M., Danks N., & Ray S. (2021). Prediction-oriented model selection in partial least squares path modeling. *Decision Sciences, 52*(3), 567–607.

Shmueli, G., & Koppius, O. R. (2011). Predictive analytics in information systems research. *MIS Quarterly, 35*(3), 553–572.

Shmueli, G., Ray, S., Estrada, J. M. V., & Chatla, S. B. (2016). The elephant in the room: Predictive performance of PLS models. *Journal of Business Research, 69*(10), 4552–4564.

Shmueli, G., Sarstedt, M., Hair, J. F., Cheah, J. H., Ting, H., Vaithilingam, S., & Ringle, C. M. (2019). Predictive model assessment in PLS-SEM: Guidelines for using PLSpredict. *European Journal of Marketing, 53*(11), 2322–2347.

Streukens, S., & Leroi-Werelds, S. (2016). Bootstrapping and PLS-SEM: A step-by-step guide to get more out of your bootstrap results. *European Management Journal, 34*(6), 618–632.

Theil, H. (1961). *Economic Forecasts and Policy*. Amsterdam: North-Holland.

Wagenmakers, E. J., & Farrell, S. (2004). AIC model selection using Akaike weights. *Psychonomic Bulletin & Review, 11*(1), 192–196.

Suggested Reading

Chin, W. W., Cheah, J.-H., Liu, Y., Ting, H., Lim, X.-J., & Cham, T. H. (2020). Demystifying the role of causal-predictive modeling using partial least squares structural equation modeling in information systems research. *Industrial Management & Data Systems, 120*(12), 2161–2209.

Hair, J. F., Hult, T., Ringle, C. M., & Sarstedt, M. (2022). *A primer on partial least squares structural equation modeling (PLS-SEM)* (3rd ed.). Thousand Oaks, CA: Sage.

Shmueli, G., Sarstedt, M., Hair, J. F., Cheah, J. H., Ting, H., Vaithilingam, S., & Ringle, C. M. (2019). Predictive model assessment in PLS-SEM: Guidelines for using PLSpredict. *European Journal of Marketing, 53*(11), 2322–2347.

Open Access This chapter is licensed under the terms of the Creative Commons Attribution 4.0 International License (http://creativecommons.org/licenses/by/4.0/), which permits use, sharing, adaptation, distribution and reproduction in any medium or format, as long as you give appropriate credit to the original author(s) and the source, provide a link to the Creative Commons license and indicate if changes were made.

The images or other third party material in this chapter are included in the chapter's Creative Commons license, unless indicated otherwise in a credit line to the material. If material is not included in the chapter's Creative Commons license and your intended use is not permitted by statutory regulation or exceeds the permitted use, you will need to obtain permission directly from the copyright holder.

Mediation Analysis

Contents

7.1 Introduction – 140

7.2 Systematic Mediation Analysis – 141
7.2.1 Evaluation of the Mediation Model – 141
7.2.2 Characterization of Outcomes – 141
7.2.3 Testing Mediating Effects – 143

7.3 Multiple Mediation Models – 144

7.4 Case Study Illustration: Mediation Analysis – 145

References – 151

© The Author(s) 2021
J. F. Hair Jr. et al., *Partial Least Squares Structural Equation Modeling (PLS-SEM) Using R*, Classroom Companion: Business, https://doi.org/10.1007/978-3-030-80519-7_7

> **Learning Objectives**
> After reading this chapter, you should:
> 1. Understand the basic concepts of mediation in a PLS-SEM context
> 2. Know how to execute a mediation analysis
> 3. Comprehend how to interpret the results
> 4. Learn to distinguish between a single and a multiple mediation analysis
> 5. Acquire the capability to use SEMinR to conduct a mediation analysis based on the corporate reputation example

7.1 Introduction

Mediation occurs when a construct, referred to as **mediator construct**, intervenes between two other related constructs. More precisely, a change in the exogenous construct causes a change in the mediator construct, which, in turn, results in a change in the endogenous construct in the PLS path model. When such an effect is present, **mediation** can be a useful statistical analysis, if supported by theory and carried out properly.

Consider ◘ Fig. 7.1 for an illustration of a **mediating effect** in terms of direct and indirect effects. A **direct effect** describes the relationships linking two constructs with a single arrow. Indirect effects are those structural model paths that involve a sequence of relationships with at least one intervening construct involved. Thus, an **indirect effect** is a sequence of two or more direct effects and is represented visually by multiple arrows. ◘ Figure 7.1 shows both a direct effect p_3 between Y_1 and Y_3 and an indirect effect of Y_1 on Y_3 in the form of a $Y_1 \rightarrow Y_2 \rightarrow Y_3$ sequence. The indirect effect, computed as the product $p_1 \cdot p_2$, represents the mediating effect of the construct Y_2 on the relationship between Y_1 and Y_3. Finally, the sum of the direct and indirect effect is referred to as the **total effect** (i.e., $p_1 \cdot p_2 + p_3$ in ◘ Fig. 7.1).

Many PLS path models include mediation effects but are often not explicitly hypothesized and tested (Hair et al., 2022). Only when the possible mediation is theoretically considered and also empirically tested is it possible to fully and accurately understand the nature of the cause–effect relationship. Again, theory is always the foundation of empirical analyses, including mediation. Nitzl, Roldán, and Cepeda Carrión (2016) as well as Cepeda Carrión, Nitzl, and Roldán (2017) and Memon, Cheah, Ramayah, Ting, and Chuah (2018) provide detailed explanations of mediation analysis in PLS-SEM.

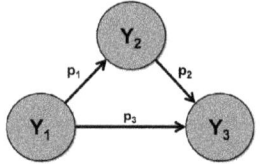

◘ **Fig. 7.1** Mediation model. (Source: Hair, Hult, Ringle, & Sarstedt, 2022, Chap. 7; used with permission by Sage)

7.2 Systematic Mediation Analysis

A systematic mediation analysis builds on a theoretically established model and hypothesized relationships, including the mediating effect. To begin, it is important to estimate and assess the model, which includes all considered mediators. The next steps are the characterization of the mediation analysis' outcomes and testing of the mediating effects. We address these three steps in the following sections.

7.2.1 Evaluation of the Mediation Model

Evaluating a **mediation model** requires all quality criteria of the measurement and structural models to be met, as discussed in ▶ Chaps. 4, 5, and 6. The analysis begins with the assessment of the reflective and formative measurement models. For example, a lack of reliability for one or more reflective mediator constructs will have a meaningful impact on the estimated relationships in the PLS path model (i.e., the indirect paths can become considerably smaller than expected). For this reason, it is important to ensure that the reflectively measured mediator constructs exhibit a high level of reliability.

After establishing the reliability and validity of measurement models for the mediator as well as the other exogenous and the endogenous constructs, it is important to consider all structural model evaluation criteria. For instance, high collinearity must not be present since it is likely to produce biased path coefficients. For example, as a result of collinearity, the direct effect may become nonsignificant, suggesting the absence of mediation even though, for example, complementary mediation may be present (see the next section). Likewise, high collinearity levels may result in unexpected sign changes, rendering any differentiation between different mediation types problematic. Moreover, a lack of the mediator construct's discriminant validity with the exogenous or endogenous construct might result in a strong and significant but substantially biased indirect effect, consequently leading to incorrect implications regarding the existence or type of mediation. After meeting the relevant assessment criteria for reflective and formative measurement models, as well as the structural model, the actual mediation analysis follows.

7.2.2 Characterization of Outcomes

The question of how to test mediation has attracted considerable attention in methodological research. Decades ago, Baron and Kenny (1986) presented a mediation analysis approach, referred to as causal step approach, which many researchers still routinely draw upon (Rasoolimanesh, Wang, Roldán, & Kunasekaran, 2021). More recent research, however, concludes there are conceptual and methodological problems with Baron and Kenny's (1986) approach (e.g., Hayes, 2018). Against this background, our description builds on Zhao, Lynch, and Chen (2010), who offer a synthesis of prior research on mediation analysis and corresponding guidelines for future research (Nitzl et al., 2016).

The authors characterize three types of mediation:
- **Complementary mediation**: the indirect effect and the direct effect are significant and point in the same direction.
- **Competitive mediation**: the indirect effect and the direct effect are significant but point in opposite directions.
- **Indirect-only mediation**: the indirect effect is significant, but not the direct effect.

In addition, they identify two types of non-mediation:
- **Direct-only non-mediation**: the direct effect is significant, but not the indirect effect.
- **No-effect non-mediation**: neither the direct nor the indirect effect is significant.

As a result, a mediation analysis may show that mediation does not exist at all (i.e., direct-only non-mediation and no-effect non-mediation) or, in case of a mediation effect, the mediator construct accounts either for some (i.e., complementary and competitive mediation) or for all of the observed relationship between two latent variables (i.e., indirect-only mediation). In that sense, the Zhao et al. (2010) procedure closely corresponds to Baron and Kenny's (1986) concepts of **partial mediation** (i.e., complementary mediation), **suppressor effect** (i.e., competitive mediation), and **full mediation** (i.e., indirect-only mediation).

Testing for the type of mediation in a model requires running a series of analyses, which ◘ Fig. 7.2 illustrates. The first step addresses the significance of the indirect effect ($p_1 \cdot p_2$) via the mediator construct (Y_2) as shown in ◘ Fig. 7.1. If the indirect effect is not significant (right-hand side of ◘ Fig. 7.2), we conclude that Y_2 does not function as a mediator in the tested relationship. While this result may seem disappointing at first sight, as it does not provide empirical support for a

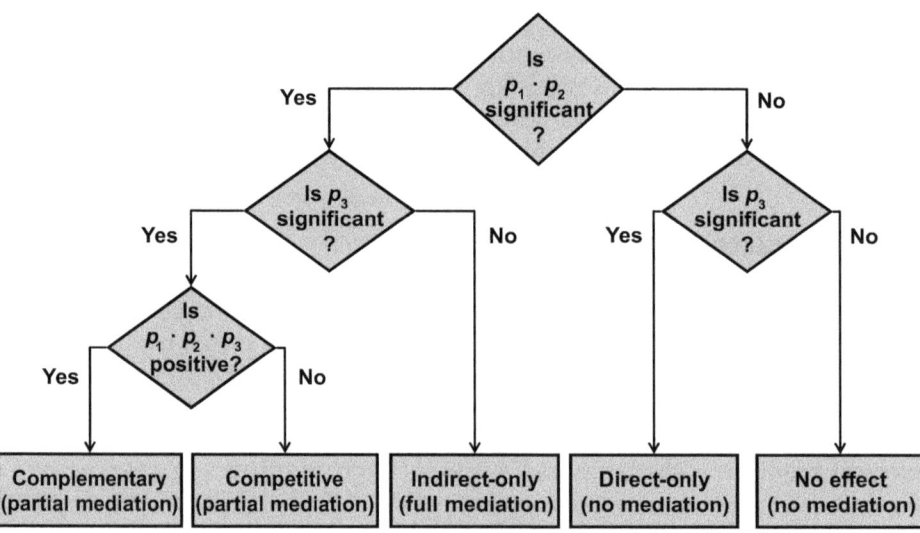

◘ **Fig. 7.2** Mediation analysis procedure. (Source: authors' own figure; Zhao et al., 2010)

hypothesized mediating relationship, further analysis of the direct effect p_3 can point to as yet undiscovered mediators. Specifically, if the direct effect is significant, we could conclude it is possible that there is an omitted mediator, which potentially explains the relationship between Y_1 and Y_3 (direct-only non-mediation). If the direct effect is also nonsignificant (no-effect non-mediation), however, we must conclude that our theoretical framework is flawed. In this case, we should go back to theory and reconsider the path model setup. Note that this situation can occur despite a significant total effect of Y_1 on Y_3 ($p_1 \cdot p_2 + p_3$ in ◘ Fig. 7.1).

We may, however, find general support for a hypothesized mediating relationship in our initial analysis based on a significant indirect effect (left-hand side of ◘ Fig. 7.2). As before, our next interest is with the significance of the direct effect p_3. If the direct effect is not significant, we face the situation of indirect-only mediation. This situation represents the best-case scenario, as it suggests that our mediator fully complies with the hypothesized theoretical framework. If the direct effect p_3 is significant, we still find support for the hypothesized mediating relationship. However, the total effect between the two constructs Y_1 and Y_3 stems partially from the direct effect p_3 and partially from the indirect effect $p_1 \cdot p_2$. In this situation, we can distinguish between complementary and competitive mediation.

Complementary mediation describes a situation in which the direct effect and the indirect effect $p_1 \cdot p_2$ point in the same direction. In other words, the product of the direct effect and the indirect effect (i.e., $p_1 \cdot p_2 \cdot p_3$) is positive (◘ Fig. 7.2). On the contrary, in competitive mediation – also referred to as **inconsistent mediation** (MacKinnon, Fairchild, & Fritz, 2007) – the direct effect p_3 and either indirect effect p_1 or p_2 have opposite signs. In other words, the product of the direct effect and the indirect effect $p_1 \cdot p_2 \cdot p_3$ is negative (◘ Fig. 7.2). It is important to note that in competitive mediation, the mediating construct acts as a suppressor effect, which substantially decreases the magnitude of the total effect of Y_1 on Y_3. Therefore, when competitive mediation occurs, researchers need to carefully analyze the theoretical substantiation of all effects involved.

7.2.3 Testing Mediating Effects

Prior testing of the significance of mediating effects relied on the Sobel (1982) test, which should no longer be used (Hair et al., 2022, Chap. 7). Instead of using the Sobel (1982) test, researchers should bootstrap the sampling distribution of the indirect effect (Preacher & Hayes, 2004; Preacher & Hayes, 2008a). Bootstrapping (see ► Chap. 5) makes no assumptions about the shape of the variables' distribution or the sampling distribution of the statistics and can be applied to small sample sizes with more confidence. Even though bootstrapping has been introduced for the mediation analysis in regression models, the approach is perfectly suited for the PLS-SEM method as well. In addition, bootstrapping the indirect effect yields higher levels of statistical power compared to the Sobel (1982) test (Zhao et al., 2010).

› There is no need for researchers to use the PROCESS routine (Hayes, 2018) proposed for regression models to analyze mediation effects in PLS-SEM (i.e., in a subsequent tandem analysis, by using the latent variable scores obtained by PLS-SEM to run a regression model in PROCESS), since bootstrapping in PLS-SEM provides all relevant results with more accuracy and precision than PROCESS (Sarstedt, Hair, Nitzl, Ringle, & Howard, 2020).

7.3 Multiple Mediation Models

In the previous sections, we considered the case of a single mediator construct, which accounts for the relationship between an exogenous and an endogenous construct. Analyzing such a model setup is also referred to as **single mediation analysis**. More often, however, when evaluating structural models, exogenous constructs exert their influence through more than one mediating variable. This situation requires running **multiple mediation analyses** for the hypothesized relationships via more than one mediator in PLS-SEM (Cepeda Carrión et al., 2017; Nitzl et al., 2016). As an example of multiple mediation with two mediators, consider ◘ Fig. 7.3. In this model, p_3 represents the direct effect between the exogenous construct and the endogenous construct. The **specific indirect effect** of Y_1 on Y_3 via mediator Y_2 is quantified as $p_1 \cdot p_2$. For the second mediator Y_4, the specific indirect effect is given by $p_4 \cdot p_5$. In addition, we can consider the specific indirect effect of Y_1 on Y_3 via both mediators, Y_2 and Y_4, which is quantified as $p_1 \cdot p_6 \cdot p_5$. The **total indirect effect** is the sum of the specific indirect effects (i.e., $p_1 \cdot p_2 + p_4 \cdot p_5 + p_1 \cdot p_6 \cdot p_5$). Finally, the total effect of Y_1 on Y_3 is the sum of the direct effect and the total indirect effects (i.e., $p_3 + p_1 \cdot p_2 + p_4 \cdot p_5 + p_1 \cdot p_6 \cdot p_5$).

To test a **multiple mediation model**, such as the one shown in ◘ Fig. 7.3, researchers may be tempted to run a set of separate single mediation analyses, one for each proposed mediator (in this case, Y_2 and Y_4) separately. However, as Preacher and Hayes (2008a, 2008b) point out, this approach is problematic for at least two reasons. First, one cannot simply add up the indirect effects calculated in several single mediation analyses to derive the total indirect effect, as the mediators in a multiple mediation model typically will be correlated. As a result, the specific indirect effects, estimated using several single mediation analyses, will be biased

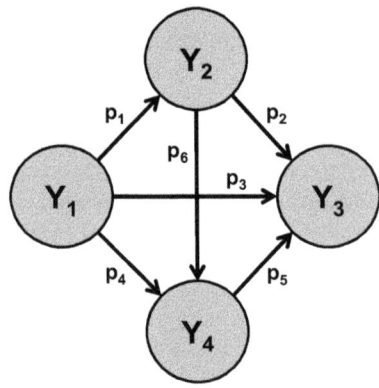

◘ **Fig. 7.3** Multiple mediation model. (Source: Hair et al., 2022, Chap. 7; used with permission by Sage)

and will not sum to the total indirect effect through the multiple mediators. Second, hypothesis testing and confidence intervals calculated for specific indirect effects may not be accurate due to the omission of other, potentially important, mediators. By considering all mediators at the same time in one model, we gain a more complete picture of the mechanisms through which an exogenous construct affects an endogenous construct (Sarstedt et al., 2020). Hence, we recommend including all relevant mediators in the model and, thus, analyzing their hypothesized effects simultaneously. In a multiple mediation model, a specific indirect effect can be interpreted as the indirect effect of Y_1 on Y_3 through a given mediator, while controlling for all other included mediators.

The analysis of a multiple mediation model also follows the procedure shown in ◘ Fig. 7.2. That is, we should test the significance of the indirect effects (i.e., each specific and total indirect effects) and the direct effect between the exogenous construct and the endogenous construct. In addition, we should test whether the total indirect effect is significant. To assess the significance of the specific indirect effects, the total indirect effect, and the direct effect, we should use the results of the bootstrap routine. Similar to the path coefficient significance test (▶ Chap. 6), we should select 10,000 (or more) bootstrap subsamples and report the 95% percentile bootstrap confidence intervals for the final result reporting. On this basis, the analysis and result interpretation of a multiple mediation follow the same procedure as a single mediation analysis. Nitzl et al. (2016) as well as Cepeda Carrión et al. (2017) and Sarstedt et al. (2020) provide additional insights on multiple mediation analysis in PLS-SEM.

7.4 Case Study Illustration: Mediation Analysis

We now perform a deeper investigation of the relationship between the two dimensions of corporate reputation (*LIKE* and *COMP*) on the key construct customer loyalty (*CUSL*). The theory of cognitive dissonance (Festinger, 1957) proposes that customers who perceive that a company has a favorable reputation are likely to show higher levels of satisfaction in an effort to avoid cognitive dissonance. Previous research has demonstrated, however, that customer satisfaction is the primary driver of customer loyalty (Anderson & Fornell, 2000). Therefore, we expect that customer satisfaction mediates the relationship between likeability and customer loyalty as well as competence and customer loyalty (◘ Fig. 7.4). To test these hypothesized effects, we will apply the procedure shown in ◘ Fig. 7.2.

To begin the mediation analysis, we need to ensure that all construct measures are reliable and valid and that the structural model meets all quality criteria. As we have conducted these evaluations in ▶ Chaps. 5 and 6 and found the model to be satisfactory, we can now move directly to the mediation analysis. If your model has not yet been thoroughly assessed, please do so before conducting the mediation analysis.

As illustrated in ◘ Fig. 7.2, we first need to test for significance of the relevant indirect effects in the extended corporate reputation model (◘ Fig. 7.4). The indirect effect from *COMP* via *CUSA* to *CUSL* is the product of the path coefficients from *COMP* to *CUSA* and from *CUSA* to *CUSL* (mediation path 1, dashed line

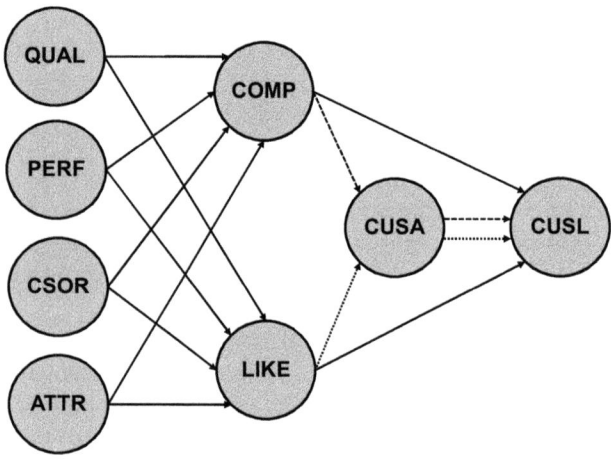

Fig. 7.4 Extended corporate reputation model with highlighted mediation effects. (Source: authors' own figure)

in ◘ Fig. 7.4). Similarly, the indirect effect from *LIKE* via *CUSA* to *CUSL* is the product of the path coefficients from *LIKE* to *CUSA* and from *CUSA* to *CUSL* (mediation path 2, dotted line in ◘ Fig. 7.4). To test for significance of these path coefficients' products, we first need to estimate and bootstrap the model and summarize the results (see ▶ Chaps. 5 and 6 for details and thorough explanation).

```
# Load the SEMinR library
library(seminr)


# Load the data
corp_rep_data <- corp_rep_data

# Create measurement model
corp_rep_mm_ext <- constructs(
  composite("QUAL", multi_items("qual_", 1:8), weights = mode_B),
  composite("PERF", multi_items("perf_", 1:5), weights = mode_B),
  composite("CSOR", multi_items("csor_", 1:5), weights = mode_B),
  composite("ATTR", multi_items("attr_", 1:3), weights = mode_B),
  composite("COMP", multi_items("comp_", 1:3)),
  composite("LIKE", multi_items("like_", 1:3)),
  composite("CUSA", single_item("cusa")),
  composite("CUSL", multi_items("cusl_", 1:3))
)
```

7.4 · Case Study Illustration: Mediation Analysis

```
# Create structural model
corp_rep_sm_ext <- relationships(
  paths(from = c("QUAL", "PERF", "CSOR", "ATTR"), to = c("COMP",
"LIKE")),
  paths(from = c("COMP", "LIKE"), to = c("CUSA", "CUSL")),
  paths(from = c("CUSA"), to = c("CUSL"))
)

# Estimate the model
corp_rep_pls_model_ext <- estimate_pls(
  data = corp_rep_data,
  measurement_model = corp_rep_mm_ext,
  structural_model = corp_rep_sm_ext,
  missing = mean_replacement,
  missing_value = "-99"
)

# Summarize the results of the model estimation
summary_corp_rep_ext <- summary(corp_rep_pls_model_ext)

# Bootstrap the model
boot_corp_rep_ext <- bootstrap_model(
  seminr_model = corp_rep_pls_model_ext,
  nboot = 1000,
  cores = parallel::detectCores(),
  seed = 123
)

# Summarize the results of the bootstrap
summary_boot_corp_rep_ext <- summary(boot_corp_rep_ext, alpha =
0.05)
```

The results for total indirect effects can be found by inspecting the **total_indirect_effects** element within the **summary_corp_rep_ext** object, **summary_corp_rep_ext$total_indirect_effects**. Specific indirect paths can be evaluated for significance, by using the **specific_effect_significance()** function. This function takes a bootstrapped model object, an antecedent construct name, and an outcome construct name as arguments and returns the bootstrap confidence interval for the total indirect paths from the antecedents to the outcome construct (◘ Table 7.1).

We use the **specific_effect_significance()** function on the **boot_corp_rep_ext** object and specify the indirect path using the *from* and *to* arguments. A separate path must be specified for *COMP*, through *CUSA*, to *CUSL*, and another for *LIKE*, through *CUSA*, to *CUSL*:

◘ Table 7.1 A list of arguments for the `specific_effect_significance()` function

Argument	Value
`boot_seminr_model`	The bootstrapped SEMinR model containing the estimated paths
`from`	The antecedent construct name
`through`	A vector of all mediating construct names
`to`	The outcome construct name
`alpha`	The statistical power in percentage to be used for determining confidence intervals. The default is 0.05 (5%) for a two-tailed test

Source: authors' own table

```
# Inspect total indirect effects
summary_corp_rep_ext$total_indirect_effects

# Inspect indirect effects
specific_effect_significance(boot_corp_rep_ext,
  from = "COMP",
  through = "CUSA",
  to = "CUSL",
  alpha = 0.05)
specific_effect_significance(boot_corp_rep_ext,
  from = "LIKE",
  through = "CUSA",
  to = "CUSL",
  alpha = 0.05)
```

> **Tip**
>
> The `specific_effect_significance()` can be used for calculating the bootstrap mean, standard deviation, t-statistic, and bootstrap confidence intervals for paths involving multiple mediators. The `through` argument can take multiple mediating constructs as arguments (e.g., `through = c("construct1", "construct2")`). Therefore, this function can be used for testing models with serial mediation.

The results in ◘ Fig. 7.5 show that the total indirect effect of *COMP* on *CUSL* is **0.074**, and the total indirect effect of *LIKE* on *CUSL* is **0.220**. When inspecting the bootstrap confidence intervals, we conclude that – since the confidence interval does not include the zero for either effect – the effects are significant at the specified 5% level. Note that the confidence intervals will look slightly different in your analysis, as they are derived from bootstrapping, which is a random process.

7.4 · Case Study Illustration: Mediation Analysis

```
Console  Terminal × Jobs ×
~/seminr/
> # Inspect total indirect effects
> summary_corp_rep_ext$total_indirect_effects
      QUAL  PERF  CSOR  ATTR  COMP  LIKE  CUSA  CUSL
QUAL 0.000 0.000 0.000 0.000 0.000 0.000 0.228 0.248
PERF 0.000 0.000 0.000 0.000 0.000 0.000 0.094 0.089
CSOR 0.000 0.000 0.000 0.000 0.000 0.000 0.086 0.105
ATTR 0.000 0.000 0.000 0.000 0.000 0.000 0.085 0.101
COMP 0.000 0.000 0.000 0.000 0.000 0.000 0.000 0.074
LIKE 0.000 0.000 0.000 0.000 0.000 0.000 0.000 0.220
CUSA 0.000 0.000 0.000 0.000 0.000 0.000 0.000 0.000
CUSL 0.000 0.000 0.000 0.000 0.000 0.000 0.000 0.000
> # Inspect indirect effects
> specific_effect_significance(boot_corp_rep_ext, from = "COMP", through = "CUSA", to = "CUSL", alpha = 0.05)
Original Est.  Bootstrap Mean  Bootstrap SD   T Stat.    2.5% CI      97.5% CI
    0.07350093     0.07443445    0.03651814  2.01272396  0.00296709  0.14620781
> specific_effect_significance(boot_corp_rep_ext, from = "LIKE", through = "CUSA", to = "CUSL", alpha = 0.05)
Original Est.  Bootstrap Mean  Bootstrap SD   T Stat.    2.5% CI      97.5% CI
    0.22001302     0.21993527    0.03687955  5.96571802  0.14917504  0.29318977
>
```

Fig. 7.5 Results of total indirect effects and specific effect confidence intervals. (Source: authors' screenshot from R)

Following the mediation analysis procedure (Fig. 7.2), we can now ascertain if the direct effect is significant for each of the two mediation effects (i.e., *COMP* to *CUSL* and *LIKE* to *CUSL*). These paths can be accessed by inspecting the `paths` element of the `summary_corp_rep_ext` object. The confidence intervals for the direct effects can be evaluated by inspecting the `bootstrapped_paths` element of the `summary_boot_corp_rep_ext` object.

```
# Inspect the direct effects
summary_corp_rep_ext$paths

# Inspect the confidence intervals for direct effects
summary_boot_corp_rep_ext$bootstrapped_paths
```

The results in Fig. 7.6 show that the direct effect from *COMP* to *CUSL* is **0.006** with a 95% confidence interval [−0.104; 0.115]. As this interval includes zero, this direct effect is not significant. According to the guidelines shown in Fig. 7.2, we therefore conclude that the relationship between *COMP* and *CUSL* is fully mediated by *CUSA*. Next, we need to consider the direct relationship between *LIKE* and *CUSL*, which has a **0.344** path coefficient with a 95% confidence interval [**0.231; 0.449**]. As this confidence interval does not include zero, we conclude that *CUSA* partially mediates the effect of *LIKE* on *CUSL*. We now need to further evaluate if *CUSA* acts as a complementary or competitive mediator for the effect of *LIKE* on *CUSL*. To do so, we need to determine whether the product of the direct and indirect effects ($p_1 \cdot p_2 \cdot p_3$ in Fig. 7.1) has a positive or negative sign. To show these paths, we use the path element

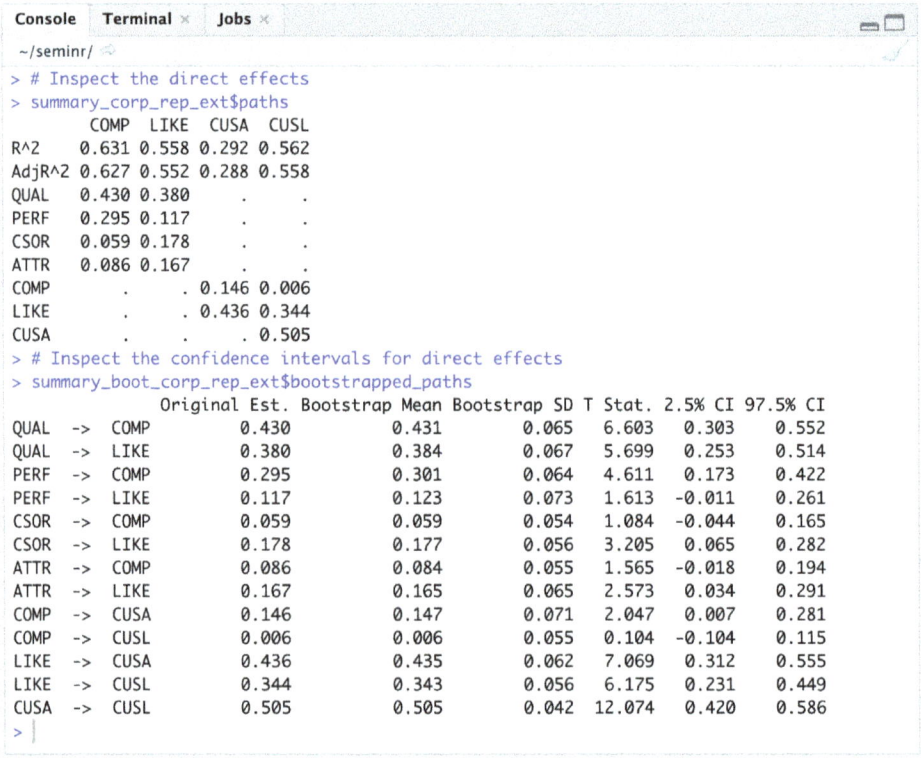

◘ Fig. 7.6 Results of direct effects and confidence intervals for direct effects. (Source: authors' screenshot from R)

of `summary_corp_rep_ext`. We can subset this path's matrix to display the path from *LIKE* to *CUSA*, `summary_corp_rep_ext$paths["LIKE", "CUSA"]`. We need to repeat this step for each of the three paths in the mediation relationship and then multiply the paths.

```
# Calculate the sign of p1*p2*p3
summary_corp_rep_ext$paths["LIKE", "CUSL"] *
  summary_corp_rep_ext$paths["LIKE","CUSA"] *
  summary_corp_rep_ext$paths["CUSA","CUSL"]
```

The results in ◘ Fig. 7.7 show that the product of the three paths is positive (**0.076**). We therefore conclude that *CUSA* acts as a complementary partial mediator in the relationship between *LIKE* and *CUSL*.

```
Console  Terminal ×  Jobs ×
~/seminr/
> # Calculate the sign of p1*p2*p3
> summary_corp_rep_ext$paths["LIKE", "CUSL"] *
+   summary_corp_rep_ext$paths["LIKE","CUSA"] *
+   summary_corp_rep_ext$paths["CUSA","CUSL"]
[1] 0.07569007
>
```

Fig. 7.7 Results of calculating $p_1 \cdot p_2 \cdot p_3$. (Source: authors' screenshot from R)

Summary

Mediation occurs when a third variable, referred to as a mediator construct, intervenes between two other related constructs. More precisely, a change in the exogenous construct results in a change in the mediator construct, which, in turn, affects the endogenous construct in the model. After theoretically establishing a mediation model and its hypothesized relationships, a systematic mediation analysis includes the estimation and evaluation of the mediation model results, their characterization, and testing for the mediating effects. Analyzing the strength of the mediator construct's relationships with the other construct(s) enables the researcher to better understand the mechanisms that underlie the relationship between an exogenous and an endogenous construct. In the simplest form, the PLS-SEM analysis considers only one mediator construct, but the model also can involve multiple mediator constructs that need to be analyzed simultaneously.

Exercise

We continue analyzing the influencer model as introduced in the exercise section of ► Chap. 3. In the model (► Fig. 3.10), SIC has a direct effect on *PI*, but also two indirect effects via *PL* and *PQ*. In the following, we turn our attention to the potential mediating effects of SIC on *PI*:
1. Is the indirect effect between SIC and *PI* via *PL* significant?
2. Is the indirect effect between SIC and *PI* via *PQ* significant?
3. Is the direct relationship between SIC and *PI* significant?
4. Which types of mediation effects are present?

References

Anderson, E. W., & Fornell, C. G. (2000). Foundations of the American customer satisfaction index. *Total Quality Management, 11*(7), 869–882.

Baron, R. M., & Kenny, D. A. (1986). The moderator–mediator variable distinction in social psychological research: Conceptual, strategic, and statistical considerations. *Journal of Personality and Social Psychology, 51*(6), 1173–1182.

Cepeda Carrión, G., Nitzl, C., & Roldán, J. L. (2017). Mediation analyses in partial least squares structural equation modeling: Guidelines and empirical examples. In H. Latan & R. Noonan

(Eds.), *Partial least squares path modeling: Basic concepts, methodological issues and applications* (pp. 173–195). Cham: Springer International Publishing.

Festinger, L. (1957). *A theory of cognitive dissonance* (Vol. 2). Stanford, CA: Stanford University Press.

Hair, J. F., Hult, G. T. M., Ringle, C. M., & Sarstedt, M. (2022). *A primer on partial least squares structural equation modeling (PLS-SEM)* (3rd ed.). Thousand Oaks, CA: Sage.

Hayes, A. F. (2018). *Introduction to mediation, moderation, and conditional process analysis: A regression-based approach* (2nd ed.). New York, NY: Guilford Press.

MacKinnon, D. P., Fairchild, A. J., & Fritz, M. S. (2007). Mediation analysis. *Annual Review of Psychology, 58*, 593–614.

Memon, M. A., Cheah, J.-H., Ramayah, T., Ting, H., & Chuah, F. (2018). Mediation analysis: Issues and recommendations. *Journal of Applied Structural Equation Modeling, 2*(1), i–ix.

Nitzl, C., Roldán, J. L., & Cepeda Carrión, G. (2016). Mediation analysis in partial least squares path modeling. *Industrial Management & Data Systems, 119*(9), 1849–1864.

Preacher, K. J., & Hayes, A. F. (2004). SPSS and SAS procedures for estimating indirect effects in simple mediation models. *Behavior Research Methods, Instruments, & Computers, 36*(4), 717–731.

Preacher, K. J., & Hayes, A. F. (2008a). Asymptotic and resampling strategies for assessing and comparing indirect effects in simple and multiple mediator models. *Behavior Research Methods, 40*, 879–891.

Preacher, K. J., & Hayes, A. F. (2008b). Contemporary approaches to assessing mediation in communication research. In A. F. Hayes, D. Slater, & L. B. Snyder (Eds.), *The SAGE sourcebook of advanced data analysis methods for communication research* (pp. 13–54). Thousand Oaks, CA: Sage.

Rasoolimanesh, S. M., Wang, M., Roldán, J. L., & Kunasekaran, P. (2021). Are we in right path for mediation analysis? Reviewing the literature and proposing robust guidelines. *Journal of Hospitality and Tourism Management, 48*, 395–405.

Sarstedt, M., Hair, J. F., Nitzl, C., Ringle, C. M., & Howard, M. C. (2020). Beyond a tandem analysis of SEM and PROCESS: Use of PLS-SEM for mediation analyses! *International Journal of Market Research, 62*(3), 288–299.

Sobel, M. E. (1982). Asymptotic confidence intervals for indirect effects in structural equation models. *Sociological Methodology, 13*, 290–312.

Zhao, X., Lynch, J. G., & Chen, Q. (2010). Reconsidering Baron and Kenny: Myths and truths about mediation analysis. *Journal of Consumer Research, 37*(2), 197–206.

Suggested Reading

Cheah, J.-H., Nitzl, C., Roldán, J., Cepeda-Carrión, G., & Gudergan, S. P. (2021). A primer on the conditional mediation analysis in PLS-SEM. *The DATA BASE for Advances in Information Systems*, forthcoming.

Hair, J. F., Hult, G. T. M., Ringle, C. M., & Sarstedt, M. (2022). *A primer on partial least squares structural equation modeling (PLS-SEM)* (3rd ed.). Thousand Oaks, CA: Sage.

Hayes, A. F. (2018). *Introduction to mediation, moderation, and conditional process analysis: A regression-based approach* (2nd ed.). New York, NY: Guilford Press.

Nitzl, C., Roldán, J. L., & Cepeda Carrión, G. (2016). Mediation analysis in partial least squares path modeling. *Industrial Management & Data Systems, 119*(9), 1849–1864.

Preacher, K. J., & Hayes, A. F. (2008). Contemporary approaches to assessing mediation in communication research. In A. F. Hayes, D. Slater, & L. B. Snyder (Eds.), *The SAGE sourcebook of advanced data analysis methods for communication research* (pp. 13–54). Thousand Oaks, CA: Sage.

Sarstedt, M., Hair, J. F., Nitzl, C., Ringle, C. M., & Howard, M. C. (2020). Beyond a tandem analysis of SEM and PROCESS: Use of PLS-SEM for mediation analyses! *International Journal of Market Research, 62*(3), 288–299.

Zhao, X., Lynch, J. G., & Chen, Q. (2010). Reconsidering Baron and Kenny: Myths and truths about mediation analysis. *Journal of Consumer Research, 37*(2), 197–206.

Suggested Reading

Open Access This chapter is licensed under the terms of the Creative Commons Attribution 4.0 International License (http://creativecommons.org/licenses/by/4.0/), which permits use, sharing, adaptation, distribution and reproduction in any medium or format, as long as you give appropriate credit to the original author(s) and the source, provide a link to the Creative Commons license and indicate if changes were made.

The images or other third party material in this chapter are included in the chapter's Creative Commons license, unless indicated otherwise in a credit line to the material. If material is not included in the chapter's Creative Commons license and your intended use is not permitted by statutory regulation or exceeds the permitted use, you will need to obtain permission directly from the copyright holder.

Moderation Analysis

Contents

8.1 Introduction – 156

8.2 Types of Moderator Variables – 157

8.3 Modeling Moderating Effects – 158

8.4 Creating the Interaction Term – 159

8.5 Model Evaluation – 161

8.6 Result Interpretation – 162

8.7 Case Study Illustration: Moderation Analysis – 164

References – 171

© The Author(s) 2021
J. F. Hair Jr. et al., *Partial Least Squares Structural Equation Modeling (PLS-SEM) Using R*, Classroom Companion: Business, https://doi.org/10.1007/978-3-030-80519-7_8

Learning Objectives

After reading this chapter, you should:
1. Comprehend the basic concepts of moderation when using PLS-SEM
2. Be able to technically execute a moderation analysis
3. Understand how to interpret the results of a moderation analysis
4. Learn how to execute a slope analysis
5. Be able to use SEMinR to conduct a moderation analysis based on the corporate reputation example

8.1 Introduction

Moderation describes a situation in which the relationship between two constructs is not constant but depends on the values of a third variable, referred to as a **moderator variable**. The moderator variable (or construct) changes the strength, or even the direction of a relationship between two constructs in a model. For example, prior research has shown that the relationship between customer satisfaction and customer loyalty differs as a function of the customers' income or age (e.g., Homburg & Giering, 2001). More precisely, income has a pronounced negative effect on the satisfaction to loyalty relationship – the higher the income, the weaker the relationship between satisfaction and loyalty. In short, income serves as a moderator variable that accounts for heterogeneity in the data. This means the satisfaction to loyalty relationship is not the same for all customers but differs depending on the income level. In this respect, moderation can (and should) be seen as a means to account for **heterogeneity** in the data.

Moderating relationships are hypothesized a priori by the researcher. The testing of the moderating relationship depends on whether the researcher hypothesizes whether *one* specific model relationship or whether *all* model relationships depend on the values of the moderator. Moderators can be either single items or multi-item constructs. In our satisfaction–loyalty example, we hypothesized that only the satisfaction to loyalty relationship is influenced by income. These considerations also apply for the corporate reputation model and its relationship between *CUSA* and *CUSL*. In such a setting, we would, for example, examine if and how the respondents' income influences the relationship between *CUSA* and *CUSL*. ◘ Figure 8.1 shows the theoretical model of such a moderating relationship.

Alternatively, we could also hypothesize that several relationships in the corporate reputation model depend on some customer characteristic, such as gender. In this case, we would run a **multigroup analysis** (Klesel, Schuberth, Niehaves, & Henseler, 2021). For a detailed explanation of multigroup analysis in PLS-SEM, see Chap. 8 in Hair et al. (2022) and Chap. 4 in Hair, Sarstedt, Ringle, and Gudergan (2018). In this chapter, our focus is on the (single) moderator analysis. More specifically, we address the modeling and interpretation of an **interaction effect** that occurs when a moderator variable is assumed to influence one specific relationship.

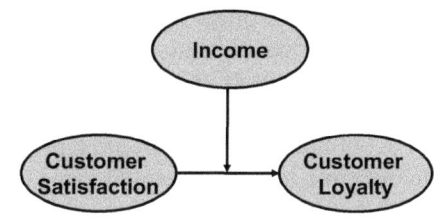

◘ Fig. 8.1 Theoretical moderation model example. (Source: Hair, Hult, Ringle, & Sarstedt, 2022, Chap. 7; used with permission by Sage)

8.2 Types of Moderator Variables

Moderators can be present in structural models in different forms. They can represent observable traits, such as gender, age, or income. But they can also represent unobservable traits, such as risk attitude, attitude toward a brand, or ad liking. Moderators can be measured with a single item or multiple items and using reflective or formative indicators. The most important differentiation, however, relates to the moderator's measurement scale, which involves distinguishing between categorical (typically dichotomous) and continuous moderators.

In our corporate reputation case study in the mobile phone industry, we could, for example, use the service-type variable (contract versus prepaid) as a categorical moderator variable. These categorical variables are usually dummy coded (i.e., 0/1), whereby the zero ("0") represents one of the two categories, called the reference category, while the value one ("1") represents the other category in a two-category situation. Note, however, that a categorical moderator can represent more than two groups. For example, in the case of three groups (e.g., short-term contract, long-term contract, and prepaid), we could divide the moderator into two dummy variables, which are simultaneously included in the model. In the latter case, both dummy variables would take the value zero for the reference category (e.g., prepaid). The other two categories would be indicated by the value 1 in the corresponding dummy variable.

Similar to regression analysis, categorical moderators can be included in a PLS path model when specifying the structural model. For example, in the case study on corporate reputation, we could evaluate whether the customers' gender has a significant bearing on the satisfaction–loyalty link. In many cases, however, researchers use a categorical moderator variable to split up the dataset into two or more groups and then estimate the models separately for each group of data. Running a multigroup analysis enables identification of model relationships that differ significantly between the groups (Hair et al., 2018, Chap. 4). This approach offers a more complete picture of the moderator's influence on the analysis results as the focus shifts from examining its impact on one specific model relationship to examining its impact on all model relationships.

In many situations, researchers have a continuous moderator variable that they theorize will affect the strength of one specific relationship between two latent variables. Returning to our case study on corporate reputation, we could, for example, hypothesize that the relationship between satisfaction and loyalty is influenced by the customers' income. More precisely, we could hypothesize that the relationship between customer satisfaction and customer loyalty is weaker for high-income customers and stronger for low-income customers. This type of moderator effect would indicate the satisfaction to loyalty relationship changes depending on the level of income. If this income moderator effect is not present, we would assume the strength of the relationship between satisfaction and loyalty is constant.

Continuous moderators are typically measured with multi-item constructs but can, in principle, also be measured using only a single item. When the moderator variable represents some abstract unobservable trait (as opposed to some observable phenomenon, such as income), however, we clearly advise against the use of single items for construct measurement. In short, multi-item scales are much more effective in terms of explaining the target construct's variance (Diamantopoulos, Sarstedt, Fuchs, Kaiser, & Wilczynski, 2012; Sarstedt, Diamantopoulos, Salzberger, & Baumgartner, 2016), which can be particularly problematic in the context of moderation. The reason is that moderation is usually associated with rather limited effect sizes (Aguinis, Beaty, Boik, & Pierce, 2005), so small (but meaningful) effects will be more difficult to identify as significant. Furthermore, when modeling moderating effects, the moderator's measurement model is included twice in the model – in the moderator variable itself and in the interaction term (see the next section). This characteristic amplifies the limitations of single-item measurement(s) in research situations involving moderation.

8.3 Modeling Moderating Effects

To gain an understanding of how moderating effects are modeled, consider the path model shown in ◘ Fig. 8.2. This model illustrates our previous example in which income serves as a moderator variable (M), influencing the relationship between customer satisfaction (Y_1) and customer loyalty (Y_2). The **moderating effect** (p_3) is represented by an arrow pointing at the effect p_1 linking Y_1 and Y_2. Furthermore, when including the moderating effect in a PLS path model, there is also a direct relationship (p_2) from the moderator to the endogenous construct. This additional path is important (and a frequent source of mistakes), as it controls for the direct impact of the moderator on the endogenous construct. If the path p_2 was to be omitted, the effect of M on the relationship between Y_1 and Y_2 (i.e., p_3) would be inflated. As can be seen, moderation is somewhat similar to mediation, in that a third variable (i.e., a mediator or moderator variable) affects the strength of a relationship between two latent variables. The crucial distinction between both concepts is that the moderator variable does not depend on the exogenous construct. In contrast, with mediation, there is a direct effect between the exogenous construct and the mediator construct (Memon et al., 2018).

◘ **Fig. 8.2** Moderation model example. (Source: Hair et al., 2022, Chap. 7; used with permission by Sage)

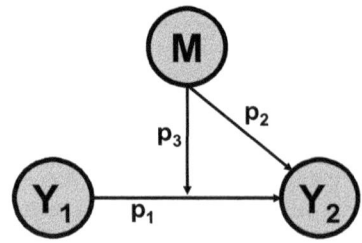

8.4 · Creating the Interaction Term

The path model in ◘ Fig. 8.2, which includes a moderating effect, can also be expressed mathematically using the following formula:

$$Y_2 = (p_1 + p_3 \cdot M) \cdot Y_1 + p_2 \cdot M.$$

As can be seen, the influence of Y_1 on Y_2 not only depends on the strength of the **simple effect** p_1 but also on the product of p_3 and M. To understand how a moderator variable can be integrated in a path model, we need to rewrite the equation as follows:

$$Y_2 = p_1 \cdot Y_1 + p_2 \cdot M + p_3 \cdot (Y_1 \cdot M).$$

This equation shows that including a moderator effect requires the specification of the effect of the exogenous construct (i.e., $p_1 \cdot Y_1$), the effect of the moderator variable (i.e., $p_2 \cdot M$), and the product term $p_3 \cdot (Y_1 \cdot M)$, which is also called the **interaction term**. As a result, the coefficient p_3 expresses how the effect p_1 changes when the moderator variable M is increased or decreased by one standard deviation unit. ◘ Figure 8.3 illustrates the concept of an interaction term. As can be seen, the model includes the interaction term as an additional latent variable covering the product of the exogenous construct Y_1 and the moderator M. Because of this interaction term, researchers often refer to interaction effects when modeling moderator variables.

So far, we have looked at a **two-way interaction** because the moderator interacts with one other variable, the exogenous construct Y_1. However, it is also possible to analyze a **multiple moderator model**. In such a model, the researcher can include a two-way interaction term for each moderator and the moderated relationship into the same model (e.g., when income and age both affect the customer to loyalty relationship in a moderation analysis). When using multiple moderators, it is also possible to model higher levels of interaction (e.g., a three-way interaction term), where the moderating effect (itself) is again moderated. Such a setup is also referred to as **cascaded moderator analysis**. The most common form of a cascaded moderator analysis is a **three-way interaction** (Henseler & Fassott, 2010). For example, we could imagine that the moderating effect of income is not constant but is itself influenced by some other variable, such as age, which would then serve as a second moderator variable in the model.

8.4 Creating the Interaction Term

In the previous section, we introduced the concept of an interaction term to facilitate the inclusion of a moderator variable in a PLS path model. But a fundamental question remains: How should the interaction term be operationalized? Research

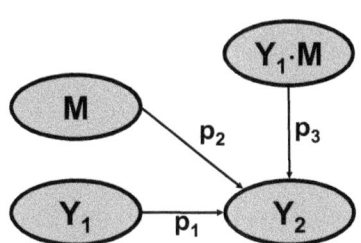

◘ **Fig. 8.3** Interaction term in moderation. (Source: Hair et al., 2022, Chap. 7; used with permission by Sage)

has proposed three primary approaches for creating the interaction term: (1) the product indicator approach, (2) the orthogonalizing approach, and (3) the two-stage approach. Simulation studies have shown that Chin, Marcolin, and Newsted's (2003) **two-stage approach** excels in terms of parameter recovery and statistical power (e.g., Becker, Ringle, & Sarstedt, 2018; Henseler & Chin, 2010). In addition, this approach offers much flexibility, as it is the only approach that is applicable when the exogenous construct (Y_1 in ◘ Fig. 8.3) or the moderator (M in ◘ Fig. 8.3) is specified formatively. We therefore recommend using the two-stage approach in most situations to create the interaction term. In the following, we discuss the two-stage approach in greater detail. See Chap. 7 in Hair et al. (2022) for a discussion of the product indicator approach and the orthogonalizing approach.

The two-stage approach has its roots in its explicit exploitation of PLS-SEM's advantage to estimate latent variable scores (Becker et al., 2018; Rigdon, Ringle, & Sarstedt, 2010). The two stages are as follows:

- Stage 1: the main effect model (i.e., without the interaction term) is estimated to obtain the scores of the latent variables. These are saved for further analysis in Stage 2.
- Stage 2: the latent variable scores of the exogenous construct and moderator variable from Stage 1 are multiplied to create a single item used to measure the interaction term. All other latent variables are represented by means of single items of their latent variable scores from Stage 1.

◘ Figure 8.4 illustrates the two-stage approach for our previous model, where two formative indicators are used in Stage 1 to measure the moderator variable. The main effect model in Stage 1 is run to obtain the latent variable scores for Y_1, Y_2, and M (i.e., $LVS(Y_1)$, $LVS(Y_2)$, and $LVS(M)$). The latent variable scores of Y_1 and M are then multiplied to form the single item used to measure the interaction term $Y_1 \cdot M$ in Stage 2. The latent variables Y_1, Y_2, and M are each measured with a single item of the latent variable scores from Stage 1. It is important to note that the limitations identified when using single items do not apply in this case, since the single item represents the latent variable scores as obtained from a multi-item measurement in Stage 1.

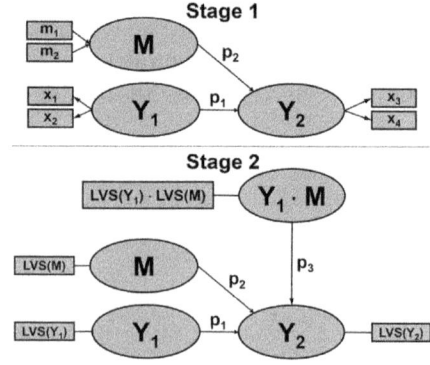

◘ **Fig. 8.4** Two-stage approach. (Source: Hair et al., 2022, Chap. 7; used with permission by Sage)

Becker et al. (2018) examined the impact of different data treatment options on the two-stage approach's performance. The results show parameter recovery works best when standardizing the indicator data and the interaction term rather than working with unstandardized or mean-centered data. Standardization is done by subtracting the variable's mean from each observation and dividing the result by the variable's standard error (Sarstedt & Mooi, 2019; Chap. 5). As indicated previously and in consideration of the above advantages, we recommend that in most situations, researchers apply the two-stage approach with standardized data when conducting moderator analyses.

8.5 Model Evaluation

Measurement and structural model evaluation criteria, as discussed in ▶ Chaps. 4, 5, and 6, also apply to moderator models. For the interaction term, however, there is no requirement to assess its measurement model since it represents an auxiliary measurement that incorporates the interrelationships between the moderator and the exogenous construct in the path model. This characteristic, however, renders any measurement model assessment of the interaction term meaningless. In addition, standard measurement model evaluation standards would not apply since the interaction term is measured with a single item. Therefore, the interaction term does not necessarily have to be assessed in the measurement model evaluation step.

> **Important**
> There is no requirement to assess the measurement model of the interaction term since it represents an auxiliary measurement that does not represent a distinct theoretical entity.

Finally, it is always important to consider the standard criteria for structural model assessment. In the context of moderation, particular attention should be paid to the f^2 effect size of the interaction effect (Hair et al., 2022; Memon et al., 2018). As explained in ▶ Chap. 6, this criterion enables an assessment of the change in the R^2 value when an exogenous construct is omitted from the model. With regard to the interaction effect, the f^2 effect size indicates how much the moderation contributes to the explanation of the endogenous construct. The effect size can be calculated as

$$f^2 = \frac{R^2_{included} - R^2_{excluded}}{1 - R^2_{included}},$$

where $R^2_{included}$ and $R^2_{excluded}$ are the R^2 values of the endogenous construct when the interaction term of the moderator model is included in or excluded from the PLS path model. In this way, one can assess the relevance of the moderating effect. General guidelines for assessing f^2 suggest values of 0.02, 0.15, and 0.35 represent small, medium, and large effect sizes, respectively (Cohen, 1988). However, Aguinis et al. (2005) have shown that the average effect size in tests of moderation is only 0.009. Against this background, Kenny (2018) proposes that 0.005, 0.01, and 0.025, respectively, constitute more realistic standards for small, medium, and large effect sizes of moderation but also points out that even these values are optimistic.

> **Important**
> Standard cutoff values for the f^2 effect size do not apply when interpreting the interaction term's impact. Instead f^2 values of 0.005, 0.01, and 0.025 should be considered as evidence for small, medium, and large effect sizes, respectively.

8.6 Result Interpretation

When interpreting the results of a moderation analysis, the primary focus is the significance of the interaction term. If the interaction term's effect on the endogenous construct is significant, we conclude the moderator M has a significant moderating effect on the relationship between Y_1 and Y_2. The bootstrapping procedure (▶ Chap. 5) facilitates this assessment. If the relationship is statistically significant, the next step is to determine the strength of the moderating effect.

In a model without moderation (i.e., without the moderator variable M) in which there is only an arrow linking Y_1 and Y_2 (see ◘ Fig. 8.3), the effect p_1 is referred to as a direct effect or **main effect**. In the case of the two-stage approach, such a main effect is, however, different from the corresponding relationship in a moderator model shown in ◘ Fig. 8.3. Here, in contrast, p_1 is referred to as a simple effect, expressing the effect of Y_1 on Y_2 that is moderated by M. More specifically, the estimated value of p_1 represents the strength of the relationship between Y_1 and Y_2 when the moderator variable M has a value of zero. If the level of the moderator variable is increased (or decreased) by one standard deviation unit, the simple effect p_1 is expected to change by the size of p_3. For example, if the simple effect p_1 equals 0.30 and the moderating effect p_3 has a value of −0.10, one would expect the relationship between Y_1 and Y_2 to decrease to a value of 0.30 + (−0.10) = 0.20, if (ceteris paribus) the mean value of the moderator variable M increases by one standard deviation unit (Henseler & Fassott, 2010). As a result, a moderator variable can strengthen, weaken, or even reverse a relationship (Gardner, Harris, Li, Kirkman, & Mathieu, 2017).

In many model setups, however, zero is not a number on the scale of M or, as in the case in our example (i.e., it is not a meaningful value for the moderator). If this is the case, the interpretation of the simple effect becomes problematic. This is another reason why we need to standardize the indicators of the moderator as described earlier. The standardization shifts the reference point from an income of zero to the average income and thus facilitates interpretation of the effects.

An important concept to understand is that the nature of the effect between Y_1 and Y_2 (i.e., p_1) differs for models with and without the moderator when using the two-stage approach. If the focus is on testing the significance of the main effect p_1

8.6 · Result Interpretation

between Y_1 and Y_2, the PLS-SEM analysis should be initially executed without the moderator. The evaluation and interpretation of results should follow the procedures outlined in ▶ Chap. 6. The moderator analysis then is executed as a complementary analysis for the specific moderating relationship. This issue is important because the direct effect becomes a simple effect in the moderator model, which differs in its estimated value, meaning, and interpretation. The simple effect represents the relationship between an exogenous and an endogenous construct when the moderator variable's value is equal to its mean value (provided standardization has been applied). Hence, interpreting the simple effect results of a moderator model as if it were a direct effect (e.g., for testing the hypothesis of a significant relationship p_1 between Y_1 and Y_2) may result in misleading and incorrect conclusions (Henseler & Fassott, 2010).

> When testing a hypothesized direct relationship between two constructs, the moderator needs to be excluded from the model.

Beyond understanding these aspects of moderator analysis, the interpretation of moderation results is often quite challenging. For this reason, graphical illustrations of results support their understanding and drawing of conclusions. A common way to illustrate the results of a moderation analysis is by slope plots (Memon et al., 2018).

> **Tip**
>
> Web pages, such as those by Jeremy Dawson (▶ http://www.jeremydawson.co.uk/slopes.htm) or Kristopher Preacher (▶ http://quantpsy.org/interact/mlr2.htm), provide online tools for corresponding computations and simple slope plot extractions.

As an example of a two-way interaction, refer to ◘ Fig. 8.3. Assume the relationship between Y_1 and Y_2 has a value of 0.50, the relationship between M and Y_2 has a value of 0.10, and the interaction term ($Y_1 \cdot M$) has a 0.25 relationship with Y_2. ◘ Figure 8.5 shows a typical slope plot used for such a setting, where the x-axis represents the exogenous construct (Y_1) and the y-axis the endogenous construct (Y_2).

The two lines in ◘ Fig. 8.5 represent the relationship between Y_1 and Y_2 for low and high levels of the moderator construct M. Usually, a low level of M is one standard deviation unit below its average (straight line in ◘ Fig. 8.5), while a high level of M is one standard deviation unit above its average (dotted line in ◘ Fig. 8.5). Because of the positive moderating effect, as expressed in the 0.25 relationship between the interaction term and the endogenous construct, the high moderator line's slope is steeper. That is, the relationship between Y_1 and Y_2 becomes stronger with high(er) levels of M. For low(er) levels of M, the slope is much flatter, as shown in ◘ Fig. 8.5. Hence, with low(er) levels of the moderator construct M, the relationship between Y_1 and Y_2 becomes weaker.

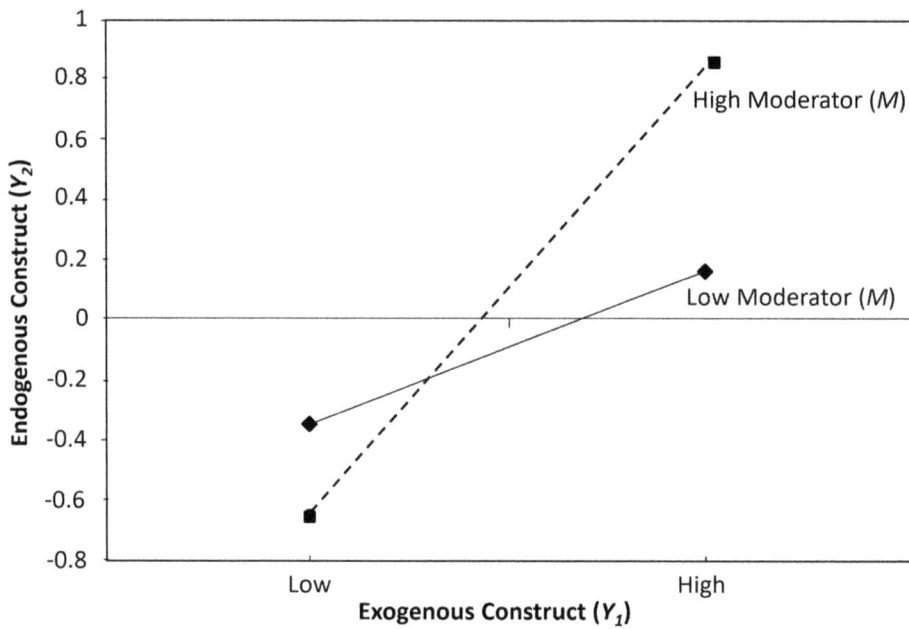

☐ **Fig. 8.5** Slope plot. (Source: Hair et al., 2022, Chap. 7; used with permission by Sage)

8.7 Case Study Illustration: Moderation Analysis

We again turn to the corporate reputation model as discussed in the previous chapters to illustrate the moderation concepts. In the subsequent discussion, we focus on the relationship between customer satisfaction and customer loyalty. Specifically, we introduce perceived switching costs as a moderator variable that can be assumed to negatively influence the relationship between satisfaction and loyalty (Hair et al., 2022; Chap. 7). The higher the perceived switching costs, the weaker the relationship between these two constructs (☐ Fig. 8.6). We use an extended form of Jones, Mothersbaugh, and Beatty's (2000) scale and measure switching costs reflectively using four indicators (*switch_1* to *switch_4*; ☐ Table 8.1), each measured on a 5-point Likert scale (1 = fully disagree, 5 = fully agree).

First, we need to update the measurement and structural models to include the new *SC* construct and its indicators *switch_1*, *switch_2*, *switch_3*, and *switch_4*. We thus need to add a new element to the list of constructs in the measurement model using the `composite()` function. We name the construct "SC" and specify the items using the `multi_items()` function and arguments "switch_" and "1:4": `composite("SC", multi_items("switch_", 1:4))`.

Creating interaction terms by hand can be time-consuming and error prone. SEMinR provides functions for simply creating interactions between constructs. In doing so, SEMinR adjusts the standard errors of the construct scores in the generation of the interaction term (Henseler & Chin, 2010). Interaction

8.7 · Case Study Illustration: Moderation Analysis

Table 8.1 Switching costs indicators

Construct name	Construct definition
switch_1	It takes me a great deal of time to switch to another company
switch_2	It costs me too much to switch to another company
switch_3	It takes a lot of effort to get used to a new company with its specific "rules" and practices
switch_4	In general, it would be a hassle switching to another company

Source: authors' own table; Jones et al. (2000)

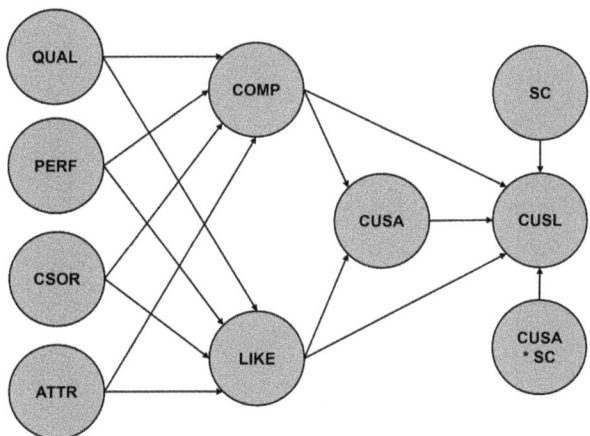

Fig. 8.6 Corporate reputation model with the added moderator switching costs (*SC*) and the interaction term (*CUSA * SC*). (Source: authors' own figure)

terms are described in the measurement model function `constructs()` using the following methods:

- `two_stage` implements the two-stage approach as recommended in our previous discussions. It specifies the interaction term as the product of the scores of the exogenous construct and the moderator variable.
- `product_indicator` generates the interaction term by multiplying each indicator of the exogenous construct with each indicator of the moderator variable.
- `orthogonal` is an extension of the product indicator approach, which generates an interaction term whose indicators do not share any variance with the indicators of the exogenous construct and the moderator. The orthogonalizing approach is typically used to handle multicollinearity in the structural model.

> The SEMinR syntax uses an asterisk ("*") as a naming convention for the interaction construct. Thus, when creating an interaction from the constructs *CUSA* and *SC*, the resulting interaction is called "CUSA*SC" in the structural model. We therefore recommend refraining from using an asterisk in the naming of noninteraction constructs.

In addition to including the *SC* construct, we need to specify the interaction term composed of the independent variable *CUSA* and the moderator *SC* using the `interaction_term()` function. The `interaction_term()` function takes the following arguments: *iv* specifies the independent variable (i.e., exogenous construct); *moderator* specifies the moderating variable; and *method* specifies the interaction calculation method (with values `product_indicator`, `orthogonal`, or `two_stage`). We now need to choose the two-stage approach to create the interaction term. We specify the interaction term as follows: **interaction_term(***iv* = "CUSA", *moderator* = "SC", *method* = two_stage). SEMinR automatically generates a name for the new interaction term by combining the exogenous construct's and the moderator construct's name separated by an asterisk ("*"), representing multiplication. Thus, the newly created interaction term will be called *CUSA*SC*. Note that SEMinR always standardizes the data when calculating the interaction term.

```
# Load the SEMinR library
library(seminr)

# Load the data
corp_rep_data <- corp_rep_data

# Create the measurement model
corp_rep_mm_mod <- constructs(
  composite("QUAL", multi_items("qual_", 1:8), weights = mode_B),
  composite("PERF", multi_items("perf_", 1:5), weights = mode_B),
  composite("CSOR", multi_items("csor_", 1:5), weights = mode_B),
  composite("ATTR", multi_items("attr_", 1:3), weights = mode_B),
  composite("COMP", multi_items("comp_", 1:3)),
  composite("LIKE", multi_items("like_", 1:3)),
  composite("CUSA", single_item("cusa")),
  composite("SC", multi_items("switch_", 1:4)),
  composite("CUSL", multi_items("cusl_", 1:3)),
  interaction_term(iv = "CUSA", moderator = "SC", method = two_
stage))
```

When the measurement model has been updated, we need to add the new structural paths. There are two new paths in the model: from *SC* to *CUSL* and from the interaction term *CUSA*SC* to *CUSL*. We therefore append the list with the two new construct names: `paths(from = c("CUSA", "SC", "CUSA*SC"), to = c("CUSL"))`. With the measurement and structural models now updated, the model can be estimated, bootstrapped, and summarized.

8.7 · Case Study Illustration: Moderation Analysis

```
# Create the structural model
corp_rep_sm_mod <- relationships(
  paths(from = c("QUAL", "PERF", "CSOR", "ATTR"), to = c("COMP",
"LIKE")),
  paths(from = c("COMP", "LIKE"), to = c("CUSA", "CUSL")),
  paths(from = c("CUSA", "SC", "CUSA*SC"), to = c("CUSL"))
)


# Estimate the new model with moderator
corp_rep_pls_model_mod <- estimate_pls(
  data = corp_rep_data,
  measurement_model = corp_rep_mm_mod,
  structural_model = corp_rep_sm_mod,
  missing = mean_replacement,
  missing_value = "-99"
)

# Extract the summary
sum_corp_rep_mod <- summary(corp_rep_pls_model_mod)


# Bootstrap the model
boot_corp_rep_mod <- bootstrap_model(
  seminr_model = corp_rep_pls_model_mod,
  nboot = 1000)


# Summarize the results of the bootstrap
sum_boot_corp_rep_mod <- summary(boot_corp_rep_mod, alpha = 0.05)
```

Following the procedures outlined in ▶ Chaps. 4 and 5, we find that all measurement models exhibit sufficient levels of reliability and validity. This also holds for the measures of the newly added SC construct, which exhibit high degrees of internal consistency reliability and convergent validity. In terms of discriminant validity, *SC* exhibits increased HTMT values only with *COMP* (0.850) and *LIKE* (0.802), but these values are significantly lower than 0.90 (Hair et al., 2022; Chap. 7).

Our next concern is the size of the moderating effect. In order to evaluate the moderating effect, we need to inspect the **bootstrapped_paths** element within the **sum_boot_corp_rep_mod** object, **sum_boot_corp_rep_mod$bootstrapped_paths**.

```
# Inspect the bootstrapped structural paths
sum_boot_corp_rep_mod$bootstrapped_paths
```

```
Console   Terminal ×   Jobs ×
~/seminr/
> # Inspect the bootstrapped structural paths
> sum_boot_corp_rep_mod$bootstrapped_paths
                Original Est. Bootstrap Mean Bootstrap SD T Stat. 2.5% CI 97.5% CI
QUAL  ->  COMP        0.430          0.426        0.065   6.654    0.302    0.562
QUAL  ->  LIKE        0.380          0.382        0.064   5.936    0.257    0.503
PERF  ->  COMP        0.295          0.303        0.063   4.656    0.184    0.427
PERF  ->  LIKE        0.117          0.125        0.068   1.713   -0.006    0.259
CSOR  ->  COMP        0.059          0.062        0.055   1.075   -0.046    0.170
CSOR  ->  LIKE        0.178          0.178        0.056   3.203    0.063    0.288
ATTR  ->  COMP        0.086          0.086        0.055   1.557   -0.015    0.200
ATTR  ->  LIKE        0.167          0.164        0.065   2.574    0.035    0.286
COMP  ->  CUSA        0.146          0.147        0.068   2.155    0.012    0.285
COMP  ->  CUSL       -0.020         -0.020        0.059  -0.346   -0.134    0.103
LIKE  ->  CUSA        0.436          0.437        0.058   7.484    0.322    0.551
LIKE  ->  CUSL        0.319          0.318        0.057   5.602    0.198    0.425
CUSA  ->  CUSL        0.467          0.464        0.047   9.962    0.368    0.554
SC    ->  CUSL        0.071          0.075        0.057   1.236   -0.038    0.190
CUSA*SC -> CUSL      -0.071         -0.073        0.031  -2.277   -0.134   -0.013
>
```

◘ **Fig. 8.7** The bootstrapped paths for moderated model. (Source: author's screenshot from R)

As can be seen in ◘ Fig. 8.7, the interaction term ($CUSA*SC$) has a negative effect on $CUSL$ of **−0.071**, whereas the simple effect of $CUSA$ on $CUSL$ is **0.467**. Jointly, these results suggest that the relationship between $CUSA$ and $CUSL$ is **0.467** for an average level of switching costs. For higher levels of switching costs (i.e., for every standard deviation unit increase of SC), the relationship between $CUSA$ and $CUSL$ decreases by the size of the interaction term (i.e., 0.467 − 0.071 = 0.396). On the contrary, for lower levels of switching costs (i.e., for every standard deviation unit decrease of SC), the relationship between $CUSA$ and $CUSL$ increases by the size of the interaction term (i.e., 0.467 − (−0.071) = 0.538). To better comprehend the results of the moderator analysis, we can use the `slope_analysis()` function to visualize the two-way interaction effect (see ◘ Fig. 8.8). This function takes the arguments shown in ◘ Table 8.2.

We apply the `slope_analysis()` function to the `corp_rep_pls_model_mod`, with $CUSL$ as the endogenous construct, SC as the moderator construct, and $CUSA$ as the exogenous construct. Finally, we assign the legend to the bottom-right corner of the plot.

```
# Simple slope analysis plot
slope_analysis(
  moderated_model = corp_rep_pls_model_mod,
  dv = "CUSL",
  moderator = "SC",
  iv = "CUSA",
  leg_place = "bottomright")
```

The three lines shown in ◘ Fig. 8.8 represent the relationship between $CUSA$ (x-axis) and $CUSL$ (y-axis). The middle line represents the relationship for an aver-

8.7 · Case Study Illustration: Moderation Analysis

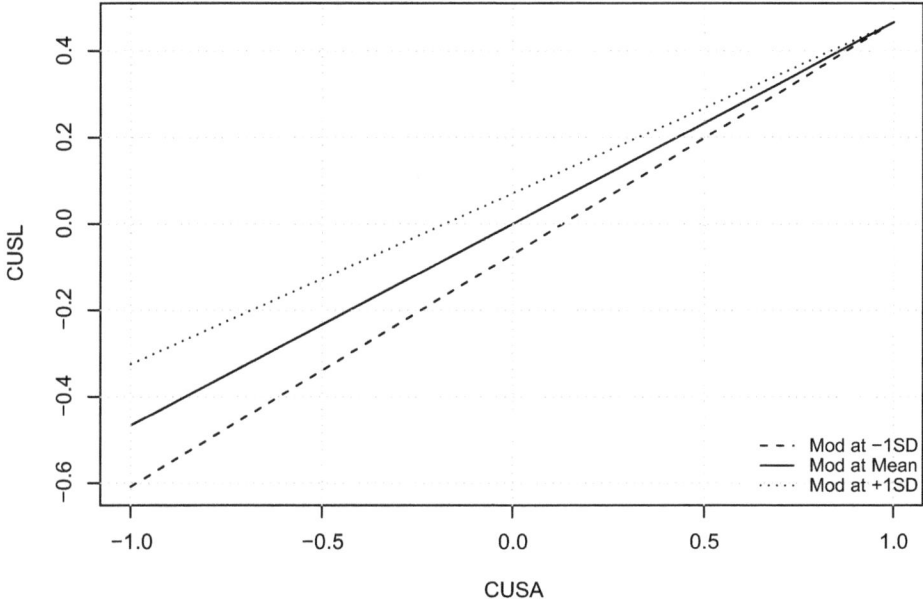

◘ **Fig. 8.8** Simple slope analysis of the two-way interaction effect CUSA*SC on CUSL. (Source: author's screenshot from RStudio)

◘ **Table 8.2** Arguments for the `slope_analysis()` function

Argument	Value
`moderated_model`	The SEMinR model containing the moderated relationship
`dv`	The dependent variable involved in the moderation
`moderator`	The moderator variable involved in the moderation
`iv`	The independent variable involved in the moderation
`leg_place`	Where to place the legend (default is `"bottomright"`, an alternative is `"topleft"`, etc.)

Source: authors' own table

age level of switching costs. The other two lines represent the relationship between *CUSA* and *CUSL* for higher (i.e., mean value of *SC* plus one standard deviation unit) and lower (i.e., mean value of *SC* minus one standard deviation unit) levels of the moderator variable *SC*. As can be seen, the relationship between *CUSA* and *CUSL* is positive for all three lines as indicated by their positive slope. Hence, higher levels of customer satisfaction go hand in hand with higher levels of customer loyalty. Due to the negative moderating effect, at high levels of the moderator *SC*, the effect of *CUSA* on *CUSL* is weaker, while at lower levels of moderator *SC*, the effect of *CUSA* on *CUSL* is stronger.

Next, we assess whether the interaction term is significant using the output shown in ◘ Fig. 8.7. The analysis yields a *t*-value of −2.277 for the path linking the interaction term and *CUSL*. Similarly, the 95% bootstrap confidence interval of the interaction term's effect is [−0.134, −0.013]. As the confidence interval does not include zero, we conclude that the effect is significant. Again, note that these results will slightly differ from yours due to the random nature of the bootstrapping process.

Overall, these results provide clear support that *SC* exerts a significant and negative moderating effect on the relationship between *CUSA* and *CUSL*. The higher the switching costs, the weaker the relationship between customer satisfaction and customer loyalty.

Summary

Moderation occurs when one construct affects the strength or even the direction of a relationship between two other constructs. As such, moderation accounts for heterogeneity in the data. After theoretically establishing a moderation model, its hypothesized relationships, and the interaction term (generated using the two-stage approach), the model evaluation follows. The moderator construct must be assessed for reliability and validity following the standard evaluation procedures for reflective and formative measurement models. However, this does not hold for the interaction term, which relies on an auxiliary measurement model to represent the interplay between exogenous construct and moderator and their joint effect on the endogenous construct. The result assessment further considers the significance and effect size of the interaction effect. In the simplest form, the analysis considers only one moderator construct, but the model also can involve multiple moderator constructs that can be analyzed simultaneously.

❓ Exercise

We continue analyzing the influencer model as introduced in the exercise section of ▶ Chap. 3. Extending the original model (▶ Fig. 3.10), we hypothesize that perceived influencer competence (*PIC*) moderates the relationship between perceived quality (*PQ*) and purchase intention (*PI*). *PIC* is measured with reflective items covering traits of the influencer – see ▶ Table 3.10 for an overview of the indicators. ◘ Fig. 8.9 visualizes the model with the *PIC* and the interaction term (*PQ*PIC*) included.

1. Do the measurement models and structural model meet all quality standards?
2. Describe the moderating effect in terms of direction and significance. Visualize the effects using a simple slope analysis.
3. Quantify the moderating effect's size using the f^2 effect size.
4. What conclusions can you draw from the moderator analysis?

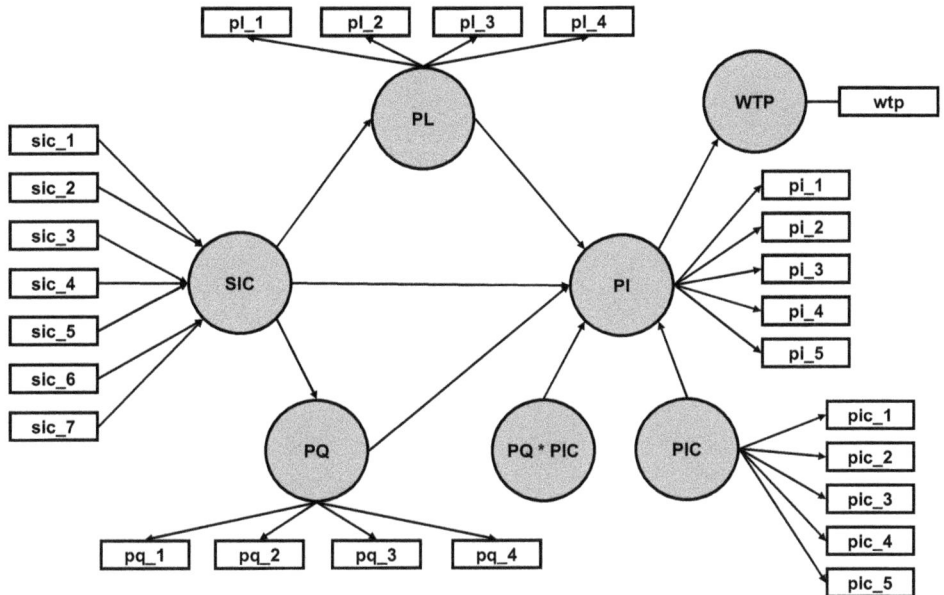

■ Fig. 8.9 The influencer model with additional hypothesized moderation effect of PIC on PQ (source: authors' own figure)

References

Aguinis, H., Beaty, J. C., Boik, R. J., & Pierce, C. A. (2005). Effect size and power in assessing moderating effects of categorical variables using multiple regression: A 30-year review. *Journal of Applied Psychology, 90*(1), 94–107.

Becker, J.-M., Ringle, C. M., & Sarstedt, M. (2018). Estimating moderating effects in PLS-SEM and PLSc-SEM: Interaction term generation*data treatment. *Journal of Applied Structural Equation Modeling, 2*(2), 1–21.

Chin, W. W., Marcolin, B. L., & Newsted, P. R. (2003). A partial least squares latent variable modeling approach for measuring interaction effects: Results from a Monte Carlo simulation study and an electronic-mail emotion/adoption study. *Information Systems Research, 14*(2), 189–217.

Cohen, J. (1988). *Statistical power analysis for the behavioral sciences*. Mahwah, NJ: Lawrence Erlbaum.

Diamantopoulos, A., Sarstedt, M., Fuchs, C., Kaiser, S., & Wilczynski, P. (2012). Guidelines for choosing between multi-item and single-item scales for construct measurement: A predictive validity perspective. *Journal of the Academy of Marketing Science, 40*(3), 434–449.

Gardner, R. G., Harris, T. B., Li, N., Kirkman, B. L., & Mathieu, J. E. (2017). Understanding "it depends" in organizational research: A theory-based taxonomy, review, and future research agenda concerning interactive and quadratic relationships. *Organizational Research Methods, 20*(4), 610–638.

Hair, J. F., Hult, G. T. M., Ringle, C. M., & Sarstedt, M. (2022). *A primer on partial least squares structural equation modeling (PLS-SEM)* (3rd ed.). Thousand Oaks, CA: Sage.

Hair, J. F., Sarstedt, M., Ringle, C. M., & Gudergan, S. P. (2018). *Advanced issues in partial least squares structural equation modeling (PLS-SEM)*. Thousand Oaks, CA: Sage.

Henseler, J., & Chin, W. W. (2010). A comparison of approaches for the analysis of interaction effects between latent variables using partial least squares path modeling. *Structural Equation Modeling, 17*(1), 82–109.

Henseler, J., & Fassott, G. (2010). Testing moderating effects in PLS path models: An illustration of available procedures. In V. Esposito Vinzi, W. W. Chin, J. Henseler, & H. Wang (Eds.), *Handbook of partial least squares: Concepts, methods and applications in marketing and related fields*. (Springer Handbooks of Computational Statistics Series, (Vol. II, pp. 713–735). Berlin: Springer.

Homburg, C., & Giering, A. (2001). Personal characteristics as moderators of the relationship between customer satisfaction and loyalty—An empirical analysis. *Psychology and Marketing, 18*(1), 43–66.

Jones, M. A., Mothersbaugh, D. L., & Beatty, S. E. (2000). Switching barriers and repurchase intentions in services. *Journal of Retailing, 76*(2), 259–274.

Kenny, D. A. (2018). Moderation. Retrieved from http://davidakenny.net/cm/moderation.htm

Klesel, M., Schuberth, F., Niehaves, B., & Henseler, J. (2021). Multigroup analysis in information systems research using PLS-PM: A systematic investigation of approaches. *The DATA BASE for Advances in Information Systems*, forthcoming.

Memon, M. A., Cheah, J.-H., Ramayah, T., Ting, H., Chuah, F., & Cham, T. H. (2018). Moderation analysis: Issues and guidelines. *Journal of Applied Structural Equation Modeling, 3*(1), i–ix.

Rigdon, E. E., Ringle, C. M., & Sarstedt, M. (2010). Structural modeling of heterogeneous data with partial least squares. In N. K. Malhotra (Ed.), *Review of Marketing Research* (pp. 255–296). Armonk, NY: Sharpe.

Sarstedt, M., Diamantopoulos, A., Salzberger, T., & Baumgartner, P. (2016). Selecting single items to measure doubly-concrete constructs: A cautionary tale. *Journal of Business Research, 69*(8), 3159–3167.

Sarstedt, M., & Mooi, E. A. (2019). *A concise guide to market research: The process, data, and methods using IBM SPSS statistics* (3rd ed.). Berlin: Springer.

Suggested Reading

Aguinis, H., Edwards, J. R., & Bradley, K. J. (2016). Improving our understanding of moderation and mediation in strategic management research. *Organizational Research Methods, 20*(4), 665–685.

Dawson, J. F. (2014). Moderation in management research: What, why, when, and how. *Journal of Business and Psychology, 29*(1), 1–19.

Fassott, G., Henseler, J., & Coelho, P. S. (2016). Testing moderating effects in PLS path models with composite variables. *Industrial Management & Data Systems, 116*(9), 1887–1900.

Hair, J. F., Hult, G. T. M., Ringle, C. M., & Sarstedt, M. (2022). *A primer on partial least squares structural equation modeling (PLS-SEM)* (3rd ed.). Thousand Oaks, CA: Sage.

Memon, M. A., Cheah, J.-H., Ramayah, T., Ting, H., Chuah, F., & Cham, T. H. (2018). Moderation analysis: Issues and guidelines. *Journal of Applied Structural Equation Modeling, 3*(1), i–ix.

Open Access This chapter is licensed under the terms of the Creative Commons Attribution 4.0 International License (http://creativecommons.org/licenses/by/4.0/), which permits use, sharing, adaptation, distribution and reproduction in any medium or format, as long as you give appropriate credit to the original author(s) and the source, provide a link to the Creative Commons license and indicate if changes were made.

The images or other third party material in this chapter are included in the chapter's Creative Commons license, unless indicated otherwise in a credit line to the material. If material is not included in the chapter's Creative Commons license and your intended use is not permitted by statutory regulation or exceeds the permitted use, you will need to obtain permission directly from the copyright holder.

Supplementary Information

Appendix A: The PLS-SEM Algorithm – 174

Appendix B: Assessing the Reflectively Measured Constructs in the Corporate Reputation Model – 177

Glossary – 182

Index – 195

© The Editor(s) (if applicable) and The Author(s) 2021
J. F. Hair Jr. et al., *Partial Least Squares Structural Equation Modeling (PLS-SEM) Using R*, Classroom Companion: Business, https://doi.org/10.1007/978-3-030-80519-7

Appendix A: The PLS-SEM Algorithm

In the following, we briefly describe the iterative algorithm employed to generate model parameter estimates (i.e., outer weights, outer loadings, and path coefficients) in PLS-SEM. In ◘ Table A.1, we describe the algorithm in pseudo-code.

The PLS-SEM algorithm comprises three stages: the initialization stage, the estimation stage, and the finalization stage. In the *initialization stage*, the data are prepared for model estimation, and the indicator weights are set to preliminary values. Specifically, the data are z-standardized (i.e., the mean is set to 0 and the standard deviation is set to 1), and each indicator weight is set to a value of 1.

The *estimation stage* comprises the iterative process which is at the heart of PLS-SEM. This is an accordion-like, back-and-forth process where the outer models (i.e., the measurement models) and the inner model (i.e., the structural model) are used to estimate each other. This process is repeated until model parameters stabilize and stop changing beyond a certain threshold.

Looking deeper into each iteration, we can recognize five distinct steps. First, construct scores (Y_i) are estimated as the weighted linear combination of the standardized indicator scores (x_{iy}) using the measurement model weights (w_{ij}). Note that in the first iteration, these weights were initialized to 1 and so construct scores are thus initially just the sum of their items.

◘ **Table A.1** Pseudo-code for PLS-SEM algorithm (source: authors' own illustration)

1 *Initialization stage:*
  1.1 Fully standardize all indicator scores (x_{ij}) across the *n* records of the given dataset
  1.2 Initialize all weights $w_{ij} = 1$
2 *Iterative estimation stage:*
  2.1 Estimate construct scores $Y_i = \sum w_{ij} * x_{ij}$
  2.2 Estimate inner structural model weights according to inner weighting scheme:
    2.2.1 Centroid: +1 or -1 for the relationship between two constructs depending on the sign of the correlation
    2.2.2 Factorial: correlation for the relationship between two constructs
    2.2.3 Path weighting: coefficients of partial regression models for the relationship between two constructs
  2.3 Re-estimate the construct scores using structural model weights
  2.4 Re-estimate the measurement model weights according to outer weighting scheme:
    2.4.1 Mode A: standardized correlations for the relationships between the construct and each of its indicators
    2.4.2 Mode B: coefficients of partial regression models for the relationship between the construct and each of its indicators
  2.5 Check convergence (the sum of measurement model weight changes is smaller than stop criterion)
3 *Finalization stage:*
  3.1 Estimate final construct scores $Y_i = \sum w_{ij} * x_{ij}$
  3.2 Estimate inner structural model path coefficients using partial regression
  3.3 Estimate measurement model loadings as simple correlations between the construct and each of its indicators

Appendix A: The PLS-SEM Algorithm

Second, the construct scores are then used to estimate the inner model weights. This estimation process depends on the researcher's choice of structural model weighting method: factor, or path weighting. The factor weighting scheme uses the (bivariate) correlation between two constructs as their path coefficient. The path weighting scheme uses the coefficients of a regression model, resulting from regressions where each endogenous construct is regressed on all its direct antecedents. Note that the methodological literature on PLS-SEM also documents centroid as a third weighting scheme. However, as the centroid weighting scheme does not offer any advantages over factor and path weighting, it has not been implemented in SEMinR.

Third, regardless of the choice of structural model weighting scheme, the relationships between constructs are then used to re-estimate the construct scores. To achieve this aim, the exogenous construct scores are multiplied by the structural model weights relating them to the endogenous construct scores to estimate a new construct score for each endogenous construct. The endogenous construct scores are simultaneously multiplied by the weights relating them to their antecedent constructs to estimate a new construct score for each exogenous construct.

Fourth, using these new construct scores, the measurement weights are estimated depending on the measurement model weighting scheme for each construct: mode A or mode B. Mode A uses correlation weights between the construct and its indicators, such that the outer weights (i.e., indicator weights) correspond to the standardized correlations between the construct and each of its indicators. In contrast, mode B uses regression weights, such that the construct is regressed on its indicators in a multiple linear regression. Hence, the outer weights (i.e., indicator weights) in mode B are the beta coefficients of a multiple regression model. The decision whether to use mode A or mode B is strongly tied to the measurement model specification. To mimic reflective measurement models, researchers typically use mode A. In contrast, to mimic formative measurement models, researchers typically use mode B. However, this default setting is not optimal under all conditions.

The fifth and final step in the estimation stage is to check whether the model has converged or whether another iteration is required. The newly estimated outer weights are compared to those at the beginning of iteration. If the summed difference between the two sets of weights is greater than a given threshold (typically 10^{-7}), then the iteration continues with the outer weights. Thus, the iterations repeat until the weights converge.

In the *finalization stage*, the final model parameters and construct scores to be reported are estimated. The final outer weights from the estimation stage are used to generate construct scores as weighted linear combinations of standardized indicator data. With the final construct scores at hand, the structural model relationships (path coefficients) are then estimated by means of least squares regressions of exogenous constructs on endogenous constructs. Similarly, all reliability and validity (▶ Chaps. 4 and 5) as well as structural model parameters (e.g., the endogenous constructs' R^2 values; ▶ Chap. 6) are estimated.

◨ Table A.1 shows a more formal description of the entire algorithm.

Further Readings
- Chin, W. W. (1998). The partial least squares approach to structural equation modeling. In G. A. Marcoulides (Ed.), *Modern methods for business research* (pp. 295–358). Mahwah, NJ: Erlbaum.
- Hair, J. F., Hult, G. T. M., Ringle, C. M., & Sarstedt, M. (2022). *A primer on partial least squares structural equation modeling (PLS-SEM)* (3rd edition) Thousand Oaks: Sage.
- Lohmöller, J.-B. (1989). *Latent variable path modeling with partial least squares.* Heidelberg: Physica.
- Sarstedt, M., Ringle, C. M., & Hair, J. F. (2021). Partial least squares structural equation modeling. In: C. Homburg, M. Klarmann, and A. Vomberg (Eds.), *Handbook of Market Research*. Cham: Springer.
- Schneeweiß, H. (1991). Models with latent variables: LISREL versus PLS. *Statistica Neerlandica, 45*(2), 145–157.
- Shmueli, G., Ray, S., Velasquez Estrada, J. M., & Chatla, S. B. (2016). The elephant in the room: evaluating the predictive performance of PLS models. *Journal of Business Research, 69*(10), 4552–4564.
- Tenenhaus, M., Esposito Vinzi, V., Chatelin, Y.-M., & Lauro, C. (2005). PLS path modeling. *Computational Statistics & Data Analysis, 48*(1), 159–205.
- Wold, H. (1982). Soft modeling: The basic design and some extensions. In K. G. Jöreskog & H. Wold (Eds.), *Systems under indirect observations, part II* (pp. 1–54). Amsterdam: North-Holland.

Appendix B: Assessing the Reflectively Measured Constructs in the Corporate Reputation Model

An important characteristic of PLS-SEM is that the model estimates will change when any of the model relationships or variables are changed. We thus need to reassess the reflective measurement models to ensure that this portion of the model remains valid and reliable before we continue to evaluate the four new exogenous formative constructs in ▶ Chap. 5. We follow the reflective measurement model assessment procedure in ◘ Fig. 4.1 (for a refresher on this topic, return to ▶ Chap. 4). The following code is used to evaluate the reflectively measured constructs:

```
# Inspect the indicator loadings
summary_corp_rep_ext$loadings

# Inspect the indicator reliability
summary_corp_rep_ext$loadings^2

# Inspect the internal consistency and reliability
summary_corp_rep_ext$reliability

# Table of the FL criteria
summary_corp_rep_ext$validity$fl_criteria

# HTMT criterion
summary_corp_rep_ext$validity$htmt

# Extract the bootstrapped HTMT
sum_boot_corp_rep_ext$bootstrapped_HTMT
```

We first evaluate the indicator loadings and indicator reliability (**summary_corp_rep_ext$loadings**, **summary_corp_rep_ext$loadings^2**). Note that the outputs contain the estimates for loadings, reliability, Fornell–Larcker criterion (i.e., FL in SEMinR), and HTMT for both reflective and formative constructs – only the reflectively measured constructs need to be evaluated. All indicator loadings of the reflective constructs *COMP*, *CUSL*, and *LIKE* have values of 0.821 and higher (◘ Fig. B.1), which are well above the threshold value of **0.708**. The indicators *comp_1* and *comp_2* have the lowest indicator reliability with a value of **0.679** (0.824^2) and **0.673** (0.821^2) demonstrating that the indicators of the reflectively measured constructs exhibit sufficient reliability (◘ Fig. B.2).

• **Fig. B.1** Indicator loadings (source: author's screenshot from RStudio)

• Figure B.3 shows the internal consistency reliability values of the reflective constructs. With rho_A values of **0.786** (*COMP*), **0.839** (*CUSL*), and **0.836** (*LIKE*), all three reflective constructs have high levels of internal consistency reliability.
• Figure B.3 shows that the AVE values of *COMP* (**0.688**), *CUSL* (**0.748**), and *LIKE* (**0.747**) are well above the required minimum level of 0.50. We conclude that the measures of the three reflective constructs have high levels of convergent validity.
• Figure B.4 documents the results of the Fornell–Larcker criterion assessment with the square root of the reflective constructs' AVE on the diagonal and the correlations between the constructs in the off-diagonal position. Overall, the square roots of the AVEs for the reflective constructs *COMP* (**0.829**), *CUSL* (**0.865**), and

Appendix B: Assessing the Reflectively Measured Constructs

```
> # Inspect the indicator reliability
> summary_corp_rep_ext$loadings^2
        QUAL  PERF  CSOR  ATTR  COMP  LIKE  CUSA  CUSL
qual_1  0.548 0.000 0.000 0.000 0.000 0.000 0.000 0.000
qual_2  0.325 0.000 0.000 0.000 0.000 0.000 0.000 0.000
qual_3  0.561 0.000 0.000 0.000 0.000 0.000 0.000 0.000
qual_4  0.441 0.000 0.000 0.000 0.000 0.000 0.000 0.000
qual_5  0.619 0.000 0.000 0.000 0.000 0.000 0.000 0.000
qual_6  0.732 0.000 0.000 0.000 0.000 0.000 0.000 0.000
qual_7  0.521 0.000 0.000 0.000 0.000 0.000 0.000 0.000
qual_8  0.393 0.000 0.000 0.000 0.000 0.000 0.000 0.000
perf_1  0.000 0.716 0.000 0.000 0.000 0.000 0.000 0.000
perf_2  0.000 0.476 0.000 0.000 0.000 0.000 0.000 0.000
perf_3  0.000 0.328 0.000 0.000 0.000 0.000 0.000 0.000
perf_4  0.000 0.514 0.000 0.000 0.000 0.000 0.000 0.000
perf_5  0.000 0.407 0.000 0.000 0.000 0.000 0.000 0.000
csor_1  0.000 0.000 0.595 0.000 0.000 0.000 0.000 0.000
csor_2  0.000 0.000 0.325 0.000 0.000 0.000 0.000 0.000
csor_3  0.000 0.000 0.703 0.000 0.000 0.000 0.000 0.000
csor_4  0.000 0.000 0.380 0.000 0.000 0.000 0.000 0.000
csor_5  0.000 0.000 0.719 0.000 0.000 0.000 0.000 0.000
attr_1  0.000 0.000 0.000 0.569 0.000 0.000 0.000 0.000
attr_2  0.000 0.000 0.000 0.256 0.000 0.000 0.000 0.000
attr_3  0.000 0.000 0.000 0.794 0.000 0.000 0.000 0.000
comp_1  0.000 0.000 0.000 0.000 0.679 0.000 0.000 0.000
comp_2  0.000 0.000 0.000 0.000 0.673 0.000 0.000 0.000
comp_3  0.000 0.000 0.000 0.000 0.712 0.000 0.000 0.000
like_1  0.000 0.000 0.000 0.000 0.000 0.774 0.000 0.000
like_2  0.000 0.000 0.000 0.000 0.000 0.755 0.000 0.000
like_3  0.000 0.000 0.000 0.000 0.000 0.713 0.000 0.000
cusa    0.000 0.000 0.000 0.000 0.000 0.000 1.000 0.000
cusl_1  0.000 0.000 0.000 0.000 0.000 0.000 0.000 0.694
cusl_2  0.000 0.000 0.000 0.000 0.000 0.000 0.000 0.841
cusl_3  0.000 0.000 0.000 0.000 0.000 0.000 0.000 0.710
>
```

Fig. B.2 Indicator reliability (source: author's screenshot from RStudio)

```
> # Inspect the internal consistency and reliability
> summary_corp_rep_ext$reliability
     alpha rhoC  AVE   rhoA
QUAL 0.878 0.894 0.518 1.000
PERF 0.747 0.824 0.488 1.000
CSOR 0.816 0.854 0.545 1.000
ATTR 0.600 0.770 0.540 1.000
COMP 0.776 0.869 0.688 0.786
LIKE 0.831 0.899 0.747 0.836
CUSA 1.000 1.000 1.000 1.000
CUSL 0.831 0.899 0.748 0.839

Alpha, rhoC, and rhoA should exceed 0.7 while AVE should exceed 0.5
>
```

Fig. B.3 Indicator consistency reliability (source: author's screenshot from RStudio)

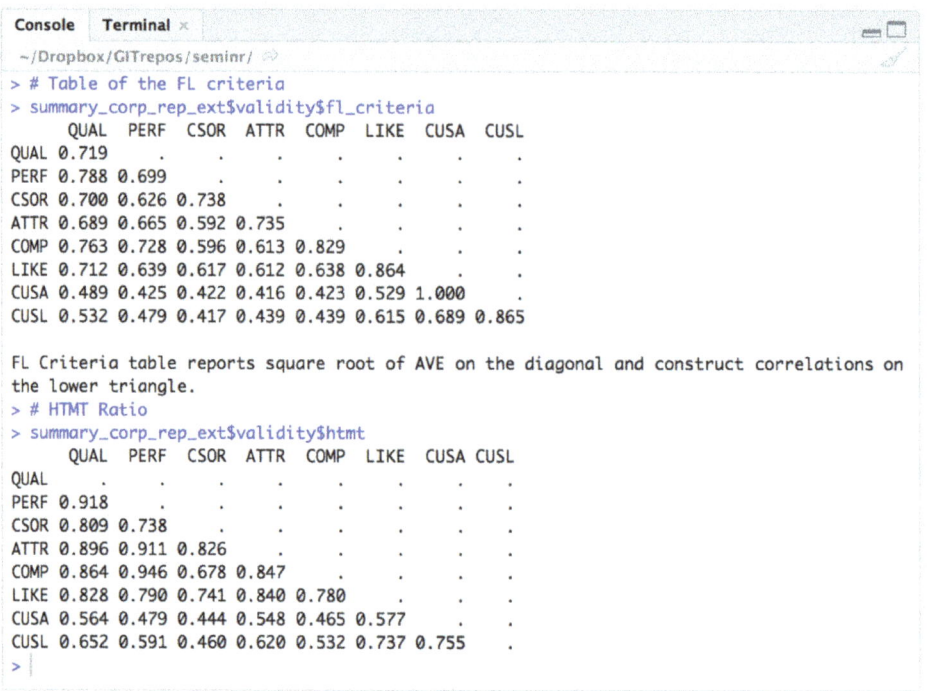

Fig. B.4 Fornell–Larcker criterion and HTMT (source: author's screenshot from RStudio)

LIKE (**0.864**) are all higher than the correlations of these constructs with other latent variables in the PLS path model. ◘ Figure B.4 also shows the HTMT values for all pairs of constructs in a matrix format. As can be seen, all HTMT values for the reflective constructs are lower than the more conservative threshold value of 0.85.

The output in ◘ Fig. B.5 displays the results of bootstrapping the HTMT metric. We consider the comparisons between the reflectively measured constructs *COMP*, *CUSA*, *CUSL*, and *LIKE* – that is, the last six rows of the table. None of the upper bounds of the one-sided 95 % bootstrap confidence intervals are higher than the threshold value of 0.90 (see ► Chap. 4). To summarize, the bootstrap confidence interval results of the HTMT criterion clearly demonstrate the discriminant validity of the constructs.

We conclude that the reflectively measured constructs in the PLS-SEM model meet the criteria for reliability and validity and therefore should be included in the path model.

Appendix B: Assessing the Reflectively Measured Constructs

```
Console    Terminal    Jobs
~/Dropbox/GITrepos/seminr/
> # Extract the bootstrapped HTMT
> sum_boot_corp_rep_ext$bootstrapped_HTMT
              Original Est. Bootstrap Mean Bootstrap SD T Stat. 5% CI 95% CI
QUAL  ->  PERF     0.918         0.922          0.034    27.000  0.866  0.978
QUAL  ->  CSOR     0.809         0.811          0.029    28.079  0.761  0.857
QUAL  ->  ATTR     0.896         0.899          0.051    17.536  0.813  0.983
QUAL  ->  COMP     0.864         0.865          0.027    31.561  0.820  0.910
QUAL  ->  LIKE     0.828         0.829          0.029    28.329  0.781  0.877
QUAL  ->  CUSA     0.564         0.562          0.043    13.253  0.489  0.631
QUAL  ->  CUSL     0.652         0.651          0.047    13.825  0.566  0.723
PERF  ->  CSOR     0.738         0.740          0.044    16.602  0.668  0.809
PERF  ->  ATTR     0.911         0.913          0.046    19.828  0.836  0.988
PERF  ->  COMP     0.946         0.948          0.037    25.925  0.888  1.009
PERF  ->  LIKE     0.790         0.792          0.045    17.724  0.717  0.864
PERF  ->  CUSA     0.479         0.477          0.058     8.245  0.383  0.567
PERF  ->  CUSL     0.591         0.592          0.057    10.463  0.500  0.684
CSOR  ->  ATTR     0.826         0.826          0.050    16.375  0.746  0.905
CSOR  ->  COMP     0.678         0.680          0.048    14.215  0.602  0.757
CSOR  ->  LIKE     0.741         0.741          0.044    16.885  0.664  0.810
CSOR  ->  CUSA     0.444         0.444          0.049     9.015  0.357  0.522
CSOR  ->  CUSL     0.460         0.464          0.053     8.610  0.369  0.548
ATTR  ->  COMP     0.847         0.850          0.059    14.244  0.749  0.947
ATTR  ->  LIKE     0.840         0.841          0.050    16.798  0.757  0.924
ATTR  ->  CUSA     0.548         0.546          0.056     9.744  0.454  0.640
ATTR  ->  CUSL     0.620         0.621          0.063     9.842  0.520  0.727
COMP  ->  LIKE     0.780         0.780          0.041    19.102  0.709  0.845
COMP  ->  CUSA     0.465         0.465          0.056     8.343  0.372  0.554
COMP  ->  CUSL     0.532         0.534          0.056     9.508  0.436  0.624
LIKE  ->  CUSA     0.577         0.578          0.043    13.558  0.507  0.643
LIKE  ->  CUSL     0.737         0.738          0.040    18.449  0.671  0.803
CUSA  ->  CUSL     0.755         0.755          0.035    21.826  0.694  0.806
>
```

Fig. B.5 Bootstrapped HTMT values (source: author's screenshot from RStudio)

Further Readings

- Eberl, M. (2010). An application of PLS in multi-group analysis: The need for differentiated corporate-level marketing in the mobile communications industry. In V. Esposito Vinzi, W. W. Chin, J. Henseler, & H. Wang (Eds.), *Handbook of partial least squares: Concepts, methods and applications in marketing and related fields* (Springer Handbooks of Computational Statistics Series, Vol. II, pp. 487–514). Berlin: Springer.
- Hair, J. F., Hult, G. T. M., Ringle, C. M., & Sarstedt, M. (2022). *A primer on partial least squares structural equation modeling (PLS-SEM)* (3rd edition) Thousand Oaks: Sage.
- Hair, J. F., Risher, J. J., Sarstedt, M., & Ringle, C. M. (2019). When to use and how to report the results of PLS-SEM. *European Business Review, 31*(1), 2–24.

Glossary

Absolute contribution Is the information an indicator variable provides about the formatively measured item, ignoring all other indicators. The absolute contribution is provided by the loading of the indicator (i.e., its bivariate correlation with the formatively measured construct).

Akaike weights Are the weights of evidence in favor of a certain model being the best model for the situation at hand given a set of alternative models.

AVE See *average variance extracted*.

Average variance extracted (AVE) A measure of convergent validity. It is the degree to which a latent construct explains the variance of its indicators; also referred to as *communality (construct)*.

Bayesian information criterion (BIC) Is a criterion for model selection among an alternative set of models. The model with the lowest BIC is preferred.

BIC See *Bayesian information criterion*.

Bootstrap confidence intervals Provide an estimated range of values that is likely to include an unknown population parameter. An interval is determined by its lower and upper bounds, which depend on a predefined probability of error and the standard error of the estimation for a given set of sample data. When zero does not fall into the confidence interval, an estimated parameter can be assumed to be significantly different from zero for the prespecified probability of error (e.g., 5 %).

Bootstrap samples Are the number of samples drawn in the bootstrapping procedure. Generally, 10,000 or more samples are recommended.

Bootstrapping Is a resampling technique that draws a large number of subsamples from the original data (with replacement) and estimates models for each subsample. It is used to determine standard errors of coefficients to assess their statistical significance without relying on distributional assumptions.

Cascaded moderator analysis Is a type of moderator analysis in which the strength of a moderating effect is influenced by another variable (i.e., the moderating effect is again moderated).

CB-SEM See *covariance-based structural equation modeling*.

Coefficient of determination (R^2) Is a measure of the proportion of an endogenous construct's variance that is explained by its predictor constructs. It indicates a model's *explanatory power* with regard to a specific endogenous construct.

Collinearity Arises when two indicators are highly correlated.

Common factor-based SEM Is a type of SEM method, which considers the constructs as common factors that explain the covariation between its associated indicators.

Communality (construct) See *average variance extracted*.

Communality (indicator) See *indicator reliability*.

Competitive mediation A situation in mediation analysis that occurs when the indirect effect and the direct effect are both significant and point in opposite directions.

Complementary mediation A situation in mediation analysis that occurs when the indirect effect and the direct effect are both significant and point in the same direction.

Composite reliability rho$_c$ Is a measure of internal consistency reliability, which, unlike Cronbach's alpha, does not assume equal indicator loadings. It should be above 0.70 (in exploratory research, 0.60 to 0.70 is considered acceptable).

Composite-based SEM Is a type of SEM method, which represents the constructs as composites, formed by linear combinations of sets of indicator variables.

Confidence intervals See *bootstrap confidence intervals*.

Construct scores Are columns of data (vectors) for each latent variable that represent a key result of the PLS-SEM algorithm. The length of every vector equals the number of observations in the dataset used.

Constructs Measure theoretical concepts that are abstract and complex and cannot be directly observed by means of (multiple) items. Constructs are represented in path models as circles or ovals and are also referred to as *latent variables*.

Content validity Is a subjective but systematic evaluation of how well the domain content of a construct is captured by its indicators.

Convergent validity It is the degree to which a reflectively specified construct explains the variance of its indicators (see *average variable extracted*). In formative measurement model evaluation, convergent validity refers to the degree to which the formatively measured construct correlates positively with an alternative (reflective or single-item) measure of the same concept (see *redundancy analysis*).

Correlation weights See *mode A*.

Covariance-based structural equation modeling (CB-SEM) Is an approach for estimating structural equation models, which assumes that the concepts of interest can be represented by common factors. It can be used for theory testing but has clear limitations in terms of testing a model's predictive power.

Critical values See *significance testing*.

Cronbach's alpha A measure of internal consistency reliability that assumes equal indicator loadings. Cronbach's alpha represents a conservative measure of internal consistency reliability.

Cross-validated predictive ability test (CVPAT) A statistical test for comparing the predictive power of different models.

CVPAT See *cross-validated predictive ability test*.

Direct effect Is a relationship linking two constructs with a single arrow between the two.

Direct-only non-mediation A situation in mediation analysis that occurs when the direct effect is significant but not the indirect effect.

Discriminant validity Is the extent to which a construct is empirically distinct from other constructs in the model.

Endogenous latent variables Serve only as dependent variables or as both independent and dependent variables in a structural model.

Error terms Capture the unexplained variance in constructs and indicators when path models are estimated.

Exogenous latent variables Are latent variables that serve only as independent variables in a structural model.

Explanatory power Provides information about the strength of the assumed causal relationships in a PLS path model. The primary measure for assessing a PLS path model's explanatory power is the *coefficient of determination (R^2)*.

f^2 effect size Is a measure used to assess the relative impact of a predictor construct on an endogenous construct in terms of its explanatory power.

Factor (score) indeterminacy Means that one can compute an infinite number of sets of factor scores matching the specific requirements of a certain common factor model. In contrast to their explicit estimation in PLS-SEM, the scores of common factors as assumed in CB-SEM are indeterminate.

Glossary

Factor weighting scheme Uses the correlations between constructs in the structural model to determine their relationships in the first stage of the PLS-SEM algorithm; see *weighting scheme*.

Formative measurement model Is a type of measurement model setup, in which the indicators form the construct, and arrows point from the indicators to the construct. The *indicator weight* estimation of formative measurement models usually uses *mode B* in PLS-SEM.

Full mediation A situation in mediation analysis that occurs when the mediated effect is significant but not the direct effect. Hence, the mediator variable fully explains the relationship between an exogenous and an endogenous latent variable. Full mediation is also referred to as *indirect-only mediation*.

Geweke and Meese criterion (GM) Is a criterion for model selection among a set of alternative models. The model with the lowest GM is preferred.

GM See *Geweke and Meese criterion*.

Heterogeneity Occurs when the data underlie groups of data characterized by significant differences in terms of model parameters. Heterogeneity can be either observed or unobserved, depending on whether its source can be traced back to observable characteristics (e.g., demographic variables) or whether the sources of heterogeneity are not fully known.

Heterotrait–heteromethod correlations Are the correlations of the indicators across constructs measuring different constructs.

Heterotrait–monotrait ratio (HTMT) Is a measure of *discriminant validity*. The HTMT is the mean of all correlations of indicators across constructs measuring different constructs (i.e., the heterotrait–heteromethod correlations) relative to the (geometric) mean of the average correlations of indicators measuring the same construct (i.e., the monotrait–heteromethod correlations).

Higher-order construct Represents a higher-order structure (usually second order) that contains several layers of constructs and involves a higher level of abstraction. Higher-order constructs involve a more abstract higher-order component related to two or more lower-order components in a reflective or formative way.

Holdout sample Is a subset of a larger dataset or a separate dataset not used in model estimation.

HTMT See *heterotrait–monotrait ratio*.

Inconsistent mediation: See *competitive mediation*.

Indicator loadings Are the bivariate correlations between a construct and the indicators. They determine an item's absolute contribution to its assigned construct. Loadings are of primary interest in the evaluation of reflective measurement models but are also interpreted when formative measures are involved. They are also referred to as *outer loadings*.

Indicator reliability Is the square of a standardized indicator's indicator loading. It represents how much of the variation in an item is explained by the construct and is referred to as the variance extracted from the item; see *communality (indicator)*.

Indicator weights Are the results of a multiple regression of a construct on its set of indicators. Weights are the primary criterion to assess each indicator's relative importance in formative measurement models.

Indicators Are directly measured observations (raw data), also referred to as either *items* or *manifest variables*, which are represented in path models as rectangles. They are also available data (e.g., responses to survey questions or collected from company databases) used in measurement models to measure the latent variables.

Indirect effect Represents a relationship between two latent variables via a third (e.g., mediator) construct in the PLS path model. If p_1 is the relationship between the exogenous latent variable and the mediator variable and p_2 is the relationship between the mediator variable and the endogenous latent variable, the indirect effect is the product of path p_1 and path p_2.

Indirect-only mediation A situation in mediation analysis that occurs when the indirect effect is significant but not the direct effect. Hence, the mediator variable fully explains the relationship between an exogenous and an endogenous latent variable. Indirect-only mediation is also referred to as *full mediation*.

Inner model See *structural model*.

In-sample predictive power See *coefficient of determination*.

Integrated development environment (IDE) Is a software that provides a set of tools to assist computer programmers in developing software, including a source code editor, build automation tools, and a debugger.

Interaction effect See *moderation*.

Interaction term Is an auxiliary variable entered into the path model to account for the interaction of the moderator variable and the exogenous construct.

Internal consistency reliability Is a form of reliability used to judge the consistency of results across items on the same test. It determines whether the items measur-

Glossary

ing a construct are similar in their scores (i.e., if the correlations between items are strong).

Interval scale Can be used to provide a rating of objects and has a constant unit of measurement so the distance between scale points is equal.

Inverse square root method Is a method for determining the minimum sample size requirement, which uses the value of the path coefficient with the minimum magnitude in the PLS path model as input.

***k*-fold cross-validation** Is a model validation technique for assessing how the results of a PLS-SEM analysis will generalize to an independent dataset. The technique combines *k*-1 subsets into a single training sample that is used to predict the remaining subset.

Latent variables See *constructs*.

Linear regression model (LM) benchmark Is a benchmark used in $PLS_{predict}$, derived from regressing an endogenous construct's indicators on the indicators of all exogenous constructs. The LM benchmark thereby neglects the measurement model and structural configurations. PLS-SEM results are assumed to outperform the LM benchmark.

MAE See *mean absolute error*.

Main effect Refers to the direct effect between an exogenous and an endogenous construct in the path model without the presence of a moderating effect. After inclusion of the moderator variable, the main effect typically changes in magnitude. Therefore, it is commonly referred to as simple effect in the context of a moderator model.

Mean absolute error (MAE) Is a metric used in $PLS_{predict}$, defined as the average absolute differences between the predictions and the actual observations, with all the individual differences having equal weight.

Measurement error Is the difference between the true value of a variable and the value obtained by a measurement.

Measurement models Are elements of a path model that contain the indicators and their relationships with the constructs and are also called *outer models* in PLS-SEM.

Measurement theory Specifies how constructs should be measured with (a set of) indicators. It determines which indicators to use for construct measurement and the directional relationship between construct and indicators.

Mediating effect Occurs when a third construct intervenes between two other related constructs.

Mediation model See *mediation*.

Mediation Represents a situation in which one or more mediator constructs explain the processes through which an exogenous construct influences an endogenous construct.

Mediator construct Is a construct that intervenes between two other directly related constructs.

Metric scale Represents data on a ratio scale and interval scale; see *ratio scale* and *interval scale*.

Metrological uncertainty Is the dispersion of the measurement values that can be attributed to the object or concept being measured.

Minimum sample size requirement Is the number of observations needed to meet the technical requirements of the multivariate analysis method used or to achieve a sufficient level of statistical power. See *inverse square root method*.

Missing value treatment Can employ different methods, such as mean replacement, EM (expectation–maximization algorithm), and nearest neighbor to obtain values for missing data points in the set of data used for the analysis. As an alternative, researchers may consider deleting cases with missing values (i.e., casewise deletion).

Missing values Are missing data (e.g., missing responses) of a variable.

Mode A Uses correlation *weights* to compute composite scores from sets of indicators. More specifically, the indicator weights are the correlation between the construct and each of its indicators. See *reflective measurement model*.

Mode B Uses regression *weights* to compute composite scores from sets of indicators. To obtain the weights, the construct is regressed on its indicators. Hence, the outer weights in mode B are the coefficients of a multiple regression model. See *formative measurement model*.

Model comparisons Involve establishing and empirically comparing a set of theoretically justified competing models that represent alternative explanations of the phenomenon under research.

Model estimation Uses the PLS-SEM algorithm and the available indicator data to estimate the PLS path model.

Glossary

Moderating effect See *moderation*.

Moderation Occurs when the effect of an exogenous latent variable on an endogenous latent variable depends on the values of a third variable, referred to as a moderator variable, which impacts the relationship. Including a moderating effect in a PLS path model requires specifying an interaction term, which represents the interplay between exogenous construct and moderator variable.

Moderator variable See *moderation*.

Monotrait–heteromethod correlations Are the correlations of indicators measuring the same construct.

Multigroup analysis Is a type of moderator analysis where the moderator variable is categorical (usually with two categories) and is assumed to potentially affect all relationships in the structural model; it tests whether parameters (mostly path coefficients) differ significantly between two groups. Research has proposed a range of approaches to multigroup analysis, which rely on the bootstrapping or permutation procedure.

Multiple mediation model Describes a mediation analysis in which multiple mediator variables are being included in the model.

Multiple moderator model Describes a moderation analysis in which multiple moderators are being included in the model.

No-effect non-mediation A situation in mediation analysis that occurs when neither the direct nor the indirect effect is significant.

Open source Is a software with source code that anyone can view, modify, and extend. The source code is made available to others who wish to view, copy, learn from, modify, or redistribute that code.

Outer loadings See *indicator loadings*.

Outer models See *measurement model*.

Outer weights See *indicator weights*.

Out-of-sample predictive power See *predictive power*.

Packages Are a collection of applications or code modules that work together to meet various goals and objectives as part of a larger software system.

Partial least squares structural equation modeling (PLS-SEM) Is a composite-based method to estimate structural equation models. The goal is to maximize the explained variance of the endogenous latent variables.

Partial mediation Occurs when a mediator variable partially explains the relationship between an exogenous and an endogenous construct. Partial mediation can come in the form of complementary and competitive mediation, depending on the relationship between direct and indirect effects.

Path coefficients Are estimated path relationships in the structural model (i.e., between constructs in the model). They correspond to standardized betas in a regression analysis.

Path model Is a diagram that visually displays the hypotheses and variable relationships that are examined when structural equation modeling is applied.

Path weighting scheme Uses the results of partial regression models to determine the relationships between constructs in the structural model in the first stage of the PLS-SEM algorithm; see *weighting scheme*.

Percentile method Is an approach for constructing bootstrap confidence intervals. Using the ordered set of parameter estimates obtained from bootstrapping, the lower and upper bounds are directly computed by excluding a certain percentage of lowest and highest values (e.g., as determined by the 2.5 % and 97.5 % bounds of the 95 % bootstrap confidence interval). The percentile method should be preferred when constructing confidence intervals.

PLS path modeling See partial *least squares structural equation modeling*.

PLS regression Is an analysis technique that explores the linear relationships between multiple independent variables and a single or multiple dependent variable(s). In developing the regression model, it constructs composites from both the multiple independent variables and the dependent variable(s) by means of principal component analysis.

$PLS_{predict}$ Is a holdout-sample-based procedure that generates case-level predictions on an item or a construct level to facilitate the assessment of a PLS path model's predictive power. The $PLS_{predict}$ procedure relies on the concept of *k-fold cross-validation*.

PLS-SEM algorithm Is the heart of the method. Based on the PLS path model and the indicator data available, the algorithm estimates the scores of all latent variables in the model, which in turn serve for estimating all path model relationships.

PLS-SEM bias Refers to PLS-SEM's property that structural model relationships are slightly underestimated and relationships in the measurement models are

Glossary

slightly overestimated compared to CB-SEM when using the method on common factor model data. This difference can be attributed to the methods' different handling of the latent variables in the model estimation but is negligible in most settings typically encountered in empirical research.

PLS-SEM See *partial least squares structural equation modeling.*

Prediction error Is the difference between a variable's predicted and original value.

Prediction statistics Quantify the degree of prediction error.

Prediction See *predictive power*.

Predictive power Indicates a model's ability to predict new observations.

R documentation Is a standard way of documenting the parameters, usage, and output of objects and functions in an R package. These files use a custom syntax and are rendered to HTML, plain text, and pdf for viewing.

R scripts Are text files containing a set of commands and comments to be executed in R. The script can be saved and used later to re-execute the saved commands. The script can also be edited so that you can execute a modified version of the commands.

R^2 See *coefficient of determination (R^2).*

Ratio scale Is a measurement scale, which has a constant unit of measurement and an absolute zero point; a ratio can be calculated using the scale points.

Redundancy analysis Is a method used to assess a formative construct's *convergent validity*. It tests whether a formatively measured construct is highly correlated with a reflective or single-item measure of the same construct.

Reflective measurement model Is a type of measurement model setup in which measures represent the effects (or manifestations) of an underlying construct. Causality is from the construct to its measures (indicators). The *indicator loading* estimation of reflective measurement models usually uses *mode A* in PLS-SEM.

Regression weights See *mode B*.

Relative contribution Is the unique importance of each indicator by partializing the variance of the formatively measured construct that is predicted by other indicators. An item's relative contribution is provided by its weight.

Relevance of the path coefficients Compares the relative importance of predictor constructs to explain endogenous constructs in the structural model. Significance is a prerequisite for the relevance, but not all constructs and their significant path coefficients are highly relevant to explain a selected target construct.

Reliability coefficient rho$_A$ Is a measure of internal consistency reliability, which considered a sound trade-off between the conservative *Cronbach's alpha* and the liberal *composite reliability* (*rho$_C$*).

RMSE See *root-mean-square error.*

Root-mean-square error (RMSE) Is a metric used in $PLS_{predict}$, defined as the square root of the average of the squared differences between the predictions and the actual observations.

Sample Is a collection of data that shall be representative for the analyzed population.

Secondary data Are data that have already been gathered, often for a different research purpose and some time ago.

Second-generation techniques Overcome the limitations of first-generation techniques, for example, in terms of accounting for measurement error. SEM is the most prominent second-generation data analysis technique.

Seed Is a number that specifies the start point when a computer generates a random number sequence. A seed is used when a computational process includes a random element in order to make the random process reproducible.

Significance of the path coefficients Tests whether a certain effect is significantly different from zero and, thereby, can be assumed to truly exist in the population.

Significance testing Is the process of testing whether a certain result likely has occurred by chance (i.e., whether an effect can be assumed to truly exist in the population). To test whether a parameter is significant, we need to compare the t-values – derived from bootstrapping – with the critical values from the standard normal distribution. Alternatively, we can inspect *bootstrap confidence intervals*.

Simple effect Is a cause–effect relationship in a moderator model. The parameter estimate represents the size of the relationship between the exogenous and the endogenous latent variable when the moderator variable is included in the model. For this reason, the main effect and the simple effect usually have different sizes.

Single mediation analysis Describes a mediation analysis in which only one mediator variable is being included in the model.

Specific indirect effect Describes an indirect effect via one single mediator in a multiple mediation model.

Glossary

Standard error Is the standard deviation of the sampling distribution of a given statistic. Standard errors are important to show how much sampling fluctuation a statistic has.

Statistical power The probability to detect a significant relationship when the relationship is in fact present in the population.

Structural equation modeling (SEM) Is a set of statistical methods used to estimate relationships between constructs and indicators, while accounting for measurement error.

Structural model Includes the construct and their relationships as derived from theory and logic.

Structural theory Specifies how the latent variables are related to each other. That is, it shows the constructs and the paths between them.

Sum scores Represent a naive way to determine the latent variable scores. Instead of estimating the relationships in the measurement models, sum scores use the same weight for each indicator per measurement model to determine the latent variable scores. As such, the sum scores approach does not account for measurement error.

Suppressor effect Describes the effect of a mediator variable in competitive mediation, which absorbs a significant share of or the entire direct effect, thereby substantially decreasing the magnitude of the total effect.

Theory Is a set of systematically related hypotheses developed following the scientific method that can be used to explain and predict outcomes and that can be tested empirically.

Three-way interaction Is an extension of two-way interaction where the moderator effect is again moderated by another moderator variable.

Total effect Is the sum of the direct effect and the indirect effect between an exogenous and an endogenous latent variable in the path model.

Total indirect effect Is the sum of all specific indirect effects in a multiple mediation model.

Training sample Is a subset of a larger dataset used for model estimation.

Two-stage approach (moderation) Is an approach to model the interaction term when including a moderator variable in the model. The approach can also be used when the exogenous construct and/or the moderator variable is measured formatively.

Two-way interaction Is the standard approach to moderator analysis where the moderator variable interacts with one other exogenous latent variable.

Variance inflation factor (VIF) Quantifies the severity of collinearity among indicators in a formative measurement model and a set of predictor constructs in the structural model.

Variance-based SEM See partial *least squares structural equation modeling.*

VIF See *variance inflation factor*.

Vignettes Are documentation that accompany software and are intended to serve as an introduction and description of functionality of the software. Typically, a vignette describes the problem the package is designed to solve and then shows the reader how to solve it. Vignettes serve as a user manual for the software.

Weighting scheme Describes a particular method to determine the relationships in the *structural model* when running the *PLS-SEM algorithm*. Standard options considered in SEMinR are the factor and path weighting schemes. The final results do not differ much, and one should use the path weighting scheme as a default option since it maximizes the R^2 *values* of the PLS path model estimation.

Index

A

Absolute contribution 94
Akaike weights 122
Average variance extracted (AVE) 78

B

Bayesian information criterion (BIC) 122
Bootstrap confidence intervals 94
Bootstrap samples 94
bootstrap_model() 64, 87, 101, 106, 107, 126
Bootstrapping 64, 94

C

Cascaded moderator analysis 159
Coefficient of determination (R^2) 118
Collinearity 117
Comma-separated value (CSV) files 54
Common factor-based SEM 8
Communality 77, 78
Competitive mediation 142
Complementary mediation 142
Composite reliability rho_c 77
composite() 57, 58, 100, 164
Composite-based SEM 9
Comprehensive R Archive Network (CRAN) 34
compute_it_criteria_weights() 134
Confidence intervals 94
Construct scores 10
Constructs 4
constructs() 57, 58, 165
Content validity 77
Convergent validity 78, 92
Correlation weights 60
Covariance-based SEM (CB-SEM) 4
Critical values 94
Cronbach's alpha 77
Cross-validated predictive ability test (CVPAT) 122

D

demo() 45, 100
Direct effect 140

Direct-only non-mediation 142
Discriminant validity 78

E

Endogenous latent variables 6
Error terms 6
estimate_pls() 61, 80, 82, 100
Exogenous latent variables 5–6
Explanatory power 118

F

Factor (score) indeterminacy 10
Factor weighting scheme 60
f^2 effect size (in moderation analysis) 119, 161
Formative measurement model 7, 60, 92
Full mediation 142

G

Geweke and Meese's (1981) criterion (GM) 122

H

head() 56
Heterogeneity 156
Heterotrait-heteromethod correlations 79
Heterotrait-monotrait ratio (HTMT) 79
higher_composite() 57
Higher-order construct 93
Holdout sample 119

I

Inconsistent mediation 143
Indicator loadings 60, 77
Indicator reliability 77
Indicators 4
Indicator weights 60, 93
Indirect effect 140
Indirect-only mediation 142
Inner model 5
In-sample predictive power 118
Integrated Development Environment (IDE) 35
Interaction effect 156
Interaction term 159

interaction_term() 57, 166
Internal consistency reliability 77
Inverse square root method 16

K

k-fold cross-validation 119

L

library() 40
Linear regression model (LM) benchmark 121
lm() 39

M

Main effect 162
Mean absolute error (MAE) 120
mean() 39
Measurement error 3
Measurement models 5, 57
Measurement theory 7
Mediating effects 140
Mediation 140
Mediation model 141
Mediator construct 140
Metric scale 19
Metrological uncertainty 9
Minimum sample size requirements 16
Missing value treatment 18
Mode A 60
Mode B 60
Model comparisons 121
Model estimation 59
Moderating effect 158
Moderator variable 156
Monotrait-heteromethod correlations 79
multi_items() 58, 164
Multigroup analysis 156
Multiple mediation analyses 144
Multiple mediation models 144–145
Multiple moderator model 159

N

names() 134
No-effect non-mediation 142

O

Open-source 34
Outer models 5
Out-of-sample predictive power 119

P

Packages 32, 39
parallel::detectCores() 106
Partial least squares (PLS)
– path modeling 4
– regression 11
Partial least squares SEM (PLS-SEM) 4
– algorithm 59
– bias 14
Partial mediation 142
Path coefficients 60
Path models 4
Path weighting scheme 60
paths() 59
Percentile method 94
plot() 84, 129
$PLS_{predict}$ 119
predict_pls() 129
Prediction 10
Prediction statistics 120
Predictive power 119
PROCESS 144

R

Ratio scale 19
R Documentation 42
read.csv() 43, 53–55
Redundancy analysis 92
Reflective measurement model 7, 60
Regression weights 60
relationships() 59
Relevance of the path coefficients 117
Reliability coefficient rho_A 78
Root mean square error (RMSE) 120
R Scripts 41
R software 35
RStudio 35

S

Sample 4
sd() 39
Secondary data 19
Second-generation techniques 4
Significance 117
Significance testing 93
Simple effect 159
Single mediation analysis 144
single_item() 58
Slope plot 163
slope_analysis() 168
Specific indirect effect 144
specific_effect_significance() 147, 148

Standard error 93
Statistical power 11
Structural equation modeling (SEM) 4
Structural model 5, 59
Structural theory 8
Sum scores 9
summary() 62, 80, 82, 87, 100, 101, 107
summary_corp_rep() 86
Suppressor effect 142
Syntax conventions 33

T

Theory 7
Three-way interaction 159
Total effect 140
Total indirect effect 144
Training sample 119
Two-stage approach 160
Two-way interaction 159

U

Uncertainty 9

V

Variance inflation factor (VIF) 93, 117
Variance-based structural equation modeling 10
vignette() 44
Vignettes 44

W

Weighting schemes 60
write.csv() 66

GPSR Compliance

The European Union's (EU) General Product Safety Regulation (GPSR) is a set of rules that requires consumer products to be safe and our obligations to ensure this.

If you have any concerns about our products, you can contact us on

ProductSafety@springernature.com

In case Publisher is established outside the EU, the EU authorized representative is:

Springer Nature Customer Service Center GmbH
Europaplatz 3
69115 Heidelberg, Germany

www.ingramcontent.com/pod-product-compliance
Ingram Content Group UK Ltd.
Pitfield, Milton Keynes, MK11 3LW, UK
UKHW021446190426
11946UKWH00022B/54